The Family as In-Patient

The Family as In-Patient

Working with Families and Adolescents at the Cassel Hospital

Edited by
Roger Kennedy, Ann Heymans
and Lydia Tischler

'an association in which the free development of each is the condition of the free development of all'

FAB

Free Association Books / London / 1987

First published in Great Britain 1986 by
Free Association Books
26 Freegrove Road
London N7 9RQ

British Library Cataloguing in Publication Data

The Family as in-patient: working with
families and adolescents at the Cassel Hospital.
1. Family psychotherapy — Great Britain
2. Psychiatric hospital care — Great Britain
I. Kennedy, Roger II. Heymans, Ann
III. Tischler, Lydia
616.89'156'0941 RC488.5

ISBN 0-946960-50-X
ISBN 0-946960-51-8 Pbk

Typeset by Rapidset and Design Ltd, London

Printed and bound in Great Britain
by A. Wheaton & Co. Ltd, Exeter

CONTENTS

PART TWO: CLINICAL WORK

Acknowledgements

The editors and contributors would like to thank the other members of staff for their support in the day-to-day work of the hospital and for their support of the book. We would also like to pay a special tribute to all the patients who participate in the life of the hospital. Ann Heymans and Lydia Tischler would like to acknowledge the fact that Roger Kennedy was the prime mover in making sure the book got off the ground. The editors would like to make clear that the work described in Oliver James's paper on the nurse/therapist relationship was the result of joint work with Louise de Lambert, former Matron of the Cassel, and Dr Alan Wilson. In addition, the concept of the nurse/therapist relationship and its supervision arose as a result of joint thinking of the Senior Staff Group between 1980 and 1982; the group included Dr Tom Pitt-Aikens, Elsie Buckenham, Dr John Denford, Oliver James, Louise de Lambert, Dr Brian Muir, Dr Philippe Ployé, Gillian Stamp, Lydia Tischler and Dr Alan Wilson.

The Editors would like to thank the League of Friends of the Cassel Hospital for their generous donation which funded the typing of the manuscript of the book; Elsie Buckenham for her superb typing; and Karl Figlio of Free Association Books for his expert guidance and enthusiastic support of the book.

We also thank the International Review of Psychoanalysis for permission to publish Oliver James's paper, 'The Role of the

Nurse/Therapist Relationship in the Therapeutic Community' and the British Journal of Medical Psychology for permission to reproduce 'A Sexually Charged Clinical Problem in the Therapeutic Community' by the same author. Anne Zachary's paper, 'A New Look at the Vulnerability of Puerperal Mothers' was first published in *Psychoanalytic Psychotherapy* Vol. 1 No. 3 in 1985, (pp.71-79).

Finally, we would like to thank Mrs D. Lawson, the Hospital Administrator, for her help in proofreading.

Contributors

Sheila Ashley. Ward Sister at the Cassel Hospital from 1978 to 1981.

Vivien Biggs. Social Work student on placement during 1979. Currently Senior Development Officer (Children's Services) in Surrey Social Services Department.

Elsie Buckenham. Assistant Administrator at the Cassel Hospital from 1965, and then Hospital Administrator from 1982 until her retirement in 1984.

Judith Burman. Senior Social Work Practitioner and, since 1977, member of the Family and Adolescent Unit Day Unit staff, and part of the Cassel Marital Clinic's staff.

Dr Luigi Caparrotta. Registrar at the Cassel from 1981 to 1984. Now Clinical Assistant at the Royal Free Hospital.

Gillian Chapman. Ward Sister at the Cassel from 1979 to 1983. Now Lecturer in Nursing Studies at King's College Hospital.

Denis Flynn. Child Psychotherapist working in the Families Unit since 1984.

Trevor Hartnup. Child Psychotherapist working in the Family and Adolescent Unit from 1975 to 1984. Now District Principal Child Psychotherapist in Wandsworth.

ANN HEYMANS. Ward Sister at the Cassel from 1978 to 1983, Nursing Officer in the Family and Adolescent Unit from 1983 to 1985. Now training as an Osteopath and Naturopath in London.

OLIVER JAMES. Clinical Psychologist at the Cassel since 1982.

Dr ROGER KENNEDY. Consultant Psychotherapist to the Family and Adolescent Unit at the Cassel since 1982. He is also a member of staff of Brent Consultation Centre and a psychoanalyst in private practice.

GEORGE LEACH. Charge Nurse at the Cassel since 1984.

Dr BRIAN MUIR. Senior Registrar at the Cassel from 1972 to 1974. He was then a Consultant responsible for different Units, including the Family and Adolescent Unit. Chairman of the Cassel Medical Executive Committee from 1984 to 1985. Now Director of Psychotherapy at the Melbourne Clinic, Australia. He is also a psychoanalyst in private practice.

MARY-ANN MUNFORD. Ward Sister at the Cassel from 1981 to 1984. Currently she is reading for a degree in Social Anthropology at London University.

Dr PETRIE THOMPSON. Registrar in Psychotherapy at the Cassel since 1984.

LYDIA TISCHLER. Child Psychotherapist on the staff of the Cassel from 1962 until her retirement in 1985. From 1964 she was Principal Child Psychotherapist and helped to establish the psychotherapeutic treatment of children at the hospital.

Dr ALAN WILSON. First joined the staff of the Cassel in 1960 as SHMO. After an absence of three years he returned to take up the position of Consultant to the Family Unit, and was also Consultant to the Day Unit for several years. He was Chairman of the Medical Executive Committee from 1979 until his retirement in 1984. He is also a psychoanalyst.

IRENE WINEMANN-MARCUS. Child Psychotherapist at the Cassel from 1981 to 1982. She is now in private practice in the USA.

JOHN WOODS. Child Psychotherapist at the Cassel on the Adolescent Unit since 1983.

Dr ANNE ZACHARY. Senior Registrar in Psychotherapy at the Cassel since 1983.

Introduction

Ann Heymans, Roger Kennedy
and *Lydia Tischler*

THE AIM OF this book is to describe recent work with troubled families and adolescents at the Cassel Hospital, a therapeutic community run on psychoanalytic lines, in the hope that our experience will be of use to other workers in the mental health field. For many years the hospital has pioneered the non-drug treatment of severe mental disturbance in adults, families and adolescents, by means of a combination of intensive psychoanalytic psychotherapy and psychosocial nursing. It has also developed a special approach to the treatment of families which have severely broken down by offering prolonged admission to a whole family, so that a family can use the hospital's facilities to attempt to restore its functioning and so return to ordinary life. The hospital does not offer asylum as such, for the life of the community is often challenging and awkward, particularly for those individuals who tend to deny their own responsibility for their actions. Nonetheless it does offer people a rare chance to face their difficulties within a therapeutic structure.

The book is a collection of papers written by several Cassel staff members. Although individual views are put forward, these papers illustrate a coherent body of knowledge and of clinical experience which can be described as the 'Cassel view'. The only previous attempt to do this systematically at the Cassel was in *Psychosocial Nursing* (Barnes, 1967) which mainly deals with the nursing work but still remains an important and pioneering study that helped to transform nursing practices in the Health Service.

Although the hospital has constantly adapted to change and has made many modifications in its theory and practice, there is nonetheless a common approach that remains central to the work. What follows is a summary of this approach.

Information about the patient comes from a variety of settings from within the hospital, and not only from the therapy sessions, unlike in most psychiatric institutions. The day-to-day work of the hospital consists of an attempt to synthesize psychoanalytic therapy with detailed and meticulous nursing work. The treatment is based on a psychoanalytically informed processing of what takes place in the course of the day in the therapy and nursing arenas, and is founded on four essential elements:

1. The active participation of patients, who are treated, as in classical psychoanalysis, as subjects with a life of their own, with conscious and unconscious intentions and motives that are respected and listened to.

2. The relationship of the patients to the hospital. The hospital provides a physical structure in terms of the bricks and mortar of the building and its layout. This structure is looked after by patients and nurses, for example in daily work groups which involve cleaning and maintenance. The structure also underpins the therapeutic work. The attitude of the patient towards the material fabric of the hospital is complicated, involving a mixture of infantile and adult elements. It can be compared to the role of the 'setting' in the consulting room in classical analysis. That is, it provides the bricks and mortar of the 'holding' and facilitating environment.

3. As well as the physical structure, the hospital provides sophisticated *therapeutic structures*. These include psychotherapeutic treatment undertaken in consulting rooms; nursing work which takes place in group and individual settings, mainly though not exclusively around activities; formal meetings for patients and staff; and supervision of the therapy and nursing. In addition, patients are involved in the life of the hospital community, which consists of their active participation in and their taking respon-

sibility for such things as cooking teams, washing-up rotas, work group areas, babysitting, and participation as patient representatives in a number of possible bodies in the daily community structure.

The expectations of functioning entailed in the daily community responsibilities provides support for, and strengthening of, patients' self-esteem, while maintaining an awareness of their need to show responsibility towards others. This expectation may include, for example, the patients sitting up all night with a distressed patient, helping others at crucial moments, and supporting others to work through important feelings and issues. Tasks and ventures at a community level are shared between nurses and patients. This illustrates how shared dependency, or rather interdependency, is normal, and not despicable or useless. The community therefore provides a picture of the possibility of help being available to counter despair, as well as the need for shared responsibility; it indicates that an individual *can* have some solution to his frustrations.

4. The hospital provides a special and complicated setting for treatment. It is not easy to make sense of what happens when a large group of people are living together. But nonetheless we attempt, both in the course of the working week and in these papers, to provide a framework for registering events and for making psychoanalytic sense of what takes place. In order to do this, we believe that *effective transmission of information* about patients is needed. The hospital has developed professional working practices to deal with the intense anxieties that are produced by the more disturbed patients. This involves sharing of strains, considerable support and supervision, as well as particular and detailed attention to the way that the nursing and therapy are linked.

The way we look at this linkage entails a radical change of approach to treatment. Nursing has always been an equal partner with therapy at the Cassel, unlike other mental health institutions. Nursing is felt to have an equally important role, with its particular emphasis on the ordinary events in the day. We have recently developed a new approach to treatment, in which there is supervision of the relationship between nurse and therapist of particular patients. This supervision is essential to the dynamics of working together in the institution. Therapy can then spread beyond the patient's individual history and problems and includes events within the hospital. Such an approach involves considerable attention to the way that patients use different staff members; patients often create splits in the staff structure where different members of staff are made to feel opposed to each other in relation to what the patient is telling them. Such splits are considered inevitable, but they are monitored and used for therapeutic ends. Thus, we have found it essential to pay attention to the working relationship between the therapist and nurse of a particular patient or family, as this provides insight into the pathological processes operating within the patients. Lydia Tischler describes in detail (p. 95) how this joint supervision is set up and monitored, how it pays special attention to the feelings in the therapists' and nurses' countertransference which patients inevitably evoke, and the effect that these feelings have on their work with patients.

Although our facilities are special, we do feel that other workers in the mental health field can benefit from our work in a variety of ways. For example, we have acquired substantial experience of severe family and adolescent breakdown, and of how such patients can be treated without drugs. The clinical descriptions here may be useful on their own in clarifying issues for the reader, or at least may open up areas for further discussion. But we have also shown how an institution can be set up with specific aims for treatment, and we believe that our innovations in working practices can be of considerable benefit in other settings. The way that we attend to the nurse/therapist relationship can readily be generalized from the Cassel experience and could become a model of interdisciplinary working in a variety of out-patient and in-patient settings, both here and in other countries. The nurse/therapist supervision throws light on the usually insulated setting of individual psychoanalysis and psychotherapy.

Finally, there is an implicit view persisting throughout the book that treatment based on psychoanalytic thought has very broad applicability, and that it should be used much more widely in other mental health institutions, as it is both more humane and more respectful of the complexity of human beings than many other approaches. We will return to this point in the book's Conclusion.

The physical and social setting of the Cassel Hospital serves at least two purposes: it provides a framework in which patients can express and understand their difficulties, and it also serves as an agent of change. The hospital occupies a large old building, parts of which date back to the late seventeenth century. It is set in spacious grounds and overlooks Ham Common in South West London. There are 55 in-patient beds as well as an out-patient department, and a Day Unit for children and adolescents. In-patients are admitted to one of three units: two for single adults, and one for families and adolescents. Within the latter, we can admit six to seven whole families; we can also admit eight adolescents aged 16 to 20 without their parents. This book will confine itself to the hospital's treatment of families and adolescents excluding the considerable amount of work with individual adults, both as in-patients and out-patients, the developing psychotherapy liaison service that takes place in the Riverside District of the National Health Service, and the hospital's considerable training and research activities.

The hospital was founded in 1919 by Sir Ernest Cassel for the treatment of people with 'nervous functional disorders' (i.e. neurotic disorders). Work with families as in-patients began in 1948 when a mother requested permission to bring her 2½ year-old son into hospital with her as she had no-one in whose care she could leave him. In time, mothers were encouraged and, finally, were expected to bring their child or children with them as the benefits of joint admission became increasingly evident and the adverse effects of separation came to be understood. For example, it was recognized that to admit a mother without her child was often to collude with her unconscious hostility towards the child or at least her wish to be separated from him or her. Although at this time only mothers and children were being admitted, fathers were not only frequent visitors but often stayed in the hospital for periods of time.

In 1963, following the appointment to the staff of a child psychiatrist and child psychotherapist to study the impact on children of their mothers' illness, the first child patient accompanied by her mother was admitted. Finally in 1967, whole families began to be treated as in-patients, a practice which continues to this day.

At the time when the first child was admitted, an experiment was taking place to transform the hospital from 'a place wherein sick people may receive shelter from the stormy blasts of life' and from an organization 'run by doctors in the interests of their own greater technical efficiency' into a therapeutic institution 'where all its members participated fully in its daily life'. As part of this process, it came to be recognized that the life of the community had to 'be related to real tasks, truly relevant to the needs of patients and staff' (Main, 1946, p. 3). Consequently, women patients who were mothers needed to remain in touch with their real tasks of mothering.

The impetus for these developments in the treatment of neurotic people owes much to the exigencies of the Second World War, as did the founding of the hospital to those of the First World War. The inherent paradox of this situation is developed here by Alan Wilson (p. 49). The impact of the Second World War and especially the evacuation of children from cities under heavy bombardment brought new insights into the effects of separation from parents on child and infant development, as described by Anna Freud, John Bowlby, Dorothy Burlingham and Renee Spitz. Little or no attention was being paid, however, to the effects on the mother of being separated from her infant or child, and on the family as a functioning unit. Although, as we have already mentioned, this was not the primary reason for admitting infants and children with their mothers, in time this became a subject of study in its own right. A number of original and important contributions to the study of mothering and the psychodynamic forces which lead to its breakdown emanated from this hospital; these are described and updated in Anne Zachary's paper (p. 184).

There were at first many misgivings that bringing children into a psychiatric hospital for adults would expose them to malign influences which could seriously affect and emotionally harm them. These fears were not borne out by events. In the experience of Lydia Tischler, over a period of nearly a quarter of a century there have only been three occasions at the hospital when it became necessary to separate a child from its mother or parents. In the first case, a boy whose mother became frankly psychotic after admission was temporarily removed to a children's home with the parents' consent. In the second and third cases, two single mothers during the course of treatment revealed their sadistic interactions with their children; they were apparently unable to modify these and so agreed to relinquish their children for adoption. Irene Wineman-Marcus describes her work with one of the children (p. 276).

Moreover, not only did we not have to separate children from their parents, but on the contrary, on admission many children began to blossom when they were relieved of the burden of trying to meet their disturbed mother's emotional demands, which they were not equipped to provide, or because they then received the attention to their own needs which their ill mothers were unable to provide (see p. 208). Monitoring and using information about the child him or herself, as opposed to the child created by parental need, turns out to be another unexpected advantage of psychoanalytically based in-patient treatment centred on every-day routines. Just as 'splitting of the transference' was turned to good use, so the 'real' child became an invaluable aspect of the child's and the parents' healing.

During the first phase from 1954-62, when the mother was the focus of treatment, psychotherapeutic endeavours were directed at understanding the specific difficulties in mothering that were central to her current problems and that were often manifested in a crisis in relation to her baby. Lomas (1960a,b) for instance wrote about the unresolved relationship with internalized envious mothers in certain young women suffering from puerperal illness.

Gluck and Wren (1959) began systematic observations on children which they recorded in the film 'Play and Personality'; this showed how, in play, children reproduce what their mothers do to them. Gluck and Wren made other valuable observations on how the mother's pathology and way of mothering could affect the child's drive towards independence; how the child could be used by the mother to hide problems and resist treatment; and also, how the child could provide staff with clues to the mother's disturbance. Thus a great deal was becoming known about the mother's unconscious conflict and how this affected her relationship to the child through her behaviour. There was, however, no comparable understanding of the child's thoughts and feelings and how he or she experienced what the mother did. This resulted in a skewed, adult-centred view of the child. The child's presence in the hospital was real enough, yet it seemed as though he or she were only a receptacle for the mother's projections and externalizations. For instance, when a mother once came to tell her nurse that her little girl of 3½ had difficulty in going to sleep, the nurse reminded the mother of her, the mother's own difficulties in this area. In this interchange, the real child with her problem was bypassed. The fact that this exchange between mother and nurse took place within the earshot of the newly-appointed child psychotherapist was not without significance. The mother probably had a number of motives for choosing to make her communication when she did. The nurse, mindful of the fact that she was there to nurse the mother and only through her the child, could not but respond to the mother like this. The child psychotherapist's response, however, was to note to herself that there was also a real child who, for whatever reason, was also having difficulty in going to sleep.

Implicit in an adult-centred view based on analysing the adult internal world, was the notion that by treating the mother she would be able to help her child. The setting up of a Family Unit came about as a result of concern for the real child and how the mother's illness might be affecting him or her. It also had its impact on the hospital as an institution which could recognize the child as an individual in his or her own right with an inner life, internalized problems, personal reactions to the mother, to the family and to the environment, all of which merit study and understanding (Tischler, née Folkart, 1964,1967). We would like to emphasize here that in all our treatment of families, we put the needs and interests of the child in the family to the fore, as they can so easily be forgotten.

No such direct line of development can be traced in the hospital's engagement with adolescent patients, which began in the 1960s. The location and relocation of adolescents within the different units of the hospital (at times with the single adults, at other times, as now, with families), reflected to some extent the uncertainty within the community at large as to where the adolescent belonged. It was left to therapists trained in work with adults but interested in the problems of adolescents to undertake their treatment. Systematic work with parents of adolescents began in 1965, when weekly meetings with adolescent in-patients and their parents were set up. The perspective from which the adolescent was viewed was of someone growing towards adulthood. Subsequently, the child psychotherapist provided an additional perspective, that of the adolescent as emerging from childhood with all the developmental hold-ups, distortions and conflicts this entailed.

Referrals to the Cassel come from a wide variety of sources; locally, in the Greater London area and nationally, from psychiatrists, general practitioners, social workers, child guidance clinics, health visitors and physicians. The families are usually in a severe state of breakdown, often having had a wide variety of treatment; those who work with them are often at the end of their tether. We are increasingly seeing socially deprived and single parent families, often where a care order on the children has been established or is in the process of being established, for example because of severe physical and mental abuse of the children. Quite often a single member of the family is the named patient; an example might be a depressed mother who has become addicted to anti-depressant or anxiety-relieving drugs, who has a chaotic family situation, with a husband who opts out of taking on his responsibilities. What distinguishes the patients we admit is the extreme nature of their pathology and the ineffectiveness of other treatments they have had. A family has to be highly motivated or desperate, or both, in order to uproot themselves and live in the hospital. There are a number of further characteristics of such families, described with clinical material in the paper by Tischler and Hartnup (p. 228). Briefly, these families tend to rely heavily on externalization and splitting; they attempt to get rid of their conflicts by trying unconsciously to change others or to force them into certain roles.

We are somewhat selective about the patients we admit. We do not treat florid mental disturbances, for example, patients suffering from acute psychoses; nor do we accept drug addicts, severe alcoholics or major crime offenders, all of whom we have found are unable to use our resources, or else have a very destructive effect on the patient group. In addition, we have to consider the safety of the children in the hospital.

In practice, most of the families who wish to come are admitted. We insist that a family has a home to go to at the weekend; patients only stay for the week, unless there are good reasons to stay in the hospital, for example, at a time of crisis, or when there is something specific that they can work on with their nurse. Given these limitations, there is a fair degree of flexibility about whom we take. A disturbed family member can often be held more satisfactorily in the context of a whole family admission than if he or she were admitted alone.

We have more recently paid specific attention to work with referral agencies over particular cases. Trevor Hartnup's paper (p. 127) addresses itself to some of the relevant issues. However, we can only touch on this area in the rest of the book. This is partly because the development of this approach in order to facilitate work with families inside and outside the hospital is a relatively recent phenomenon, and also because the topic merits detailed consideration in its own right, perhaps in a separate book.

After referral and possible consultation with the referring agency (particularly with complicated cases involving, for example, the possibility of a care order, or with those families who have needed the intervention of many agencies), the family's admission proceeds through one or more consultations with therapy staff, to two home visits if the family show interest in the idea of admission. The purpose of the first visit is to make a nursing assessment of the family's suitability for in-patient treatment. The criteria for suitability hinge on the family's motivation in seeking help, their willingness to form a relationship with nurses, and their ability to look at their own difficulties. Emergency domiciliaries are undertaken where appropriate, for example in cases of acute puerperal breakdown, as described in Anne Zachary's paper (p. 188). Otherwise, immediately prior to admission, the family is visited by their admitting nurse and a patient from the unit to discuss practicalities, such as what to bring into the hospital, and to explain hospital routine. Nurses are allocated a caseload of up to three families with whom they will be specifically involved.

All patients spend a preliminary assessment period of three to five weeks in the hospital before there is a commitment on either side to long term treatment. At a diagnostic meeting, chaired by the consultant, detailed written reports are presented from the various workers, after which a decision about treatment is made, including a decision on the immediate *focus* for treatment. The focus unifies psychodynamic understanding of the pathology and the nursing plans, and is usually formulated in relatively simple language. For example, a treatment focus for both the therapy and nursing of a mother in a state of puerperal breakdown would usually be the mother/baby relationship, with special attention to the feeding process. This might change some months later, when the focus might become how the father and mother deal with their relationship. With adolescents in treatment, the willingness of their parents to support treatment and come to a weekly group consisting of all parents and adolescents is a vital factor.

Our assessment procedures may lead to different modes on handling different family groups. We believe strongly in offering a choice of psychotherapeutic treatment modes, depending on individual needs, rather than a blanket approach. We have the facility to offer individual treatment for members of the family including the children, for marital therapy, and for mothers and children in sessions where focus is on difficulties with physical and emotional contact. Regular family meetings with the family's nurse and therapist are built into the treatment plan. These focus on current day-to-day issues.

The usual length of the patients' stay is between nine and fourteen months; quite often, there are six month follow-ups after discharge. The fact that treatment is of limited duration emphasizes the need for a constant focus of treatment to be maintained, we do not have time to 'see what happens' in an open-ended way, as in individual psychoanalysis. Nor would this approach be appropriate in an in-patient setting, for after some 18 months of admission there arise the problems of institutionalization, and the inability to ever effectively separate from the hospital and leave the 'sick role'.

There have not yet been formal follow-up studies of families, but the hospital has undertaken formal follow-up research of adults, which show both a significant success rate and highly cost-effective care. Thus, in spite of the fact that in-patient care as practised at the Cassel is labour intensive and costly, the overall cost actually saves the taxpayer many thousands of pounds. (Denford et al. 1983). This is especially important when comparing psychoanalytic treatment with other apparently more efficient methods.

Families are currently housed on the second floor of the building. Single mothers share rooms with two and three beds, while couples have their own rooms. Children are accommodated as close as possible to their parents, usually in an adjoining room. Children from different families may share bedrooms. In the same area as the bedrooms, there is a small sitting room with a colour television and facilities for making hot drinks and babies' feeds. In another part of the hospital, unfortunately some distance away from the bedroom area, is a small kitchen for preparing children's suppers, a large sitting room and a children's playroom. The large sitting room is also used for various meetings during the day.

During the assessment period, children of school age attend the hospital Day Unit for three full days and two half days per week, a full day being from 9.30 a.m. to 3 p.m. This unit is staffed by a qualified teacher and three nurses, and managed by the principal child psychotherapist. At the end of the assessment period, a decision is made, in collaboration with the parents, as to whether or not a child will benefit from continuing to attend the Day Unit. If not, it may be more appropriate for the child to attend an ordinary school locally, or to return to his or her school if it is nearby.

In the Family and Adolescent Unit, patients and nurses share responsibility for cleaning, maintaining and decorating the living areas; they are also both involved in childcare, shopping, cooking and generally maintaining the necessary routine of daily life. As Macklin (1978, p.1) says, 'It may seem that when patients are capable of taking such responsibility and carrying out such work, they do not need a nurse to work with them. But if the nurse leaves the patients to work alone, she has missed the point of her job. She does not join the patients in work necessarily because assistance is needed, but rather as an opportunity to make a relationship which is the basis of their work together and which is an area of study for the patient, the nurse and the therapist.' As we shall discuss fully later, the nurse makes a valuable observational and therapeutic contribution through involvement in everyday activities which become the focus of therapeutic work, and through joint work and supervision with the therapist.

As well as doing things together, patients and nurses on each unit meet in a group each day. The group's purpose is to provide a setting in which the coming day's events can be anticipated, the previous day's events explored and understood and information shared. In short, it is a setting in which the necessary thinking can be done to support the ordinary processes of living. In one of the families nursed some years ago, this particular daily event was taken on by a family at home. The 'B' family spent a couple of weeks away from the hospital towards the end of their treatment period, to see how they managed prior to thinking about discharge. At the last minute, Mrs B had to go to the north of England to be with her ill mother. Mr B and the three children, aged six, four and two, were left at home to fend for themselves, something that Mr B had in the past found extremely stressful and sometimes overwhelming. On their return to the hospital, Mr B reported that he had managed quite well in his wife's absence. It transpired that he had had a meeting with the children each morning, to decide what they would do for the day.

When families come to the hospital, they are expected and encouraged to take part in the life of the patient community. Here, it is hoped, the difficulties that they may have been trying to avoid can re-emerge, this time in an environment which is safe and open enough for anxieties, conflicts, hostilities, fears and also strengths and successes to be explored. Therefore, rather than colluding with the patients wishes that the conflicts be removed, we try to support them in owning and making sense of their feelings and experiences.

For example, in one family it was very painful for the mother to look after her younger daughter, a baby of five months. The mother reported that she was afraid she might hit or in some way damage the baby, and that one of the most dangerous times was around feeding. She made it clear that she expected the nurses to have an efficient technique at their disposal, a formula that would make her feel better. She made it equally clear that she would not trust other patients to help her.

In order to support her in continuing to care for the baby, and so as to create a safe enough environment for this to happen, we arranged for a nurse and patient to be with her and the baby at feeding times. Although this did not fit in with her wishes, the presence of other people usually helped her to contain her feelings enough to function. It also enabled other patients to be in touch with her difficulties. She was encouraged to use a weekly parents' meeting, as well as her psychotherapy sessions, to explore the situation further.

Keeping patients in touch with one another is, in our opinion, an essential aspect of treatment in a community which strives to be therapeutic to its members. Such an approach implies some recognition that people with disabling neurotic difficulties also have skills and resources, perceptions and experiences, the sharing of which can contribute greatly to the life of the hospital community and to the treatment of individuals. The nursing task in supporting the daily work of the hospital is to create an environment where patients can be involved with one another in a way that recognizes and uses these resources. We think that the degree to which these relationships promote responsibility for oneself and concern for others, rather than passive dependency, institutionalization and regression, is a measure of the community's therapeutic potential.

An example of our approach to dependency is in how the hospital deals with night time. Only one nurse is on duty in the hospital; she is expected to go to sleep after 11.30 p.m. That is, there is an expectation that the community goes to sleep and does not have its 'therapy' outside daytime sessions. The duty nurse can be called up by a night orderly but the nurse then takes off time from the following day shift, thus discouraging her from being called. In cases of emergency, there is an on-call team including senior medical and nursing staff. The nurse may feel it necessary to call a community meeting of all patients to deal with a crisis, or may arrange a rota of patients to stay up with an acutely suicidal patient.

In order to make in-patient treatment possible and effective, specific techniques have been developed by the hospital over many years, some of which have already been mentioned. Interpretation of *transference phenomena*, however, remains central to the thinking involved in treatment, as it does in classical psychoanalytic treatment. Moreover, attention is given to a variety of transference phenomena not usually looked at by psychoanalysis. There is for example transference to the hospital structure, transference to various groups and to individual workers. And far from being a distorting intrusion into the analytic process, these 'split' transferences become valuable therapeutic tools. As Brian Muir discusses in his paper (p. 64), in-patient psychotherapy can be a highly sophisticated activity 'because it is possible to get a whole view of the patient and then choose different transference interpretations to evoke or leave out,according to what seems most facilitating of reality testing'. However, it is also a very complicated business, requiring considerable skill, constant monitoring of day-to-day events in a daily staff meeting (chaired by the consultant, who is a psychoanalyst, or a senior nurse), and regular supervision by experienced senior staff. A main task of the latter is to help tease out major themes in the hospital and unit at any one time, and relate these themes to individual patients. Another task is to 'metabolize' staff anxieties and to support the staff, who are daily subjected to intense emotional pressure in dealing with disturbing and disturbed patients. They will also use staff anxieties and induced disagreements as observational and therapeutic tools.

Brian Muir and Lydia Tischler (p. 97) also touch on the question of confidentiality and the complicated issue about how much can be kept secret with safety in the hospital. As Muir explains 'the classification and reclassification of patient material of a private kind from individual sessions is a complicated and vital aspect of the work at the Cassel. A difficult matter is the amount and detail that the the therapist tells the patient's nurse about what is said in sessions, and also what the patient believes the therapist will or will not tell the nurse'. As Tischler describes, in nurse/therapist supervisions, what is most useful is not that the therapist tells the nurse the exact content of session material, but that the therapist is in touch with the various countertransference issues, as well as the fantasies that the patient may have about the nurse, or about the relationship between nurse and the therapist. Although fear of betraying confidences is common amongst therapists new to the hospital, in practice it is rarely a major problem, in the sense that there do not often arise situations in which a major confidence is asked to be kept. As it happens, when it does occur it is just as likely that the nurse will be the confidante as the therapist. In fact, it has been found time and again that maintaining secrets with individual staff members leads to dangerous and sometimes suicidal situations for the patient; that the staff member is not acting in the patient's best interests in keeping the secret, for the secret is usually indicative of an attempt to create unhealthy splits in the staff group. This is a reflection of the patient's pathology. Thus, confidentiality of issues often resolve into therapeutic rather than ethical issues.

We will now outline the main themes of each of the papers we have collected. Roger Kennedy's paper, 'Work of the day', opens Part One, the theoretical section. Its aim is to link the work of the hospital with the classical thought of Freud, in particular relating the significance of everyday activities to the place and function that Freud ascribed to the day's residues and waking thoughts in the formation and interpretation of dreams. In addition, the paper describes, with clinical examples, the central occupations of the hospital's treatment of families, the nature of family breakdown, how the hospital pays focal attention to the work of the day in the treatment situation, and how everyday life becomes the focus for the detailed work of analyzing sources of disability and distress. This paper sets the tone for the rest of the book, which will in various ways elaborate on its themes.

Alan Wilson's 'An outline of work with families at the Cassel' gives a resumé, in an historical context, of the hospital's basic work with families, emphasizing how such work is an integral part of the total psychotherapeutic community of the hospital. He describes, with a clinical example, how the real events of the day in terms of ordinary living give rise to the therapeutic work on the Family Unit, and how our aim is to undertake a style of focussed or focal therapy, the focal formulation making it possible to unify and adjust staff work with the family and other patients, both in terms of content and level of work at any particular time.

Brian Muir's paper, 'Is in-patient psychotherapy a valid concept?' does not deal specifically with families or adolescents, but addresses itself to some of the basic questions about in-patient therapy, relevant to all patients. For example, he discusses the effect of admission on a patient, the assessment of the patient in the setting of the hospital, the aims, objects and limits of therapy, the place of nursing and the function of the community, the question of regression including its management and containment, and the nature of psychotherapy with special reference to transference in the in-patient setting.

Oliver James' paper, 'The role of the nurse/therapist relationship in the therapeutic community' describes in mainly theoretical terms the model of the nurse/therapist relationship. James uses Winnicott's concept of using and relating to objects to show how the nurse is the object of progress in relating. He describes how psychotherapy in the in-patient setting should take as its *primary* task the facilitation of the nurse/therapist relationship.

Lydia Tischler's paper, 'Nurse/therapist supervision' concludes the theoretical section. Her paper is clinically-orientated. It describes how we monitor the nurse/therapist relationship in special supervisions, and how this becomes an integral part of the patients' treatment. Tischler's paper deals with a theme that is now at the heart of the work of the Cassel and which will come up repeatedly in the book: the creation of an overall therapeutic strategy unifying psychosocial nursing and psychotherapy, continuously supported by an analysis of inter-staff strain and perception, especially between nurse and therapist.

Part Two on clinical work opens with Richard Burman's paper, 'Regressive distortions in a psychotherapeutic community'. He describes, with clinical illustrations from work with families, how patients may regress on admission and the form the regression may take. As Brian Muir points out in his paper, one of the dangers in hospital is that of encouraging patients to regress into dependency; this may relieve professional anxiety, but it will not foster change. The aim of treatment is to accept a degree of 'regression to vulnerability but a retaining of responsibility'.

Burman describes the inevitable results of admission, that of a regressive disturbance, and shows how one needs to pay close attention to this if a 'useful' regression is to be maintained. He also discusses some of the pressures that staff are subjected to by patients, such as demands for sudden changes in the existing treatment arrangements, or for a particular staff member to go against expected arrangements. He shows how staff can be seduced into believing that they are being flexible, but how they really may be identifying with an unconscious attack on their own structures. The staff at the Cassel are daily subjected to such pressures, which reflect the extreme pathology of the patients we treat: the inevitable pull of regressive forces is an attempt to undermine the process of facing conflicts. Rather than shying away from such forces, pretending that they do not exist or drugging patients so that there is no need for them to think, we believe it imperative to face the problem head on, but we do so with a firm if flexible and constantly adaptable therapeutic structure.

Trevor Hartnup's paper, 'Psychotherapy or placement for the troubled adolescent', came out of a conference we arranged for social workers in the North West Thames Regional Health Authority. As he describes, 'both the paper and the title of the study day sprang from the experience of in-patient psychotherapy, where the adolescents referred and treated are both troubled in themselves and often so troublesome to parents or residential social workers that the question of placement is under consideration'. Through examination of the nature of adolescent pathology and development and the hospital's working structures, Hartnup attempts to provide a model of how other professionals may achieve an effective working partnership. He addresses himself to the inevitable tensions that arise among staff at the hospital because of the nature of their expectations and because of the pathology of the troubled adolescent. In particular, he deals with the tensions arising between the nurse and therapist, explaining how we can attempt to face these tensions and use them therapeutically. This is very much the theme of most of our current work and forms a considerable part of the content of this book.

John Woods, in 'An adolescent patient's relationship with her nurse as a focus for treatment' describes in clinical detail the application of the hospital's ideas on the nurse/therapist relationship to the treatment of a disturbed adolescent girl, Joan. He focuses on three particular areas of work: Joan's signing on for unemployment benefit, the difficulties Joan experiences over a change of bedrooms, and her leaving the hospital. The description aims to show the value of maintaining the nurse and therapist's distinct but connected modes of functioning, and how alterations in the nature of the nurse/therapist relationship exposed Joan's inner conflicts. Woods feels that there is a parallel in this work with the work of the individual psychoanalyst: 'Nurse and therapist together perform the task undertaken by the analyst that is the measuring of what the analyst is being 'made to feel' by the patient's projections against the analyst's own reality'.

George Leach's nursing study focusses particularly on the way that nurse/therapist supervisions affected the nursing work and helped the family he describes to become engaged in treatment. Although the family was admitted as an emergency, they came to regard the hospital itself as the source of their problems. Their ambivalence about treatment was reflected in supervisions, which provided an insight into the dynamics of the family, and enabled the nurse to work with issues of distancing, denial and splitting.

Mary-Ann Munford's care study, 'Working with a disturbed adolescent boy in a psychotherapeutic community', shows the nursing management of a patient, John, who needed a considerable amount of time and detailed planning to help him through his treatment. On admission, John was on large doses of major tranquillizers; when these were removed, he revealed considerable difficulties, with periods of suicidal depression. The account shows in vivid detail how careful nursing care plans are developed to help deal with and hold such deeply disturbed patients without drugs.

Anne Zachary's 'A new look at the vulnerability of puerperal mothers' deals with the effects of families on the staff, the staff's countertransference feelings, and how the staff carry on and respond to powerful projections. She reviews previous writings about work at the Cassel with puerperal mothers, and gives a vivid and detailed account of two patients recently treated with their families. The emphasis of the paper is on the therapy material, but the nursing and community structures around the family are also described, using nursing observations.

Denis Flynn's paper 'The child's view of the hospital: an examination of the child's experience of an in-patient setting', examines the rationale of focussing on work with the children at the hospital. He gives a number of illustrations of the child's view of the hospital, and how listening to the child's view within the family is fundamental to our work with families, as well as being an integral part of the wider therapeutic community treatment. He also examines his theme within the context of a description of the psychotherapy of a six-year-old boy admitted with his family.

His paper leads on to 'Observations on family functioning in an in-patient setting' by Lydia Tischler and Trevor Hartnup, which focusses on family dynamics but with the child's point of view in the foreground. Staff dynamics are not specifically discussed here. What distinguishes work with families at the Cassel, and what our work has in common with the Tavistock Clinic's family therapy workshop (see Box et al, 1981), is an analytic approach to therapy, and also an attitude whereby we respect the child's point of view and his or her inner world. Tischler and Hartnup emphasize the importance of this attitude, and describe what makes the hospital setting therapeutic: the integration of nursing, educational and consulting room settings.

Sheila Ashley's paper 'Good baby, bad baby: exploring a mother's perception', describes in detail an aspect of the nursing work of a mother and one of her children. She examines the difficulties for both parents and staff in working with parents who have experienced a deprived childhood, and the difficulty such parents have in avoiding the repetition of deprivation with their own children.

Petrie Thompson's paper, 'An account of the early stages of treatment with an in-patient family', is a summary of the treatment of a difficult family who had exhausted all previous forms of treatment, and who tried to repeat this in the hospital by attempting to split the staff. He charts how the staff attempted to resist the family's pressures and encourage a therapeutic relationship.

The paper by Luigi Caparotta and Judith Burman, 'Notes and vicissitudes of a confused and confusing family', is a brief account of the treatment of a family who constantly induced in the workers a sense of confusion and boredom. The authors, confining themselves to therapy material, illustrate how these feelings were put to therapeutic use; in particular, they show how, through the use of the Cassel's therapeutic structures, the parents were able to become more separate from each other and then attend more appropriately to their children's needs. Although not dealing specifically with community or nurse/therapist issues, the authors aim to illustrate one aspect of the treatment of families at the Cassel: the basic psychotherapeutic work.

In the paper by Irene Wineman-Marcus, 'Facilitating a child's removal into foster care', the process of allowing a child to enter into foster care because of inadequate parenting is described. The author also discusses the specific way the Cassel deals with such a stressful and difficult task.

The section on clinical work closes with Vivien Bigg's paper, 'The in-patients' views of the Cassel experience', which describes the results of her interviews with 11 in-patients after their discharge from the Family Unit. She describes how patients recall and value the life of the hospital community more vividly than the individual therapy they have had. We return to this theme in the Conclusion of the book.

The last section of the book, Part Three, comprises two papers which cover more general, theoretical aspects of the therapeutic community, although both papers also use clinical material drawn from work with families. We felt it important to include these papers, as they illustrate ongoing thinking of the hospital and provide the backdrop to the ordinary day-to-day work.

The paper by Oliver James and Alan Wilson, 'A sexually charged clinical problem: social, structural and classical psychoanalytic approaches', is one of a series of papers produced as a result of a collaborative study between members of the Brunel Institute of Organizational and Social Studies and staff and patients at the Cassel. Durkheimian and psychoanalytic functionalist views of the role of social structure in therapy are contrasted; a unifying social psychological position is offered as an alternative which is appropriate to the Cassel's attempt to unify psychotherapeutic and social structures.

Gillian Chapman's 'Social action theory and psychosocial nursing' offers a different viewpoint to that proposed by James and Wilson. She poses a theoretical model of nursing, and explores the coincidence of interests and intents between social action theorists such as Giddens and Silverman, and therapeutic community structure and psychosocial nursing. She believes that their theory focusses on areas such as everyday functioning that are particularly relevant to the Cassel's nursing work. She illustrates her views through the examination of the nursing care of an in-patient family. She also focusses on the central role of everyday activities and on the sophisticated and complex task of nursing which calls upon a number of different responses.

Elsie Buckenham's short paper, 'Hospital administration in a therapeutic community', gives an outline of the way that administration is seen as an integral part of the clinical work at the Cassel. It also illustrates how we try to examine splittings in every area of institutional work, including that between administrative and therapeutic staff.

We end the book with a Conclusion which summarizes our views and ideas, and attempts some discussion of their application.

One area of special importance is the continual discovery that problems thrown up by intense in-patient psychoanalytically-orientated treatment not only do not disturb the analytic frame, but rather contribute to a deeper understanding of analytically-orientated treatment in general. This is because they bring to a focus issues such as splitting of the transference, confidentiality, and disrupted analytic settings which are met in all analytic practice in a less intense form. What we have had to deal with, as a necessity, has forced us to grapple with both theoretical and practical issues that could be more easily put aside in individual practice. We have, of course, emphasized here the enormous contribution that psychoanalysis makes to institutional treatment of severe disturbances; the former point needs, however, to be equally well-established.

Part One
Theory

[1]

Work of the Day
Aspects of Work with Families at the Cassel Hospital

Roger Kennedy

The work of the day

I WISH TO DISCUSS some aspects of recent work with families in the Cassel Hospital, an in-patient therapeutic community run on psychoanalytic lines. Some of these ideas may be relevant to the psychoanalytic treatment of individuals and families as out-patients. This paper is deeply indebted to the previous work at the Cassel Hospital of Dr Tom Main. One of his achievements was to transform a model of in-patient treatment of mental disturbance in which regressed patients were being attended to and passively nursed to that of the active patient, actively involved in psychotherapy and the nursing process. I put forward the simple idea in this paper that central to this new model is the notion of what I call the ordinary *work of the day* around which is focussed both psychotherapy and the nursing work. I am limiting the concept of the work of the day so that it does not refer merely to everything that happens in the day, but only to those events which are significant in some way to the individual and his or her family, or which have precipitated some kind of thought process and/or action. Thus, the work of the day would include unsolved problems, major worries, overwhelming experiences, undigested thoughts, forbidden or unsolved thoughts, what has been rejected and suppressed and what has been set in motion in the unconscious by the activity of the preconscious and consciousness. It refers to all the significant, and at times deceptively indifferent, thoughts, feelings and experiences that have occupied us during the day, and which provide the raw material for thinking and for dreaming. The work of the day is what gives material for thought and provides the basic framework of living.

Much of this work normally carries on automatically without the subject being particularly aware of its regular occurrence or of its 'everydayness', and without the subject giving it much attention. The work is normally taken for granted, and yet it is far from simple in nature, as one can see from the treatment of disturbed families and individuals where such basic work has broken down. The work of the day is normally focussed around essential activities and events such as eating, sleeping and working. Such events, ritualized and structured to a varied extent, provide the emotional context that drives practical life. Our reliance on everyday structures and rituals, however sophisticated, to hold us together may have something to do with the nature of our emotional life, in which feelings are often fleeting; we seem to need something solid and relatively unchanging to help us pin our feelings down in order that we may acknowledge or study them. It would appear, then, that a major task of the work of the day is, as it were, to enable us to 'discover' our emotions through ordinary events. Such events, even though they may seem trivial, form common human intercourse, and provide the basis for intimacy. Indeed, one could say that true intimacy between people often consists of being with each other in ordinary, everyday situations without feeling awkward.

Normally one performs the activities of the day without thinking about their basic structure; rather, the basic structure provides material for thinking. However, in the patients I am discussing, the things most people do without thinking are charged with emotion and conflict, and this involves the breakdown in continuity and consistency of daily life. The life of the day is not 'held together'. One could describe this in Winnicott's terms as a breakdown in the family's 'holding' environment.

There are some similarities between what I have called the work of the day and the place and function that Freud ascribed to the day's residues and waking thoughts in the formation and interpretation of dreams. Freud emphasized the importance of recent events and the relevance of waking thoughts in the instigation of dreams. The significance of recent events and fresh impressions has not had time to be lost through the processes of repression. The instigating agent of a dream is found among the experiences which the subject has not yet 'slept on', i.e. these are often undigested experiences. Freud described how the material that has occupied us during the day dominates the dream, and how one can understand dreams as a continuation of waking life. Displacement and the use of indirect representation are mainly responsible for the dream's puzzling appearance which disguises this continuity. Freud wrote (S.E.4, p.177) that the 'analysis of dreams will regularly reveal its true, psychically significant source in waking life, though the emphasis has been displaced from the recollection of that source onto that of an indifferent one'. Freud also wrote that the day's residues (S.E.12, p.273) 'have the most numerous and varied meanings; they may be wishes or fears that have not been disposed of, or intentions, reflections, warnings, attempts at adaptation to current tasks, and so on'. The day's residues are thus the psychical material for the dreamwork to act upon.

The unconscious wish is the essential additional factor in the construction of the dream. This wish can come to expression in the day's residues and can supply them with a force which enables them to press their way to consciousness. Particular unconscious conflicts can be, as it were, 'hooked' or 'transferred' onto the recent material; and the latter can provide a point of attachment for such conflicts. Similarly, returning to the theme of the paper, one could say that the unconscious weaves its connections around the work of the day. In psychoanalytic treatment, one may be looking for past conflicts through the processes of reconstruction and interpretation of the transference, and yet one hopes very much that one is working with fresh material from recent events, that is, from the work of the day, as such material has not yet been bogged down by the processes of repression, and is often rich in content. Indeed, one could go so far as to say that as long as the present and the ordinary events of a patient's life are in the treatment, one can more easily uncover the repressions of the past. As Freud demonstrated in *The Psychopathology of Everyday Life* (S.E.6) one is often led from the commonplace to the psychically significant. However, I am also emphasizing the psychical significance of ordinary events, not only as a point of attachment for unconscious conflicts, but in their own right as the framework for living.

The breakdown of the work of the day

The Cassel Hospital provides a unique opportunity for looking at the day-to-day, week-to-week living arrangements of families. The families we treat are in general in an extreme state of breakdown and are often barely able to cope with the ordinary tasks of living together. One often also notices that they have begun to drain the resources and patience of involved professionals in the world outside the hospital. There is often, for example, the threat or reality of a care order to one or more members of the family, or the threat that a member of the family will leave home. During our assessment procedures we try, among other things, to look at how families bring in their own pathology and 'living space' into the hospital; that is, how they bring in the pieces of their reality and repeat their breakdown within the hospital. This breakdown, both in an individual and his or her family, can be seen as a piece of inner reality that has not stood up to social reality, where there has been a conflict between the family and their milieu. This is obviously repeated on admission to the hospital in one way or another; however, it takes different families a different span of time for this repetition to occur. The repetition seems to have a time course of its own.

There are many factors leading to family breakdown. These include individual factors such as an important member of the family who is strained, who may have an individual breakdown or illness. There may, on the other hand, be group factors in the family; that is, the family may not function effectively as a group. There may be chance events or important life events; there may also be developmental factors, for example, the challenge to the family's functioning that is made by the maturing of an adolescent child. One often finds in such families that the work of the day has broken down in the outside world and that ordinary tasks are not given enough attention. When this occurs, the family or particular vulnerable members of the family may well be subjected to overwhelming anxieties. The work of the day may break down when there has been severe social stress or when there has been what I call 'malignant splitting' in the family, i.e. a repeated and intense use of primitive splitting mechanisms in the family's object relations, common to most of the families we happen to treat, which interferes in a major way with the family's capacity to attend to normal functions, or a breakdown of the normal social barriers, for example, when there has been sexual abuse by one member of the family of one or more other members.

Although we see a wide range of both individual and family psychopathology, I think one can make the general point that in a number of these families one can see a breakdown in the process of working over or metabolizing thoughts and feelings from hour to hour, day to day and from week to week. That is, there is a breakdown in the day's structure that provides the material for thinking and enables the subject to discover his or her feelings. Normal events are then experienced as persecutory and lacking in continuity; thinking about them seems painful and useless. The physical and psychic 'bricks and mortar' of the family home become loose and fragmentary, and the capacity to keep partners and children in mind becomes eroded. An increasingly wide gap appears between the parents' knowledge of their family life and their capacities to use this knowledge. Some families reach a point where they seem hardly able to attend to events such as organizing mealtimes or bedtimes; in addition they often resort to impulsive actions as a way of trying to get the environment to respond to their needs.

As is well known, one often finds that one or more parents of such families have suffered from fairly severe emotional or physical deprivation in childhood. In more theoretical terms, one could speculate that there has been an absence of the primary infantile experience of satisfaction, what Freud called the 'bedrock of psychic life' (S.E.5,p.602). These parents seem to have experienced a repetitious absence of satisfaction in their childhood, as a result of parental or social deprivation. As adults, they often try to seek some satisfaction, but in unsatisfactory ways. For example, many deprived patients feel desperately needy, and have a hope or a fantasy that the damage done to them can be totally made up. This may lead to a desperate search for resources, for example from professional workers, but the patients will never feel that what they get is good enough. They thus tend to drain the patience and capacities of those who try to help them, and so end up repeating the absence of satisfaction which they were apparently so desperately seeking to avoid. It is noteworthy in this context that we often find a family, on admission to the hospital, to be in severe financial debt, with a related housing crisis.

On this topic, I think that one can describe at least two kinds of debt. Firstly, there is the debt in which one owes something to someone which has to be repaid: one could call this a negative, owing debt. Secondly, there is positive debt, in which one is indebted to somebody but there is no need to pay back what one has received. One could perhaps see a negative debt in families when there is a rigid, repetitious link with a deprived past; this can, in fact, never be really paid back or done away with, that is, when there is always an overdraft to the past. A positive debt obviously refers to an experience of effective parenting and is linked to some hopeful prospect about the future, when there is some kind of positive balance in the family's resources.

In the members of the families that I am describing, who to all intents and purposes have never had much basic experience of satisfaction, rational thinking has in Freud's terms never come to 'safeguard' the primary processes. Freud (S.E.12, p.223) wrote that 'the substitution of the reality principle for the pleasure principle implies no deposing of the pleasure principle, but a mere safeguarding of it: a momentary pleasure, uncertain in its results, is given up, but only in order to gain along the new path an assured pleasure at a later time'. However, with the families we treat there is often a fantasy present that thinking interferes with their life and is both persecutory and unhelpful. Putting the situation simply, the patients avoid the possibility of acknowledging their distress and of allowing themselves to have thoughts. In addition, there may be a pattern of turning to an inner, precarious fantasy object or attempting to make an external object fit in with the inner fantasy object; there may be also sometimes a turning to 'alternative resources' such as drugs or perverse sexual excitement. What such patients do to their objects can also be seen as an agressive attack on their own internal parents. This latter attack may be contained in their symptoms. For example, when real parents neglect their real children this may represent an attack on the internal parents. This could also be seen as turning a passive childish experience into an active adult one. We often see this in those adult patients in the hospital who apparently want constant parenting, or appear very needy, and yet, in spite of considerable efforts by staff and other patients, avoid effectively using hospital structures or any kind of out-patient psychotherapy. Instead, they constantly and desperately bite the hand that feeds them; at the same time, they seem unaware of the aggressive aspect of their demands. Such patients are well described by Tom Main in his classic paper, 'The ailment'.

Another major theme, central in trying to understand the origin of the breakdown of the work of the day, is how the parents in these families often feel they cannot take on their role as parents, at least for a whole day. This may occur for a variety of reasons, such as a lack of their own parenting, their immaturity, the envy they may feel towards their children, or social pressures. One could in general say that the birth and presence of a child are highly complex and powerful for the adult. A child may awaken past conflicts and re-open old narcissistic wounds; the adult may be quite capable of inter-adult relations, but quite incapable of responding to the child. One often sees in families in the hospital how difficult it may be for some parents on the one hand to keep their adult capacities and ability to respond to their children separate and intact, and on the other, to satisfy their own child-like dependency needs. In extreme situations, the child's presence may precipitate such a disruption in mental functioning that the child will be subjected to primitive and unmodified psychic or, indeed, physical attacks at the hands of the adult, who can no longer distinguish the child from the unwanted bad parts of themselves. The child may also become the object which unites or divides a family; the child will then be, as it were, a 'child object' for the family, a mere function and not a person. One might also speculate that the breakdown in the parents' parenting and in their ability to attend to the basic events around the child's day is linked to an earlier breakdown in their own parenting, either at adolescence, or perhaps at the period of primary parental pre-occupation, when the parents had to keep the child actively in the front of their mind for much of the day. There would often seem to be the repetition of a basic gap in the parents' thinking as it concerns the child.

The work we do at the Cassel hospital with families involves a unification of psychoanalytic psychotherapy and psychosocial nursing. The purpose of this paper is not to describe the details of this work, except insofar as they are relevant to the main theme. In general one could say that the hospital pays particular and focal attention to the work of the day in the total treatment of individuals and families. It becomes the focus for the detailed work of analysing sources of disability and distress. In particular, we look at what happens during the day, at events such as eating, feeding of babies, night time preparation tasks such as cleaning, and structured meetings. The achievements and conflicts from day to day and from week to week around these events become a central focus of attention. Neuroses, like dreams, have a preference for belittling the importance of the details of working life and neglecting them to a realm of indifference. As Freud wrote

(S.E.12,p.218) 'every neurosis has as its result the forcing of the patient out of real life'. However, the Cassel hospital focuses on these details; all the penumbra of resistances, denials, associa tions and material that occupies the hospital during the day be comes a main agent of treatment and hopefully of change; and it is hoped that such material provides the focus, or at very least the background, for both the individual psychotherapy and the detailed nursing work. Severe splitting mechanisms, common to many of the patients we treat, have a tendency to obscure individual emotions and conflicts. For this reason, we put particular emphasis on the details of what has happened to particular individuals and what they have experienced, and on what work the nurse and therapist of a particular patient are doing. We also try to find out about the nature of the particular nurse/therapist relationship (see Oliver James, p. 78); we emphasize the individuality of the patient's feelings and provide a framework for individualized thinking. At the same time, there are a number of different group activities in the hospital. We do not believe in the idea of the function of the group as an analyst; however, we see the group has certain useful functions: for example, it may serve as a mediator of projections, as well as the unique source of information of unconscious processes. In general, through individual and small group supervision, staff meetings, and, in particular, the supervision of the relationship between the nurse and therapist of particular patients, we aim to provide a setting for the patient's reflection on him or herself and for the registration and understanding of distorted communications and distorted relations. At the same time, as Alan Wilson puts it (p. 63) 'the psychotherapeutic community is not a stable, polite society: it is a prescription of uncertainty...free association, but free association observed with focal attention'. The hospital does not, on the one hand, provide rigid rules nor, on the other hand, does it believe in free-for-all, unbounded chaos. It aims to provide daily structures in which uncertainty and indeterminateness can be tolerated and worked with. In particular, in our treatment of families we aim to work with and support the parents' 'authority'. This refers to the parents' capacity to allow and tolerate a child to be dependent on them and to appreciate the child's world, with its need for good enough security, flexibility, warmth and understanding on a day-to-day, hour-by-hour basis. It is our experience that there are a number of disturbed families who need in-patient treatment because such basic daily work has broken down in the outside world, making them no longer viable as a unit. Our major aim is often to enable such families to recover or discover their capacities to deal with the 'bricks and mortar' of their physical and psychic home. To a greater or lesser extent, such therapeutic work may be more important to these families, at least at the time of their admission, than more traditional understanding of the psychopathology of the individual members, although this work, also usually continues during admission.

Clinical examples

The following examples attempt to show how essential activities in the families' functioning can break down.

'A' family : feeding time

This family was admitted as an emergency following a domiciliary visit. The problem was that the mother was suffering from a severe post-natal depression after the birth of her second girl baby. Mrs A was depressed, distraught and said that she felt unable to stay in her own home. Although the birth was satisfactory, Mrs A said that she had problems feeding the baby. The baby refused to take anything from the bottle and would cry as if in anger. The mother described this supposed failure at feeding as the trigger of her problems and she started to feel anxious, panicky, inadequate and tearful, with increasing intensity, until her admission when the baby was five months old. 'I feel so guilty', said Mrs A, 'I'm not giving her what she wants, I'm not special to her; after all, anyone can give her a bottle'.

The crisis point was reached when Mrs A lost control and shut herself in the bedroom screaming, not able to deal with the baby's crying. She felt she was on a knife edge; she was afraid of losing control and afraid of slipping into madness; at the same time, she felt it would be nice to regress to a childlike state and to be looked after. Mrs A was able to respond quite well to both her children, but only separately. There were major problems at feeding time, when she seemed unable to cope with the two children together. In addition, the two year old would rush around at meals trying to get her mother's attention; indeed when Mrs A was feeding the baby the older child used to writhe around on the floor screaming. Mr A in general felt inadequate and unable to support his wife in the way she felt would be helpful. This made him feel angry, but he was unable to express this anger.

Most of Mrs A's anxieties were increased at feeding times. These anxieties included a feeling of wanting to run away, thoughts of disappearing in a puff of smoke, and suicidal preoccupations. She felt trapped when the baby wouldn't feed; the baby's demands made her feel inadequate and overwhelmed. While disappointed at giving up breast feeding after two months she was also concerned at her own weight loss. In therapy sessions she at first disclosed how closely she identified with the baby; she said how she wished to become very much like a little girl herself and admitted that she wanted to be held, cuddled, fed and looked after.

The first area of attention in treatment was the mother/child relationship, with particular emphasis on feeding, as so many of the family's problems seemed to arise at this time or at any rate to be increased in intensity. It is interesting that as treatment proceeded, Mrs A revealed her own 'feeding' difficulties: a predominant feature of the family's early admission was the feeling of deadness that they provoked and evoked in other people. There was a massive denial of feelings of attachment to the hospital and to each other. Anything we offered the family was not accepted as good enough; Mrs A arranged a special kind of vegetarian meal for herself, and managed to arrange to have her meals before the other patients, which seemed to be indicative of her increasing social isolation in the hospital. She then revealed in detail a number of sadistic fantasies she had in relation to the baby. The family became outsiders in the Family Unit; they were unpopular, and would not accept our help as of any use. They constantly maintained the idea of discharging themselves in a month's time. They maintained this idea, in fact, for a number of months.

Staff at the Unit found that they were being intimidated by Mrs A's threats to leave, and exploited by her demands to be given very special treatment. While staff were disagreeing with each other, the family itself seemed to be doing very little in the hospital. However, when this was realized by the staff and then raised with the family, the treatment began to move. There was considerable work done on the theme of mourning, on difficulties in the couple's relationship as well as on work with the children. When a staff member produced the concept of presenting the family with a 'staying date' rather than a leaving date the treatment turned the corner. The family settled down to detailed work and there seemed at last to be a reasonable 'feeding' relationship between the family and the hospital; the family was considerably improved on discharge and at the six months follow-up.

'B' family : from crisis to crisis

The 'B' family was particularly hard to treat. Mrs B, the only available parent, had great difficulties in all areas of the work of the day. The family consisted of Mrs B and her three children, a boy aged six, and two girls aged four and five. Mrs B presented as if there were no severe problems; however, these periods of apparent calm were punctuated by repeated crises, which made it impossible for work to continue on an out-patient basis with several different agencies.

A main problem seemed to be the behaviour of the boy, who was administering medicine to his younger sisters; on two occasions the children had to be taken to hospital. The boy's behaviour was also difficult at school where he had become miserable, apathetic, unco-operative and unable to concentrate. In addition, he had also begun to soil. On consultation, the family were quite chaotic, with the children trying to run wild while the mother sat back passively.

Mrs B showed a very inconsistent attitude to the children, particularly towards the boy; she found it difficult to assert her authority with him. When she saw the failure of her inconsistent efforts to be obeyed, she resorted to physical violence. She then felt very guilty, afraid of being overwhelmed with anger and battering the boy to death. Mrs B and her son seemed locked in a projective system, in which he intended to represent the bad unwanted parts of his mother. Mrs B's own father was alcoholic and rejecting and had himself taken a number of overdoses, while her mother was weak and inconsistent. Her mother died when she was 13 and Mrs B then ran away from home. She and her siblings were not infrequently physically beaten.

It was particularly difficult to define a focus of work for the family after the initial assessment. Mrs B presented as mindless and not knowing what to do with her own children, although well able to look after other people's children. This feature of mindlessness, which at times seemed calculated, persisted throughout the admission. Instead of thinking about what to do, she tended to get other people to think for her, by her acting out. She would often impulsively return home, causing the children considerable distress and confusion. Typical of her attitude was the way she dealt with a bill for her water supply at home. The water had been turned off by the Water Board as the bill had not been paid for three years. Mrs B expressed surprise as she assumed that Social Services had been automatically paying it, in spite of her having had many reminders. Rather than negotiate with the authorities or with professionals, she wished to remain in the hospital over the weekend, because there would be no water at home. When this idea was challenged, she said that it did not matter anyway as she had a way of turning on the water without the authorities knowing – which she apparently succeeded in doing. She displayed little anxiety or insight about the episode, which was typical of many.

The episode illustrates firstly, her tendency to take flight from difficult situations; secondly, her difficulty in anticipation and planning; and thirdly, her difficulty in understanding the effects of her behaviour on the children, who felt confused by her. In addition, there was a sadistic quality to this denial of their needs and of her own authority as a parent. It was also noticeable that Mrs B had great difficulty in keeping the children in mind when they were not in her presence.

The psychotherapy sessions were also particularly difficult, as she tended to see interpretations and understanding as merely an attack on her capacities; the transference had an almost psychotic feel to it. Particularly distressing was the fact that as long as a programme for the boy's soiling took place in the hospital he was clean, but as soon as the family went home, Mrs B was unable to continue to follow the programme, and he returned to soiling.

The family improved in the hospital, where a structure was provided. However, Mrs B had great difficulty in taking the structure with her. Various attempts were made to understand this fact in psychodynamic terms, for example, means of interpretation in terms of her splitting and of her defence against overwhelming anxiety. Considerable efforts were made to help the family deal with day-to-day issues. However, there was only quite limited success.

'C' family : connecting and playing together

Mrs C, a woman in her early twenties, and her son James, aged 5, were referred in order to attempt to bring them together after a number of separations. Mrs C had been hospitalized following an overdose, and had shown great difficulties in coping with her son. Indeed, he had been put into care twice and was being fostered prior to admission.

Mrs C showed evidence of severe psychopathology with marked schizoid features, and a tendency to lapse into primary process thinking and action. For example, following her consultation, she shaved her head completely bald and mused about looking like a baby. Mrs C came from a large family of mixed race; her father was described as very strict and used physical punishment to discipline the family, who were expected to come at his beck and call. Her mother was described as sacrificing her life for her children; she still behaved as if they were all babies. Mrs C was intelligent and did well at a good school, but married aged 18; this interrupted her education. Her husband walked out when she became pregnant and did not take part in their subsequent life. James was a bright child, but difficult to manage because of his behaviour difficulties; in particular he had a large vocabulary of abusive language, which he often used.

An important dynamic in the mother/son relationship seemed to be a *faulty connection*. This was illustrated not only by their difficulties in staying together before admission, and Mrs C's incapacity to attend to James' needs, but also from birth, when there was a difficulty in breastfeeding. The story was that Mrs C was told that her nipples were not long enough; she attributed the great difficulty that she had in trying to feed James to this. She described how somehow James could never take the breast, and later on, how he was not interested in taking food from her.

In psychotherapy sessions in the hospital with Mrs C, there was also great difficulty in the 'connecting up' of the therapist and Mrs C. There were long silences; the therapist had a countertransference feeling that she was being shown what it felt like not to be in touch with what was going on in Mrs C's inner world. Mrs C often spoke in disjointed unfinished sentences, especially when describing her angry feelings with James, and she often talked as if she and the child were merged as one. She described the feeling that because she had James she must not talk about herself; however, she also realized that this was perpetuating her own mother's view of the world.

Initially, Mrs C was somewhat isolated in the hospital; she somehow missed being included in the community rota for washing up, breakfast duty and cooking. However, she worked efficiently in her work area which was the children's playroom and at children's teas; but it was difficult to share a task with her, and she gave people the feeling that she was just going through the motions. Her nurse felt that he had to do all the work in making contact with Mrs C. she brought nothing to him. James settled down to some extent in the Day Unit, but could only be managed on a one-to-one setting; his abusive swearing irritated both the staff and other children. As admission proceeded, Mrs C found a useful niche for herself in community cooking, and seemed to derive a genuine sense of personal validity from this role. Her sullen withdrawal from people and her resentful 'going through the motions' was challenged over the issue of how she managed children's tea time. In addition, a major piece of work, which facilitated Mrs C and James 'connecting up', was done when her therapist and nurse met both Mrs C and James for regular play sessions for a few weeks. Mrs C's capacity to play with James was encouraged, and some limited interpretation of symbolic material was made. Individual psychotherapy was subsequently arranged for James.

There were many improvements in the relationship between Mrs C and James. Attention to both the psychodynamic meaning of the resentment about being a mother and a capable adult, and attention to the basic work of being a mother during the day, seemed fundamental to the changes that took place; this enabled both of them to live together once more on a more stable footing.

'D' family : unsafe family

This family consisted of a mother and father in their thirties, a two-year-old boy and a six-month-old girl. The family were admitted because the baby was at risk from being battered, or at least from coming to some physical harm. Mrs D had had quite serious depression following the premature birth of the baby girl. It had been a very traumatic time in which the baby was in an incubator for long periods and had had a considerable amount of medical attention. Following this, the mother began to show clear signs of wanting to harm the baby, for example by tampering with the baby's feeds and shaking the baby very severely. Although there seemed a reasonable attachment to the two-year-old boy by both parents, the girl was handled, in particular by the mother, with very little interest and attachment.

The two main issues, initially and subsequently, were on the one hand to provide a safe network both in the hospital and outside, and also to provide a focus of work on the relationship between the parents and the children, in particular the lack of attachment between mother and baby. In order to facilitate both these aspects of the work, a considerable amount of attention was paid to the parents' own problems about dependency.

Both parents were educated, middle class professionals. Unfortunately, both of them had suffered major losses in the recent past; the only living close relative was the maternal grandmother, who was described as possessive and not interested in helping her children. Mrs D was herself the younger of two siblings.

We had to provide a constant focus of attention throughout the whole day, particularly for the mother and baby, which meant that, initially, she was not left unaccompanied at feeding times, although this subsequently was not necessary. Mrs D herself had a devouring quality to her; nothing seemed to her to be sufficient or good enough. She acidly rejected anything which she was offered, describing how qualified people in the helping professions seemed only to enjoy the privileged position because they had power. She also tended to stimulate in people fantasies of rescuing a helpless lost soul, but when anybody tried to help she tended to find it crushing and denigrating, and hence had to reject it.

Mr D had found that his own parents made him feel impotent and helpless; he felt he had an over-protective, all-giving, but essentially devaluing mother and a distant father. Both Mr and Mrs D looked down on the staff and on the therapy and did not want to show any feelings of dependency on them. They talked quite openly about how resentful they felt at having to be in the hospital. They made staff feel that there was something quite vicious and uncomfortable about them, and they also talked for a considerable amount of time about wishing to leave the hospital and so bring to a premature end their treatment.

We tried to foster, in a relatively non-persecuting way, an attempt by them to share what each of them had observed separately, so that they could use it together. We attempted to do this by providing a non-persecuting model of noticing and talking. It was discovered that one of the dynamics in the family was that taking notice of one thing seemed to imply ignoring something else. For example, Mr D felt that he was dropped if notice was being paid to his wife's anxieties. At the same time, Mrs D felt like dropping the baby, because if improvement was noticed, she feared that the family would be discharged.

The main focus of work became more and more the parents' inability to focus on the problem of separation and loss, linked in particular to their weekends at home. For example, they would consistently come back very late on a Sunday night, which meant that they were not able to have the Sunday meal with the other patients; it also meant that on the Monday morning the two-year-old boy was difficult to handle, and became quite disruptive for a while.

Therapy was primarily individually based, with both individual therapists coming together for occasional marital meetings; there were also occasional meetings of the whole family. The treatment was a success in that the situation of risk disappeared, and the family were able to leave feeling that they had got something constructive from their stay. The staff also felt that this was a success. However, the whole treatment had required considerable attention to almost every aspect of the work of the day, certainly for the first six months or so while the safety of the baby was doubtful. The treatment also necessitated the staff having to deal with considerable amounts of verbal attack from the parents. These attacks had to be metabolized and fed back in appropriate form, and this required that the senior staff paid particular attention to looking after the therapists.

EVENTS IN THE HOSPITAL

I have commented that material occupying the hospital during the day is used for therapeutic purposes for individual patients and families; the following example is designed to illustrate this theme.

In the weekly whole hospital staff group meeting, the following themes arose:

It was early September just after the summer break. It had recently been discovered that various consulting rooms had been broken into, which was quite an unusual occurrence at the hospital. There was talk of doors being left open and rooms being emptied or feeling empty. There was a query about whether or not confidential material had been seen. There was a feeling that this was one example of intrusions into private areas which perhaps were taking place in other areas of the hospital, outside the consulting rooms. There had been one or two major staff changes recently; people were feeling that boundaries between members of staff were shifting and new boundaries being made. In addition, there had been a recent increase of night time disturbances in which the duty nurse had been put under considerable stress and had to do more work than is customary in order to help patients settle for the night.

In the staff group, a specific family then became the focus of discussion. This family whom I shall call the 'E' family consisted of a mother, father and baby aged nine months. This particular family had been admitted as an emergency following a domiciliary visit, as the mother was in a severe state of post-natal depression and could no longer look after the baby.

They had a rather horrific history in that their first child was born severely brain damaged; this was probably related to a severe ante-natal haemorrhage in the pregnancy. Although the doctors looking after this first child felt that it should be allowed to die as it was so severely damaged, Mr and Mrs E managed to keep the baby alive for some eight months by means of intensive nursing care, in which they would take turns for virtually 24 hours in a day to keep it alive. The baby finally died when Mr and Mrs E gave it back to the hospital to care for for a week or so, so that they could have a rest. Just at this time Mrs E conceived a new baby. She subsequently had great difficulty in attaching herself to it and could hardly differentiate the dead baby from her live baby. In addition, there was both a violent marital relationship with constant rows, as well as severe obsessional near psychotic psychopathology in Mrs E.

Following the general themes in the staff group, it was then discovered that the E family had become special patients. It was recognized that they did not attend any of the daily work groups in which all patients participate with nurses, to look after areas of the hospital. They had not been going home on weekends for many weeks, so that there had been absolutely no differentiation of boundaries between the week and the weekend. This was also most unusual, as it is an expectation that families go home for the weekend in order to maintain contact with their outside world, unless there is a very special reason for them not to be doing so. The family were not on a community cooking rota; other patients had become fed up with doing everything for them, and in addition there were quite marked differences of opinion in the nurse and therapist of Mrs E, resulting in the therapist realizing that she should take up much more of the patient's hostility towards her in the transference.

It was realized that by coupling the general themes of the group with this particular family, there was something to be learnt about the family's psychopathology and how the hospital were (or perhaps were not) dealing with it. The empty rooms in the hospital seemed to be related to the empty space in Mrs E in which there was no new baby. Mr and Mrs E wished for special intensive care with no boundaries, with no return home on the weekend. They also wished to remain in their own private world, which was against the expectations of living in a community. They felt that sharing their private world was an intrusion into their rigidly held private space, rather than a chance to be able to share anxieties.

After this meeting, the staff from the Family Unit was able to take up much more vigorously what the family had been doing and what they had been avoiding until then.

For my last example, I have chosen to give a number of typical general themes which arise in the Families Unit and become the focus of attention.

Towards the end of one particular week approaching the Christmas holidays, it had been noted by the hospital administrator as well as some of the nursing staff that a number of cigarette ends had been found around the hospital. The place was beginning to look quite untidy, and there was doubt about whether or not these cigarette ends belonged to the patients, the staff, or the group of electricians who were in the process of re-wiring the hospital. This re-wiring process had entailed knocking a number of large holes, probably at times rather unnecessarily, into the plaster, so that the place was beginning to look a mess. There was a general feeling that the fabric of the hospital had been interfered with in a damaging way. Members of staff as well as patients had mixed feelings about what was happening; some people feel that this was the price one had to pay for modernization and others felt that the whole job had been botched.

In general, in the patient group and in various meetings throughout the hospital, there was a fear of latent madness getting out of hand and wish for staff to take over responsibility. In addition, there was quite an angry, defiant independence; for example, many patients were not returning for their Sunday supper. This resulted in the children making it difficult for the parents to put them to bed on Sunday night, and they also became quite disruptive in the Monday morning playgroup. The parents' wish to be looked after seemed to become greater than their wish to be adults and parents for their children. There were general rather typical complaints that there were not enough staff or that the nurses were not available, and that staff had too high expectations of what patients were able to do.

However, it was generally felt by staff that a number of patients at this moment were avoiding issues in their own treatment. It was also discovered that there was an interference in the way that milk was being supplied; a number of bottles of milk had gone missing. Suddenly, the Families Unit found themselves without enough milk. It turned out that individuals were plundering the milk without letting anybody know. In addition one mother, Mrs C in the previous example, had been taking off the cream from the milk, and had been feeling quite guilty that no one had discovered this until that week.

These various themes and observations are of course complex, and one cannot very easily link all the themes to particular individuals. However, the fact that the fabric of the hospital had been interfered with, as well as the fact that there was a coming break, obviously precipitated feelings of rage, helplessness and a wish to be looked after on the part of the patients as a whole. Such feelings in the hospital are interpreted to some extent on a group level and more generally on an individual therapy basis, while the expectation is maintained that whatever parents' feelings are about wanting to be looked after, they are still expected to maintain their authority as parents to their children. Any other attitude on the part of the staff would really be a perversion of their work, and inappropriate use of their resources. Mrs C's own particular plundering of the cream of the resources in terms of the bottles of milk was taken up quite vigorously in her individual therapy sessions with some success.

Conclusion

In this paper I put forward an idea which I call 'The work of the day' around which psychotherapy and nursing can be focussed. The theoretical considerations are illustrated by clinical examples.

[2]

An Outline of Work with Families at the Cassel Hospital

Alan Wilson

This account is based on the theoretical concepts of a 'paranoid schizoid position' and a 'depressive position' in psychic development and function. The historical introduction uses these concepts to relate 'inner world' and 'outer world' events. The account goes on to suggest the influence of these positions, through projective mechanisms, in forming relatively stable zones of group function which acquire qualities of intimacy, familiarity and strangeness. The structural aspects of privacy and publicity are referred to. The place of resistance and a capacity to ignore is described in giving a particular view of focal family work.

History

Two events in the world at large have had particular significance for the Cassel Hospital. In the First World War, the breakdown of personal function in conditions such a shell shock, led directly to the founding of The Cassel Hospital for Functional Nervous Disorders. Psychotherapeutic treatment of individual neurotic conditions progressed on an in-patient basis under the eminent direction of Dr T.A.Ross. The Second World War again plunged the world into organized hostilities as a paradoxical technique for 'survival'. Individuals displaced from intimate relationships within a familiar context failed to maintain integrated personal functioning within organized fighting services seeking survival through a planned process of war. Studies such as the Northfield experiment proved to be major developments in the treatment of individual neurotic breakdown. They provided the basis for the new direction taken by work at the Cassel Hospital from 1946, under the leadership of Dr Tom Main. The real, persecutory, lethal, quality of these world-at-large wars provided a congruence with inner world persecutory anxiety, which in health is dealt with by the ordinary defensive aspects of personality and character structure. Treating the outcome of this congruence in the breakdown of personal function permitted the development of thoughtfully-arranged group living structures, facilitating the work of individual psychotherapy. At the Cassel Hospital these group living arrangements have come to be known as the psychotherapeutic community.

The beginning of family work at the Cassel

In 1946, the Cassel hospital began accepting patients again on its new site at Ham Common, Richmond. The in-patient work was with individual patients, men and women. The work which eventually led to the establishment of the Families Unit began when a woman patient asked if she could bring her child into hospital with her. Accepting this request to come into hospital with part of the family proved successful and it became possible to extend the practice so that mothers and children in difficulties from puerperal breakdown onwards could become part of the routine clinical work of the hospital. Once mothers and children were using the in-patient facilities, the next step to admitting husbands was a relatively easy one. Husbands were first admitted in a special category, known as 'healthy adults lodged', but it was not long before their part in treatment became an active one and work with whole families was established. It is now 38 years since the first mother and child were admitted at Cassel. The relevance of this telescoped account is to stress that work with families has evolved in the interaction between patients and staff in the psychotherapeutic community, and a body of practice has been built up, rather than a theoretical blueprint put into operation. We have often come to understand how practices are useful and how they work *after* they have become recognized as happening, as well as actively trying out new ideas and technical approaches.

By 1960, nursery groups within the hospital had been established, and the part played by mothers and children in the work of the hospital became such a constant factor that a nursery school was established and the appointment of a psychoanalytically trained child psychiatrist, child psychotherapist, and consultant paediatrician became possible. This had particular significance for the whole hospital in that not only was ordinary ego development from infancy to adolescence represented by children within the hospital, but also by a specialized group of professionals, i.e., the educationalist, psychologist, child psychotherapist, consultant paediatrician and child psychiatrist. This made possible the study of 'healthy' developmental processes that influenced the community function, alongside the impact of regressive processes under the influence of psychopathology which also made an impact on the total community function.

At the time of these appointments, work with families went on throughout the hospital although the Ross Unit came to be regarded as the place in the hospital where families were most appropriately treated. This allowed the professional staff specializing in work with children to have closer professional relationships with nurses and therapists treating the adult members of families; the family unit team became a more discrete professional group. This formation of discrete professional groupings proceeded further when it was decided to admit and undertake work with adolescents unaccompanied by their parents. Work with adolescents ready to move away from parents is not the central concern of this account, but early experience with the adolescent groups highlights some important points in maintaining the facilitating interaction between group function and individual treatment. Early experience of the adolescent group, as a group socially and territorially defined only by the hospital authority, led to polarized, conflictual situations between the adolescents and the rest of the community. Some time later, after changing the social and territorial division within the hospital by housing the single adolescent patients within the family unit, it became possible for the adolescents to become a group, rather than be forced into a group situation. The result was a marked change in how the group as a whole behaved.

This illustration makes it possible to clarify a similar point in relation to work with families at the hospital. *Work with families is an integral part of the total psychotherapeutic community of the hospital.* The work can only proceed by engaging with the stress and necessity of maintaining the total community, in a moment-to-moment, hour-to-hour, and day-to-day functioning form. Thus the *psychotherapeutic community* is not an institution with rules and procedures securing its progress, rather it *is a prescription for uncertainty allowing the law of necessity (necedere,* not going away) *sired by free association, to become the mother of invention.* The prescription of community is what is common. Service, office and duty are all related to necessity, that is, to not going away, but going into. This entails inventing, experiencing the peril of experimental relationships between people and things, and discovering the nature of danger and security, of jeopardy and safety.

In the process of building up this account of work with families in a psychotherapeutic community, I have already begun to employ the etymology of words alongside their current usage. This provides a ready historical and developmental means of illustrating the psychoanalytic principles involved alongside a manifest description of the work. The Latin word *hostis* means a stranger or a foreigner. In fact an enemy (*inamicus*, 'not a loved one') is specifically a private enemy, not a public one. This distinction of private and public when placed in the series intimate private and strange public, identifies areas of group activity within which distinct psychological functions or mechanisms can operate.

ADMISSION PROCEDURE

During a time of war or open hostilities, at first only two classes of people exist: friend or foe. Something can sometimes help distinguish between them, usually a uniform. The etymology of the word 'thing' in Old Saxon means a meeting place or legislative assembly. Visitors to the Cassel Hospital feel acutely the need to distinguish between patients and staff; they feel at a total loss without anything to help discriminate. This 'total loss' is an immensely valuable point of admission in all senses of the word. At this point only the input of fantasy into the process of reality testing ('re-al' thing classification) can invent a friendly participation, tolerate strangers, and with careful nursing maintain the physical absence of foes and warlike behaviour.

Coming to understand the immense value of this 'indiscriminate' period of admission has helped adhere to a policy whereby families do not visit the unit before admission. If a family accepts admission after a domiciliary visit or initial outpatient consultation followed by nursing assessment, the family should be admitted directly to the Unit at a specified time, for example, (Tuesday, 5 June at 11.30 a.m.). Only a further nursing home visit is necessary to help choose the intimate and familiar things to bring with them, i.e. clothes, photographs, toys. They can come as if hostile people into a hostile environment. In this way, they are able to find their hosts hospitable; the patients and staff acting as hosts can welcome the strangers. These last events bring in the antithetical meanings derived in the etymology of the word *hostis*.

Families who visit before admission have been found, at the end of this visit, to welcome the opportunity that is available to them. However, when they get home, they show great facility in devising an unstable improvement, which allows them to cancel the admission. Subsequently, they again request admission when the improvement breaks down.

The operation of the reality principle in an individual personality develops and continues to be based in the intimate relationship between the individual and other people and the psychological and physical functions their relationship serves. The development of intrapersonal object relations, from part object to whole object, takes place in the nuclear intimacy between human beings whatever cultural form the familiar quality of that nucleus takes. The importance and necessary privacy of that intimacy, supporting the organization of a capacity for concern, is generally accepted. Anatomically and physiologically established differences, as between mother/child, father/child, genital woman/genital man, sleeping/waking and grooming/nutrition, are the substrates of a psychological process of private intimacy, upon which rests the creative function of reality testing, when the opportunity of strange unknown people and things presents itself.

Entering into the meeting structure of the Cassel Hospital soon enables those who accept admission to surround themselves with familiar conventions and rituals of social living, passing beyond the reality of the situation into an illusion of security; there can develop a sinister privacy, which can pass over into interpersonal neglect. Fortunately, there is considerable truth in the saying that familiarity breeds contempt, also that in the process of daily living things more readily display neglect than people.

Creating a familiar arrangement in a strange place

It is difficult to conceive of a family without a system of physical things to support the intimate business of family living. This system of things, often referred to as 'home', can be developed to a complexity of function that serves to detach and isolate rather than to extend the boundaries of familiar function. This complexity of operation is often a defensive elaboration in withdrawal from the unresolvable stresses of intimacy between parent and child or husband and wife. The system of things begins to fail under the influence of behaviour problems in young children, together with anxiety, depression or other specific neurotic symptoms complained of by the mother. The father if in work may be taking time off, and the situation may reach a crisis where doubts about continuing the marriage are being expressed. In particular, the mother may be seeking some help. Alternatively, the family may have become a problem to someone else, usually a health visitor, or social worker, or other professional, who sees that the children may be in danger or neglected. The parents may admit to being unhappy together and wish to change the situation.

The accommodation offered to such a family within the Family Unit is deliberately limited. In a room for parents, there is a double bed, (or if they arrange to change this, two single beds), a wardrobe, a dressing table, a handbasin, upright chairs, a rug or two on the floor, and a door to the room which does not lock from the inside. The children will be accommodated in a room nearby, siblings possibly together, possibly having to share with children of other families depending on their ages. The parents' room is a room where the family can wash and dress, though for bathing and going to the toilet the general facilities of the Unit have to be used. Similarly, for family laundry there is a smallish common washroom and ironing room. Next door there is a small kitchen with a fridge, gas stove, cupboards and washing up facilities. Small meals such as breakfast for anyone needing an early start before hospital breakfast time, tea for the children when they come home from school, or babies' feeds and small snacks during the day can be prepared in the kitchen. What is technically the Nursing Officer's Office is a large room which he or she makes available to the whole Unit as a meeting and common room. It has a television and fairly comfortable chairs in it. The whole Unit accommodates about 30 people and is centrally heated. Fortunately, it is by no means soundproof, thus making isolation much more difficult.

Admission to the Unit often presents a very sharp transition from isolation to threatening exposure. Alongside this, patients on the Unit have prepared for the new family coming in, made up their beds and so on. The opportunity for reality testing between people, through these urgent and necessary activities will be great and relieving. The parents in the new family may have feelings of hostility which are likely to be expressed against staff, and particularly nursing staff, who will be blamed for the nature of the provision and for not providing continuous care and reassurance. These complaints are seldom made directly. The new children will usually accommodate fairly quickly, having other children to relate to and places to be active in. They engage during the day, but at first, they often have problems at night.

Initial assessment

Admission to the Unit is always for assessment, and the assessment is openly and clearly a two-way process between all members of the family, the rest of the patients and the staff of the Unit. The family is there to assess whether what they see as being available on the Unit is likely to be of any use to them, just as the staff and the rest of the patients will also attempt to make such an assessment. All members of the family will be assessed by the professional workers assigned to work with families. A member of the nursing staff on the Unit will have been assigned to the family before admission and from the home visit will have nursed the family into hospital. The nurse's work with the family, during the period of assessment, will be a continuation of this. The nurse works with the family to support the processes of ordinary living while in hospital, and to look at the practical problems of doing this with the rest of the Unit. In the three to four weeks of assessment, through his or her observation of all members of the family, the nurse will be able to report on the quality of family function, the individuals' ability to use relationships, and the difficulties in relating which get in the way of healthy functioning. The nurse will develop a view of the possibility of achieving nursing objectives while the family is in hospital. Adults and children in the family will be assessed by the Adult and Child Psychotherapists.

We aim to make available two hours per week of individual psychotherapy time for adult patients. For the children, developmental and educational needs must be taken into account, as well as provision for psychotherapy. All children are seen and also assessed educationally by the teachers in the hospital educational unit and by the psychologist. The work is co-ordinated by the child psychotherapist. Every member of the family has a general physical examination. For the children, this is carried out by a GP contracted to work with the hospital; for adults, by a hospital doctor who is not working as the particular patient's psychotherapist.

A typical day begins when children wake their own or others' parents with their play. The business of getting up, washing, dressing and having breakfast takes place. Sleep the previous night, once begun, has usually proceeded more steadily on the Family Unit than in the rest of the hospital. Most of the rounds of the night orderly passed unnoticed. Getting up and having breakfast are halting, sticky, difficult times. Bravely, the young children 'play in' the day, evoking in adults a cranky wakefulness; they fiddle and fret the jigsaw bits into a shape that fits with yesterday, because they have troubles that do not vanish overnight. Leftovers in the kitchen, a room in disarray, an absence more than half expected, but now confirmed, will lead the sensitive and observant nurse to feel let down and to suspect a sinister content to private events of which she does not yet know the details. Mrs X and her family had been admitted because she felt depressed and was dieting compulsively. Her little boy of three was having behaviour problems. Her daughter of six seemed to be doing reasonably well and had a good relationship with her father, a businessman who, in a worsening marital situation, had stayed at home largely because of his daughter. In psychotherapy, Mrs X's superficially compliant relationship with her dominating mother was beginning to open up, as was her relationship with her father whom she admired, but felt ignored by. Certainly, her father offered no protection from a demanding mother who favoured her younger sister. With the admission of the new family, Mrs X began to appear more tense and silent in her psychotherapy sessions. Interpretation of her resentment and anger towards the new family and the hospital for admitting them led to Mrs X talking more about her sister at the time when this sister was ill, and Mrs X's wish that she would die. She also talked about her secret anger towards her mother for nursing her sister and expecting Mrs X to help.

A new family, the Ys, have been admitted a week ago. The nurse has been on a home visit, and brought the mother, Mrs Y, back with her into the hospital with a new one-month-old baby. This new mother is at times confused, suspicious and anxiously overactive; at other times she sits stuck, and unable to know what to do. Mr Y is doubtful about coming in with his wife; he could have stayed with his parents. His job in the accounts office of his firm was a key one and his boss depended on him. Mrs Y is four years older than him, the projects organizer in the graphics department of a firm that his firm used as a subcontractor. They got to know each other through work, went on holidays together, got married and got a flat, but they had not expected to have a baby so soon. Mrs Y had stopped feeding the baby before admission as she found feeding very difficult, with a cracked, sore nipple. Since admission, Mr Y had begun to take on making up the feeds; he could now feed the baby. With the nurse and other patients' support, it had been possible to keep the family intact and functioning. Mrs Y was beginning to settle down. In fact, she had taken a surprisingly active part in a group which had come together out of a community meeting to look at plans for new curtaining in one of the common rooms.

Mrs X had been very supportive during the new patients' admission and first few days in the hospital. She had helped get the room ready for the Y family, and made useful suggestions with the nurse about arrangements for the baby. The nurse had not done midwifery, so it was helpful to her to have Mrs X's thinking as an experienced mother.

The Y family were also patients of Mrs X's nurse and therapist. However, two days ago, the nurse had suggested to Mrs X that she would be on duty early this particular morning and they could get together about arrangments for dealing with the children's teas on the Unit, and buying in food for them. They would then be able to go into this in further detail with the rest of the mothers on the Unit in the 'firm meeting' that morning. Having discovered Mrs X's absence, the nurse met Mr X returning from having taken their older daughter to school in the hospital. Mr X was about to go off to work. He was going by public transport. His wife had taken the car for a dental appointment that she had to keep for the younger child. It subsequently transpired that Mrs X had arranged the dental appointment the day before and that she and Mr X had had a row the night before. He had slept on a couch in the common room. They had not spoken to each other that morning.

Going on to the Unit meeting of patients and nurses, these events could be pieced together and the sinister aspect of the privacy begin to be engaged with. The whole Firm's relationship with the Xs begin to be looked at. Its competent controlling distance, experienced as a lack of warmth, could be thought about, in preparing for Mrs X's return from the appointment with the dentist which she had so revengefully arranged by successfully manipulating her son. In the staff meeting, these events could further be examined, bringing the notion of revenge more directly into the psychotherapy. The unconscious hostile attack by Mrs X on the hospital and nurse, making the nurse feel let down, left out and worried, along with the therapist, could be looked at. This was a way of getting the nurse and therapist to feel what Mrs X had experienced as a girl, (feeling angry, ignored and forced to be compliant in relation to her mother), in order to test out whether it would provoke the same quality of angry retaliation from the staff as it had from her mother and father. Mrs X could not perceive her mother and father as helpless, frightened people with a dying daughter; angry in their impotence.

Somewhat later in the day, shortly before the nurse was due to go off duty, Mrs X returns to the hospital. The understanding of these events, springing from the nurse's own observations and her work with patients and with colleagues during the meeting structure of the day, enables the nurse to welcome Mrs X back to the hospital with equanimity and say accurately how glad she is to see Mrs X back; the nurse can also acknowledge calmly that Mrs X's timing of her return falls just when she, the nurse, is going off duty. They will have to make a time when they can get together again about children's teas tomorrow; perhaps Mrs X did not feel that the arrangement they had made for this morning was either specific enough or gave enough time. They fix a time and the therapeutic process can now move on to the next sequence of events to be analysed, at community, Unit, group, family and individual levels.

This clinical example gives some idea of how the real events of the day in terms of ordinary living give rise to the therapeutic work on the family Unit. It leaves out specifically work with children, and the sessions that Mrs X's little boy has with the Child Psychotherapist, and the threatening dimension this poses to the family in hospital. It also leaves out the other reason why he was taken to the dentist; he was late for his session with the Child Psychotherapist.

This account of the work with families has only mentioned the work with the teacher, the Psychologist, the Child Psychotherapist. It has given some further description of the work of the nurse relating to the family and the therapist treating one of the parents. It may well be that another therapist is working with the other parent. This is the group that works closely at first hand with the family. It is principally to this group that the nursing officer and consultant on the Unit relate in conceptualizing and supervising and therapeutic work. The aim is to undertake a style of focal or focussed therapy, the focal formulation making it possible to correlate and adjust staff work with the family and other patients, both in terms of content and level of work at any particular time. *Thus the focal formulation with the X family might be the family's demands for performance as a defence against dependency.*

Taken out of context with the observations reported and discussed during the formulation of the focus, the words themselves have little meaning or general usefulness. They are as private to the professionals who fashioned them as family names or nicknames are to the family concerned. 'The demands of performance as a defence against dependence' has the ring of jargon. It may be recognizable as a sort of psychodynamic focus; it gives little indication, to an outsider, of how it would operate. It has a diagnostic quality and function and, if well worked through in formulation, serves to regulate, co-ordinate, and focus professional work throughout a period of time and sequence of events.

The Latin word meaning 'a hearth' is the etymological root of focus. A hearth may be defined as an apparatus which makes possible the safe use of fire because it is resistant to heat and combustion. In a psychological sense, the focus also represents an important functionally-organized aspect of resistance, that is, resistance to instinctual forces, resistance to processes which the focus makes it possible to use.

The focus is a structure formulated selectively out of the substance of theory, relevant and adaptive to current work tasks of the professional group working with the family on the unit. It relates, understandably, absence to presence, nursing activity engaged in to activity avoided, psychodynamic areas manifestly engaged with to those left latent. This subtle integration in focal work is difficult to convey in words, because it means talking about what one is carefully 'not talking' about. We can attempt to do so by labelling this process 'the work of ignorance', in the sense that something can only be ignored if it is known about. If there is an important reason, over a period of time, to ignore an acquaintance at a party, it can only be done successfully when you are sure he or she is present at the party. When you are sure he or she is at the party there are three alternatives: leave the party; engage in a damaging confrontation; or stay at the party and do the 'work of ignorance' until safe recognition is possible.

Earlier in this account, engagement with the process of age, appropriate ego maturation and development, and processes of regression under the influence of personal psychopathology were referred to. Frustration, discomfort, distress, pain and suffering are experiences common to maturation and regression. The 'work of ignorance' as a function of focal work aims to assist in achieving the engagement and working through of these painful areas of experience within the limits of what is 'hurtful', as distinct from an intensity or form of experience that is damaging. The aim is for reality testing to proceed rather than reaction formation to take place. This is as important in the care of staff as in the care of patients. The quality and content of demands, confrontations and interpretations, the nature of possible denials, collusions, seductions, of forms of 'acting out' and 'acting in', must be understood and managed with an articulate awareness of these limits of pain. This is essentially what makes the work safe, psychologically and physically, enabling conflict to inform reality rather than distort or destroy it, as it does in war.

This account began by relating the origins of the contemporary Cassel Hospital to the events of the First and Second World Wars. The disintegrating potential of a congruence between the outer reality of total war and the inner reality of individuals ruthlessly exposed, (oedipus) by disruption from intimate familiar surroundings, may result in breakdown of personal function. This congruence of outer and inner 'ruthlessness' leads to a breakdown in the psychic work of depression, and leaves only the individual's capacity to be ill as the basis for recovery.

The voluntary status of all patients at the hospital is an indication of the capacity to be ill, and includes the understanding of the 'necessity' to be in hospital. The capacity to be ill rests on there being present established elements of depressive capability. The hypothesis 'there is something wrong with me' can be used for the experiments of reality testing, and the necessity not to run away while working through the findings can be tolerated.

The *established focus* can be said to define the possible *experimental programme.* The work of ignorance, with its other side, the work of attention, is closely involved with *supervision.* Supervision is an integral part of the therapeutic process, making it tolerable to the nurse and the therapist to look afte patients, rather than intrusively attempt to cure. It is analogous to the tasks undertaken by unconscious processes within the individual who is comfortable in 'polite society' and informed by a functioning sense of guilt (i.e. where politics can perform a synthesising function, containing danger).

The psychotherapeutic community is not a stable, polite society, it is a prescription of uncertainty, of free association, but free association observed with focal attention.

In daily living within the hospital, functions of office and duty (community) relate to issues of identity continuity: how to be recognized as friend or foe, or both, in the field of projection systems operating at a level where 'things' or 'objects' are being invented.

Out of the amorphous arrangements of admission, areas of intimacy, familiarity are constructed providing the apparatus for the experimental programme of focal family work.

[3]

Is In-patient Psychotherapy a Valid Concept?

Brian Muir

In this paper, I shall attempt to outline the essential features of in-patient psychotherapy at the Cassel Hospital. I shall discuss the special modifications of technique which have been evolved in our hospital, in order to ensure as far as possible that the experience of in-patient psychotherapy is a genuine and efficacious process which utilizes and takes advantage of the special features of the in-patient setting. As a corollary of this, I shall describe some of the consequences of this setting which are particularly likely, unless due attention is paid them, to render psychotherapeutic engagement a futile and meaningless experience. These negative forces are manifest in both individuals and groups, and in staff as well as patients. Although this paper represents an attempt to formulate my own thoughts, understandings and orientation regarding this rather difficult topic, I would nevertheless like to pay tribute and acknowledge my debt to the many colleagues, both teachers and pupils with whom I have worked during the past 15 years at the Cassel Hospital. In using the term psychotherapy, I am referring specifically to psychoanalytic psychotherapy with *interpretation of transference phenomena* as a central technique. The aim of this is to bring about internal dynamic change in the patient in terms of improved reality testing, better self control, richer emotional life, more independence, and better capacities to function in personal, social and practical realms. The objective is more specific for each patient, and is defined as a limited focus and goals. Furthermore, my remarks relate predominantly to psychotherapy with individuals, but the same arguments can be applied to conjoint marital and family work as practised in the hospital, bearing in mind other technical modifications required.

Other areas that I will examine here are the effect of admission on the patient, the assessment of the patient in the setting of the hospital, the aims, objects and limits of therapy, the place of nursing and the function of the community, the question of the management and containment, regression and, in particular, the nature of psychotherapy with special reference to the transference in the in-patient setting.

In attempting to review the literature, the most striking thing to emerge is how very little has been written specifically about the special techniques, constraints and difficulties which psychotherapy with in-patients requires and imposes. Some reference, although fairly minimal, is made to this problem in the Menninger Foundation Psychotherapy Research Project (1972), but the most pertinent work remains Tom Main's various papers written over a period of nearly 30 years working in the hospital; notable among these is his paper, 'The ailment'.

I would like to pursue the question posed by the title of this paper by trying to answer a number of subsidiary questions. Firstly, 'Why in-patient psychotherapy?'. Many psychotherapists would argue that the idea of in-patient psychotherapy is actually antithetical to the establishment of a psychoanalytic psychotherapeutic relationship. Others would maintain that hospital management may be necessary while psychotherapy goes on outside the hospital, during a period when a patient is too ill to manage his or her own life in the real world. But it is not this latter situation to which I am referring, nor to the simple application of ordinary techniques of psychotherapy with an in-patient by a hospital doctor, who leaves all the management problems to another doctor and to the nursing staff. It is my assertion that the above practices are all subject to serious disadvantages. I think the answer to my first question is best dealt with by thinking about the kind of patient population that is provided for using this particular treatment technique.

It would be fair to say that, in Britain at least, there exists in every large mental hospital, and probably in most in-patient psychiatric units in general hospitals, a number of patients apparently not psychotic but unable to cope with real life and its demands, and for whom little or nothing can be done by conventional psychiatric treatment methods. These patients' psychopathology and clinical phenomenology has over the last ten or twenty years been variously described as severe characterological disorder, personality disorder, and more recently, in psychoanalytic literature, as severe narcissistic and borderline personality organization. Thus, in answer to my first question, there exists a group of patients ill enough to need hospital admission, who are estranged from themselves and from relationships with others, crippled in their capacity for creative work and environmental adaptation. For them, psychotherapy is often felt to be the only source of possible help, as other psychiatric methods and support have usually been tried and have failed.

Secondly, we must ask 'What is the effect of adulterating the classical psychoanalytic one-to-one situation?' How does the therapist find a technique to cope with the fact that he or she has a group of patients in individual psychotherapy who know one another, who talk about their session material and who see the therapist in situations other than their sessions, such as in community or other meetings, chance encounters in corridors and so on? Perhaps even more importantly, we should ask 'What kind of technique needs to be employed to deal with the fact that the therapist has daily contact with the patient's nurse and talks with him or her about the patient, just as the patient talks to the therapist about the nurse and other patients?'.

Thirdly, there is the question of the length of the psychotherapeutic process: 'Should this be an open-ended process with all the attendant risks of long-term hospitalization, such as the well-known phenomena of institutionalization and the promotion of dependency of the malignant kind in the patient? Or can the process be effective if it is relatively short term, such as the Cassel Hospital, by and large, offers?'

Fourthly, we may ask, 'What is the purpose of hospitalization as such other than giving the patient support and shelter that he or she needs because of the nature of his or her illness, and if there is any other purpose, what is its relevance to the psychotherapy?'. In other words, 'Is the purpose of hospitalization merely holding, so that psychotherapy can take place, or could it be further described as an experience in living which is in itself illuminating and a form of free or not so free behavioural association?'.

I shall try to address these last three questions in order. Let us return to the question of what modifications of techniques are required to meet the special conditions imposed by in-patient status on psychotherapy. Here, the joint notions of the transference to the institution as a whole and to the various human beings experienced by the patient in his or her life within it, along with the notion that the patient's free associations consist of more than verbal utterances in the consulting room, are both important and relevant.

The key feature that distinguishes individual psychotherapy with in-patients is that the reality of the objects of transference are known directly to the therapist. In out-patient work, the therapist does not usually have first-hand knowledge of the significant events, people and material reality in the patient's life. He or she only knows what the patient tells him. With in-patient work, the therapist either knows or can find out about the realities and can check the patient's perceptions and attributions against his or her own and other staff members' accounts. The therapist can choose either to ignore these 'extraneous' sources of material, or to utilize them to advantage and further the treatment.

Manifest and interpretable transference phenomena become fairly quickly evident with most patients soon after admission. These phenomena occur at several different levels: in the patient's attitude towards the material fabric of the institution, (i.e. to the building with its furniture and fittings), in the patient's attitude towards the relationship with the larger community as a whole, and in the patient's relationship with his own unit. Finally, the transference will appear in relation to individuals, especially to the nurse, to the therapist and to the therapist's other patients. The more primitive aspects of the transference are generally manifest in behavioural terms: these may include inability or refusal to engage with assigned household tasks such as keeping one's bedroom clean, taking part in the general care of the servery or other work groups, or avoiding community meetings. Relevant interpretations may be to do with exploitation of a providing maternal figure, manifestations of a neglected, dirty or unwanted self in relation to a maternal figure, or paranoid anxieties involving projected jealousy and envy and consequent work difficulties.

Primitive defensive mechanisms of splitting and projective identification are most evident in the community and unit setting, in the form of perceptions either by the group or individuals within it, of good and bad figures and the location of good or bad aspects of the self in others.

Now when I speak of behavioural free association, it will become immediately obvious that the quality and nature of the patient's behaviour in the hospital both towards himself, other people and the furniture and fabric of the building will be decisive in terms of whether treatment engagement is possible or not. Clearly some behaviour is incompatible with a treatment relationship being pursued.

If the therapist makes it clear to the patient that he or she is in receipt of constant information from the nurse and other sources, and that he or she is prepared to use this information with the patient to clarify and interpret free associations in the sessions in terms of the patient's transference to the whole hospital as well as to him or herself, the various problems of adulteration of the traditional therapist/patient dyad by the intrusion of other persons and extraneous factors tend to fade away. They may even become useful enrichments of the therapeutic process. The therapist is concerned to interpret and understand the here and now in terms not only of what is going on in the consulting room, but what has been going on in the hospital as a whole over the previous 24 hours or more. This understanding and interpretation of the patient's life events, both those that are successful and those that fail in the setting of the hospital, are then related in the usual manner to the past, to the repetition compulsion and to its accompanying maladaptive life techniques. Thus, the potential material available in the in-patient setting is considerably more rich and varied than would be possible in the classical out-patient or private office situation.

What is attempted is an examination in a sharing way with the patient, of the important areas of failure in the patient's functioning and reality testing. The patient looks at his or her skill at utilizing other people's craziness as a means of relocating or disguising one's own. The patient's skill at manipulating reality is exposed and the motive for the manoeuvre understood.

The question of privacy and confidentiality, which is so important in psychotherapy, poses immediate problems in the in-patient setting. Most obviously, difficulties arise when we consider communications between nurse and therapist. The passing on of information by the nurse to the therapist is not too difficult to manage, but what of information in the reverse direction, and what would be the purpose of such an exchange?

Clearly, there must be good definition of what is public and what is private, and within the community of the hospital there are few secrets concerning *behaviour*. Most behaviour becomes public property, and patients should be made aware of this from the outset. Fantasy is another matter, and communications of a private nature are respected, obvious examples being masturbatory fantasies.

Nurses frequently, though not regularly, need to know something from the therapist about the patient, particularly the difficult patient, in order to be able to continue nursing the patient by understanding the basis of his or her behaviour, without condoning it or being falsely tolerant of it. If fantasies of a kind involving harm or loss to the self or others, or involving risk to life, seem in danger of erupting into action, and the patient is evincing little or no responsibility, the therapist must feel free to discharge the patient if the latter refuses to allow the community knowledge of the risk he or she poses.

What then is likely to happen if the therapist attempts to do orthodox psychotherapy with interpretation of the transference solely to him or herself? My experience is that although there is a small minority of patients who are able to engage with benefit in a therapeutic relationship of this kind, the majority of in-patients, for reasons I will come back to later, are inclined to form a false or compliant engagement with the therapist. They view the therapeutic process as a fascinating exercise in self-study, but are devoid of any commitment to real understanding or change. They undertake to enter into this compliant relationship as payment of a kind which they feel qualifies them to remain on in the environment of the hospital in which they have usually carved out a very firm niche enabling them to perpetuate their illness.

There are some dangers involved in interpreting the transference hospital-wide, and the unintentional fostering of aggressive acting-out is one of these. This is brought about by the patient feeling rejected by the therapist if the therapist does not acknowledge and interpret negative and positive feelings towards *himself or herself* as well as to the institution, the building and others in it. It is particularly important not to *deflect* strong transference feelings from the person of the therapist to others in the hospital when those feelings are clearly experienced primarily in relation to the therapist; this is especially tempting for younger and less experienced therapists working with patients whose affect is primitive and intensely uncomfortable. Here there may be a temptation to 'dilute' transferences, especially those of a regressive hostile dependent kind, by spreading them over the hospital.

Using the right techniques, in-patient psychotherapy can be highly sophisticated, because it is possible to get a whole view of the patient and then choose different transference elements to evoke or leave alone according to what seems most facilitating of reality testing. By and large, transference interpretations which have a sense of relevance and immediacy will be those which most enhance the patient's capacity to be ill, or in other words, to engage with psychic pain and tolerate the disruption of the narcissistic self-image.

I would like to emphasize at this point that the classification and re-classification of patient material of a private kind from individual sessions is a complicated and vital aspect of the work at the Cassel. A difficult matter is the amount and detail that the therapist tells the patient's nurse about what is said in sessions, and also what the patient believes the therapist will or will not tell the nurse. The blurring and redrawing of private/public classificatory boundaries is an important process which can act against, as well as in favour of, the goals of treatment. It is vital that both patients and staff are clear about what is private, what is public and which private matters can be expected to be made public, by whom, to whom and in what contexts.

We turn now to the third subsidiary question, which asks, 'What are the relative merits of long-term stay and shorter-term stay of six months to a year, or at the outside eighteen months?'. At the Cassel Hospital we have no experience of very long term treatment, but there is a general feeling that even if the psychotherapeutic community of the hospital maintains the patient in a fairly realistic life situation, the returns from long term hospitalization are likely to be rapidly diminishing after a certain optimum period. The reason for this is that in spite of all efforts to ensure that the hospital environment does not protect or give asylum too much from real life, that it does so in some measure is undeniable. Thus my experience at the Cassel is of relatively short term treatment involvement. In psychotherapeutic terms, this means in effect that the treatment lasts, in the majority of cases for between ten and fourteen months. Because of this somewhat standardized length of treatment and in-patient stay, the psychotherapy is focal in nature. The focus most usefully delineated in the first instance, though it may be refined at later stages during the patient's stay, is the real reason for admission in human terms. Such reasons may involve situations like the following: the family could no longer tolerate the patient and eventually excluded him or her; the patient showed inability to relate to and negotiate with authority figures at work; there was inability to sustain work effort at university; there was failure to perform adequately the task of mothering and to meet the demands of young children; there was inability to begin to become a separate person as an adolescent. Such foci, if vigorously pursued, can lead to a very rewarding treatment outcome and usually become refined to more specific areas of psychopathology, whether oedipal or pre-oedipal.

Turning now to subsidiary question four, we ask, 'What is the purpose of hospitalization as such, and what is its relevance to psychotherapy?'. Before I embark on this particular issue, I think it would be useful to say something aboiut the general effect of admission. It is, time and time again, a clinically observable phenomenon that the offer of admission has a remarkably regressive effect on the majority of patients. The concrete gratification of bed and full board provided in a rather gracious building with lovely gardens as a guest of the National Health Service, proves very seductive. Patients come into hospital, no matter how well prepared, with powerful conscious and unconscious expectations and longings to be totally looked after. They consequently feel angry, duped and cheated when this fantasy does not materialize more concretely still. The fantasy of being the possessor of an all-providing mother, taking charge of her body, her provision of food, and indeed her sexual functions including the capacity to have more babies, (i.e. to admit more patients), is a powerfully insistent one on the part of the patient, and is accompanied by a regression of behaviour. This regression generally becomes more autistic or solipsistic and exploitative with increasing concreteness of transactions. Now, from the psychotherapist's point of view, if there is a purpose to the hospitalization that is relevant to psychotherapy, it is certainly not to bring about this state of affairs. Thus, the climate and established culture of the community needs to be of a nature and powerful enough to counter and eventually win out over these regressive forces (which I have described as being predominantly a feature of new patients, but which in fact are present in all patients to some extent or other throughout their stay). How does such a climate and culture discourage malignant regression, and establish and maintain this? How are the values of responsibility for oneself, self-appraisal, thought and enquiry preserved and judged over mindless and impulsive behaviour usually in the service of needs to be instantly gratified? The short answer to this question is that this is brought about by psychoanalytically informed nursing and by the maintenance of a psychoanalytically supervised therapist/nurse relationship, which ensures that the therapist is not able to withdraw from the vicissitudes of everyday life during the 'other 23 hours', but must be available daily to participate in a mutually supportive free exchange with the nurse about his patient, with all the inherent possibilities of splits and quarrels, on the one hand, and mutual respect, support and understanding on the other. Nursing, whether it takes place at the level of facilitating the more healthy functioning of the whole hospital community at nights and weekends or at the level of the firm or Unit during the working weekday, is the vehicle by which the experience and experiment of living in the hospital can become the source of material for useful psychoanalytic work. There are areas of ego failure and strength in both individual and group functioning which become evident in the day-to-day nursing of ordinary human working-together tasks and situations; these afford the patient the opportunity not only to reappraise his or her strengths but to come to terms, albeit painfully, with areas of inadequacy and failure. This exercise in turn may offer the possibility of change. Of course, all this involves the increased tolerance and working through of depressive as well as persecutory anxieties, and often there is an escape into regressive behaviour, such as drug taking, alcohol abuse or suicidal gestures, as a means of escape from psychic pain.

This brings me to a brief discussion of the management of regressive behaviour in the hospital. I have described above how the community is, in my view, primarily a crucible specifically designed to offer an experience and experiment in living, from which learning from experience can occur. This does not mean a democratic society in which patients can make up their own rules and take over the total government of the community. On the contrary, it is seen as a tool devised and used primarily by nursing staff, psychotherapists and patients. Patients can, if able and willing, use this tool in order to facilitate their own and others' understanding of themselves and thereby hopefully to instigate some change. But there is another function that the community performs; this is that of holding. These two functions are to some extent complementary, just as the overall functions of the psychotherapeutic community and psychotherapy are complementary, one not being of much value without being informed and enlightened by the other. The limitations of holding of more severely ill and regressed people in the community are dictated by the quantity and quality of the behavioural communications the patient makes. But holding can occur at many levels and be implemented by anything from an apparently casual glance or word to an organized rota system to ensure the safety of a suicidal patient over a period of 24 hours or maybe longer. At this level, the holding function of the community occasionally needs to be reinforced by the ancillary use of psychotropic drugs. Thus great value is afforded to caring as long as it takes place in an ordinary, dignified human manner. It must never be patronising or infantilizing and certainly must never demand the dependence of a patient. It must rather respond to certain regressive or dependent needs if it is judged that these should be met in the interests of the patient's health. An example might be where a nurse or another patient washes a patient's hair or encourages a self-neglecting young man or woman to change their linen and take a bath. Such a climate of fair shares and mutual concern is difficult to maintain. There is constant pressure, especially at the level of the Unit group, to collude with and conceal ill behaviour and sick aspects of personal functioning under the guise of holding and care, in such a way as to make the behaviour less accessible to examination and enquiry. One of the dangers in the hospital is that of *seducing* the patient to regress to dependency, which may have the psychological effect of relieving anxiety in all members of the professional team. But if a degree of regression is not the result of seduction, it has a painful or uncomfortable quality for the patient and those around him or her. This can be engaged with in therapy as a supportive setting for its ultimate usefulness as 'regression to vulnerability but retaining responsibility'. This regression has a humanizing and healing effect, and allows the patient a more benign expression of his illness. It enables the patient to make maximum use of his or her experience in the hospital. Thus, malignant regressive urges involving dependency are regularly recognized and struggled with in endeavouring to help the patient to maintain some level of adult functioning. However, there are, mixed up with these, less healthy dependency needs and longings, the ordinary universal attachments we all need to make with one another in the course of life. Therefore, if the patient has been well enough to make a useful engagement with the hospital and some of the people in it, the issue of separation and termination and the setting of a leaving date becomes as important a focus as the reason for admission. The work done on this focus will, if it is genuine, consolidate the experience and all the patient has learned from it.

This brings me to the question of assessment. All in-patients are admitted initially for a period of in-patient assessment lasting about four weeks. During this time, the staff concerned are making an assessment of the usual factors such as motivation, capacity for self-responsibility and self-appraisal, extent of dependency needs and type of regression to be expected, quality of object relations, ego strengths, and so on.

But perhaps most important of all is to have a well-formulated initial focus and clearly defined treatment goals related to this focus. This avoids an ever-broadening extension of the original focus about the real reason for admission, and confines the work to this focus and to termination issues which are likely to be sharply delineated when a leaving date is set. The less benign regressive forces in the community can powerfully impair the capacities of the workers to keep their focus and goals constantly in mind. Without a reasonably modest and clearly formulated focus and goal of treatment in every case, the omnipotent notion of cure is likely to creep into the minds of both patients and staff with consequent escalating mutual expectations and eventual decline of staff and patient morale. If the goal is explicit and realistic from the outset, hope may then be a possibility rather than a day-dream; the work put in by the patient and staff towards the achievement of this goal will be experienced as a re-affirmation of that hope and will be of real value. The corollary of this is that, inevitably, some painful truths will need to be faced up to. These are truths about permanent damage which cannot be undone; however, this is damage which, if faced up to, may make for the possibility of a more creative adaptation to real life and more realistic expectations of oneself in that life.

To finish, I would like to scrutinize the individual and collective aspects of the psychotherapeutic process at the Cassel. The list below is an artificial separating out of individual and collective aspects of the treatment for clarity of exposition. But I want to emphasize that almost all the characteristics found in one are also found in the other. Individual and collective work are *not* competing and conflicting processes, but they are of different orders. It is the thesis of my paper that psychoanalytic in-patient psychotherapy would be far less effective without the collective work and vice versa.

The collective work is dependent upon psychoanalytically informed nursing and upon a psychoanalytically supervised nurse/therapist relationship (the 'care of the caretaker'). In this way, the nurse/therapist relationship has evolved along lines similar to the historical development and application of the concepts of transference and countertransference. It has shifted from being a nuisance and an undesirable interference to being a valuable tool which enriches and enhances the clinical work.

THERAPEUTIC PROCESSES AT THE CASSEL HOSPITAL

	Individual	*Collective*
1.	Providing therapeutic support (perhaps for vulnerability) and understanding associated with mothering.	Challenging (anti-social and self-destructive) behaviours associated with fathering.
2.	Interpretation of transference towards achievement of aims (psychological dimensions).	Positive and negative reinforcement of healthy and unhealthy behaviours towards achievement of objectives e.g. satisfactory sexual relations, capacity to work.
3.	Focus on primitive sources based in early experience.	Focus on the reality-ego of the immediate present.
4.	Exploration of distorting influences of the past on the present.	Exploring the immediacy of responses from others.
5.	Discovery that 'others', apart from the therapist, exist as mental representations of people from the past.	Discovery that 'others' exist as real, currently actual people.
6.	Exploration of private and secret experience 'alone' (the therapist does not 'count' as the public).	Exploration in public. The private or secret may be made public to a real, judging public.
7.	From experience to behaviour.	From behaviour to experience.

[4]

The Role of the Nurse/Therapist Relationship in the Therapeutic Community

Oliver James

In his paper 'The ailment' Main (1946) showed how failures in communication between nurse and psychotherapist can allow a splitting of 'good' and 'bad' objects by the patient which splits nurse and therapist and leads to anti-therapeutic pairings.

This paper shows that the different tasks of nurse and therapist create a danger: each is liable to undermine the work of the other in order to maintain their own effective functioning.

The Cassel Hospital moved from a 'separation system', in which the therapist was kept totally separate from the patient and his nurse outside the consulting room, to a mixed system, in which therapist, patient and nurse did have contact outside therapy (Ployé, 1977). This shift followed the successful suicide of a patient who had created a split between nurse and therapist.

In this paper, we show that it is vital for the nurse and therapist to meet regularly if the therapeutic opportunities provided by the patient's residence in a community are to be used properly; but we also show that these meetings must be handled carefully if anti-therapeutic distortions in the relations between the nurse and therapist, and between them and the patient, are to be avoided.

The first part of this paper briefly outlines a conceptualization of the community which has been made at the Cassel Hospital, to set the context in which the nurse/therapist relationship exists.

The second part explores the different roles played by the nurse and the therapist in promoting 'desired mutative processes' in patients. The third part examines the relationship between nurse, therapist and patient, employing Winnicott's (1972) distinction between using, and relating to, objects. This analysis produces two important propositions: the nurse must be protected from the therapist's way of working, and vice versa, through well-focussed supervisions; and that the principal role of the therapist emerges as the facilitation of the change from relating to using in the patient's relationship *to the nurse.*

The theoretical basis for Cassel hospital treatment of in-patients

Rationale for in-patient individual psychotherapy

In a sense, this needs no introduction, but it seems worth locating here the hospital's particular orientation to psychoanalytic psychotherapy in an in-patient setting.

Techniques and theories may be drawn from classical psychoanalysis, represented by Melanie Klein, Anna Freud, and their disciples such as Bion and Segal. However, the principal source influences are 'middle group' clinicians such as Winnicott and Balint. Specific application of psychoanalytic thinking to brief psychotherapy is pursued, along the lines described by Malan and Balint. The therapist is expected to interpret, and to help the patient to reconstrue his transference to the social entities of the community and to his nurse, as well as to the person of the therapist. This increases the complexity of the therapist's task since he must consider his countertransference to these (of which he has first-hand knowledge), as well as to his patient.

Rationale for therapeutic utilization of the social entities of the community

In the absence of any integrated explanatory theoretical framework within which to conceive of the therapeutic utility of the social entities of the community, we have embarked on an attempt to develop one, using the various fragments which do exist, and developing others where they were lacking. Our basic propositions may be summarized as follows:

(i) That as social entities increase in size:
- their characteristic modes of psychodynamic functioning change;
- their modes become more primitive, corresponding to ever earlier psychobiological stages in individual development;
- the appropriate media for communication in them change;
- the knowledge regarding their therapeutic effectiveness decreases in quantity and quality.

(ii) That the therapeutic potentiality of the community mode requires further investigation of a systematic type before any of its therapeutic and anti-therapeutic effects can be assessed or stated with a theoretical explanation thereof.

We argue that the patient's personal and social, strucural relation to the occupants of the roles and the social entities of the community *is diagnostic of the vicissitudes of particular aspects of his psychodynamic functioning, and is the medium for changes in these aspects.*

The patient's response to his nurse demonstrates (among other things) his capacity to be cared for. His response to other patients demonstrates this also, as well as his capacity to nurse others. His response to his therapist demonstrates his capacity to understand verbal interpretations of his defences and reconstructions of his past, and to develop the capacity to do these for himself. The aspects are evoked by these relations, which are diagnostic and the potential medium for change.

We suggest that:

- The small group mode corresponds to the mode of the person at the adolescent stage of psychobiological development.
- The large group mode corresponds to the mode of the person at the infant stage of psychobiological development.
- The community mode corresponds to the mode of the per-

son at the late foetal/early neonatal stages of psychobiological development.

Just as each of the patient's relations to his nurse, therapist and to the other patients is demonstrative of particular aspects of his personality development, so it is with his relation to the different sizes of social entity (organized by the social structure) in the community: his relation to the small group is diagnostic of, and a medium for change in, the vicissitudes of his adolescent stage of development. His relation to the large group is diagnostic of, and a medium for change in, the vicissitudes of his early childhood and infantile functioning; and his relation to the community, of his late foetal and neonatal functioning. That is, each of these entities sheds light on, and is a possible means of change in, these aspects of the past-in-the-present of the individual. A principal means of diagnosis of patient functioning in these aspects is his capacity *to use the modes of communication appropriate to the entity and to the psychobiological stage to which it corresponds.* Thus, a patient who treated a large group as if it was a dyadic social entity might demonstrate this relation to his early childhood/infantile functioning by using words as signs; he might show an incapacity to use words as symbols or to adopt the non-verbal means appropriate to large group functioning. Again, he might consistently use words only symbolically, or even not use words at all, communicating by non-verbal media only in a small group, thereby demonstrating a developmental blockage in adolescent functioning.

On the basis of this, we propose that a systematic scrutiny of the form (that is, the mode of communication) and the content of the patient's relation to the nurse, therapist, other patients, and the small group, large group and community social entities should be attempted at an early stage in the in-patient's stay. This is in order to review what the patient reveals about his psychobiological history in these relations. Such a practice would increase the staff's awareness of the whole psychodynamic picture of the patient, of the likely areas in which difficulties could occur, and in which change is desired. It would also provide staff with a systematic theoretical perspective within which to place the patient, and would maximize the therapeutic effectiveness of in-patient community treatment.

THE RATIONALE LINKING INDIVIDUAL AND COMMUNITY THERAPIES. THE NURSE/THERAPIST/PATIENT RELATIONSHIPS

The integration of what happens between the patient and the nurse (P-N), the patient and the therapist (P-T), and the nurse and therapist (N-T) is central to the effectiveness of the individual and community therapies described above. If the patient's relationships are to be scrutinized adequately, then it is vital that the N-T relation is functioning with a minimum of distortion.

In what follows we examine the individual and joint roles of the nurse and therapist in fostering the desired initiative psychological processes for patients.

Definition of mutative processes in the Cassel Hospital

Firstly, the *holding, containment and actual care of patients,* by each other, by staff, by the structure and culture of the firms and by the community:

(i) This *can be a new experience for patients,* either as donor or recipient, which allows them for the first time to value and understand their need for dependence, and that of others;

(ii) This *provides a degree of a feeling of certainty and safety* which holds the patient's level of anxiety to a level which is possible to tolerate.

Secondly, the *recovery and understanding of thoughts, feelings and acts* (that is the consequences of them, and responsibility for them) which exist in the present and/or arose in the recent or long distant past, and have been lost.

This is achieved by the *registration* of the patient's thoughts, feelings and acts by other patients and staff in firms and in the community, and their *interpretation* in psychotherapy, individual and group, *as distorted or inappropriate relating* in the transference to the psychotherapist, and to members, activities, expectations and places of the firm and the community.

This definition can be condensed as follows: 'Holding, containment and actual care of and by patients can be a new experience for them and provides a degree of certainty and safety which makes it possible for them to tolerate the recovery and understanding of forgotten thoughts, feelings and acts which hitherto have distorted behaviour. This is achieved by their registration and by their interpretation as distorted or inappropriate relating.'

Similar and different roles played by nurse and therapist in fostering mutative processes

Both nurses and therapists *hold* and *contain* patients:
(i) by 'being there', reliably, as people who the patient knows will be present at certain times and in certain places;
(ii) by drawing the patient's attention to the existence of temporal, spatial and social realities of their world;
(iii) by being people whom the patient knows are concerned with his welfare.

The nurse and therapist may differ in the way they provide holding and containment. Usually the nurse will not perform this function by an interpretation of her words or deeds, whereas the therapist may do so.

The nurse provides *actual care,* in the sense of doing something for a patient as a more or less token gesture of holding or containment.

The therapist never actually does something for the patient in this sense. For example, whereas the nurse may suggest that the patient has an early night, and take him a cup of hot chocolate as a token of holding (doing two actual things: organizing the patient's time and space and providing a physical token), the therapist will not make suggestions or do things for the patient, but rather, will attempt to draw the patient's attention to the dependent needs which he is expressing.

Generally, nurses do more *registering* of a patient's distorted or inappropriate relating, and therapists do more *interpreting.* However, both sometimes do either. Both are concerned to help the patient recover and understand 'lost' thoughts, feelings and actions by the processes of registering and interpreting.

However, a number of important and clearcut, if not always recurrent, differences do exist between the ways in which nurses and therapists do these things.

Because of his training, his orientation and the mode of work of psychotherapy, the therapist is more self-conscious about giving interpretations of the discrepancy between how the patient views him (the transference) and how the therapist has behaved. That is, in therapy the patient and therapist talk with the particular focus on the patient's past and its relationship to the way the patient relates to the therapist and the present. The nurse and patient may discuss his past and its relationship to how he relates to the nurse, but this is not their primary focus. Furthermore, the nurse and patient do not meet regularly in a consulting room whereas the therapist and patient do. This structure is specifically designed, as is the rule that the patient must say what is in his mind, to facilitate the revelation of the transference of the patient to the therapist. Thus, although the therapist and patient may discuss transferences to people other than the therapist, the transference to the therapist will be more frequently and more powerfully evident. It will be the focus of interactions, owing to the structure and function of the meetings between therapist and patient, more than will those between the patient and the nurse.

Both nurse and therapist may draw attention to inappropriate affect (for example, smiling and laughter by a patient when describing something painful or upsetting). However, the therapist does not draw attention to inappropriate behaviour, apart from in psychotherapy groups, *as it is happening.* The nurse does so, frequently. Both nurses and therapists will register, from time to time, the way the patient makes them feel. By and large, the therapist will self-consciously and explicitly do this, to draw attention to transference phenomena. In contrast, the nurse does not do so self-consciously for this reason; rather, she will tell the patient how he is making her feel, so as to help him to grasp the reality of the consequences of his actions. She may help the patient to realize, for example, that being beastly and manipulative makes people feel beastly and manipulated. In addition, of course, the nurse will register this because she does not like feeling beastly or manipulated! This is quite different from the therapist, because although the therapist does act as a litmus paper for how the patient makes him feel, he also, more than the nurse, aims to 'merge' or empathize with the patient to discover what his experience is like as well. The nurse does this less, because she is in a real relationship in a less artificial (although, since it is in a hospital designed to be therapeutic, it is artificial to this extent) social context than that of the consulting room. In real relationships the kind of subject matters for discussion, and the psychic boundary-breaking characteristic of the therapist/patient relationship, are not frequently evident.

Both nurse and therapist draw attention to, or register, patient contraventions of expectations. Nurses frequently report that they feel that patients experience them as 'nagging', whilst therapists do not. This may be explicable in terms of the different reasons why nurses and therapists draw attention to breakage of expectations. They share the reason that both wish to help the patient to be aware of his relationship to the social reality of the rules of living of the hospital. However, the nurse does so because, especially at night, she has a hospital to run; patient contraventions of expectations make this job harder. The therapist, on the other hand, does not have this job and can concentrate on the psychic significance of such contraventions.

We might summarize the differences between the nurse and therapist roles in fostering the mutative processes with the example of their different relations to the activity of smoking. By and large, the nurse will not interpret the symbolic significances of a patient's cigarette smoking, whereas the therapist may do so because his primary task is to discover and help the patient to use knowledge of, the meaning of his deeds, words and experience. Confronted with a cigarette smoker, rather than interpreting it, and dependent on context, the nurse will be more likely to draw attention to the consequences or effects of the activity: to ill health, to the rules against doing so in particular contexts, to the fire risk at night in bedrooms, to the distress caused by a cough to someone nearby, and so forth. It is even possible that the nurse might accept a cigarette if the patient offers her one.

Nurse/therapist/patient relations

The above account of individual roles does not explore what goes on between them. The following is a formulation of the psychodynamics of these relations, using the ideas of Winnicott.

Relating, using and transitional using

The distinction between the use of objects and relating to them is a means for analysing the relationship between nurse and patient and therapist. Winnicott (1972, p.104) describes the difference between these as follows:

> For the time being, may I leave it that relating can be described in terms of the individual subject and that usage (of objects) cannot be described except in terms of acceptance of the object's independent existence, its property of having been there all the time.

Developmentally, the infant moves from object-relating to usage, and this latter is essential if the further development of transitional object usage is to occur.

Nurse and therapist techniques for effecting these changes

Both nurse and therapist, whether consciously or not, should be seeking to enable the patient to move from relating, to usage, to transitional usage. However, they will use different methods to achieve this. The nurse uses the countertransference which the patient evokes in her, as the means. Her real feelings, often expressed by sentences beginning, 'You make me feel . . .', are adhered to and expressed to the patient. If the patient is relating to her, this fact will sooner or later, *if he is capable of developing usage,* impress itself upon him. In the act of recognizing that the nurse has real feelings and that these are not the same as those which he attributes to her, the patient moves from relating to usage. Out of this change, transitional usage may develop.

The therapist, on the other hand, uses verbal registration and interpretation as his principal tools for drawing the patient's attention to not only the fact of relating (where it occurs in place of usage) but also, the patterns of relating (transference patterns). The therapist constantly seeks awareness of his countertransference; he may permit and is unable to avoid some of it directly impinging on the patient's consciousness. However, the use of these feelings as a direct, if non-verbal, way of saying, 'You are not treating me as separate from your magical wishes' is not his main technique. This is not to say that the therapist does not obtain information about the patient from the way he makes him, the therapist, feel.

Nurse and therapist countertransference

A nurse who is being related to rather than used by patients is under some strain. She is the persistent recipient of projections, and it is hard for her to sustain the reality of her feelings and keep expressing them whilst under such a barrage. To stop doing this, however, is to fail to insist on the patient's recognition of them (which inherently is an act of usage when the patient does so). The nurse may give way in two main ways: by accepting the patient's projections to the extent of introjection, and becoming as the patient perceives her in fantasy; or by erecting defences. Two clear means of defence are described by Menzies (1959) and Tonnesmann (1979). For Menzies, the defence is a resort to the nurse's social structural position, with an emphasis on her role's artefacts, such as her uniform, her authority, and an impersonal professionalism. For Tonnesmann, the defence is a collapse into 'niceness' in which all value judgements, whether personal or professional, are superseded by an 'unconditional positive regard' which denies the existence of separateness and impoverishes reality testing. Either defence impedes patient recognition of relating.

Whereas the nurse must express her countertransference spontaneously and largely without subjecting it to conscious scrutiny whilst doing so, the therapist must bring his under control and use it carefully and sparingly, if his interpretations are to effect the desired change in the patient from relating to usage.

These differences in the clinical use to which nurse and therapist put their countertransference create a major problem in their relationship. They are doing the opposite of each other, and the danger is that the nurse's attempts to be spontaneous and straightforward in her expression of her feelings threaten the therapist's need to examine and control his expressions of his feelings, and vice versa. When nurse and therapist meet to discuss a patient there are nearly always the following tensions: a desire on the part of the therapist to interpret the nurse's feelings about the patient to her; a desire on the part of the nurse to suggest to the therapist that he does not understand what the patient 'is really like' and that his understanding is 'too theoretical'.

Whilst the therapist is protecting himself against uncomplicated expression of his feelings towards the patient, the nurse is trying to avoid interpreting and failing to express hers (always a big temptation for a nurse in a psychoanalytically oriented institution). Both are avoiding that which the other seeks to achieve.

The problem is particularly acute for the therapist. He may be defending himself from massive patient projections, and these may have aroused powerful countertransferences in him. When he meets with the nurse, the temptation to offer interpretations of her countertransference is correspondingly great; it is an attractive and obvious way of interpreting his own to himself, *but by proxy,* and as a defence from doing so. Likewise, the temptation is great to criticize the nurse for expressing her feelings towards the patient; he must not do so himself, so he tells himself not to by prohibiting her. Again, the therapist may be highly defended against certain projections of the patient; this may lead him to criticize the nurse for adopting defences against her patient's projections.

Such actions on the therapist's part inevitably increase the nurse's difficulties and decrease the likelihood of her being able to sustain the reality of her feelings in the face of patient projections, and relating rather than use. Excessive self-awareness of her own countertransference may inhibit the spontaneity of expression thereof, always assuming that the therapist's interpretations do not turn out to be incorrect and are not, still further, intrusive projections to be added to those already emanating from the patient. Interpretation of (or projection on to) the nurse's defences are unlikely to enable her to relinquish them, since they are a real response to real projections whose illumination does not alone remove them.

Supervising the nurse/therapist dyad

The foregoing suggests a need for meetings between the nurse and therapist, but also for monitoring of their relationship. The meeting is required so that the two can discuss the differences and similarities in the way the patient is relating to and using each of them. 'Ailment' types of splitting would be revealed by these discussions, but, in addition, the therapist obtains valuable information regarding the conditions under which the patient was able to use rather than relate to; the nurse can receive reassurance and support for her attempts *to obtain recognition and use of the reality of her feelings in the countertransference.*

However, it is essential that the therapist is aware of, and helped by a supervisor to understand, his self-defensive wish to interpret and project on to the inevitably threatening mode of functioning by which the nurse works. Thus, for example, the therapist may be helped to understand that a nurse who is defending herself against a set of massive projections from his patient needs to do this. He can use this knowledge and work with the patient on his relation to the nurse (hopefully stemming the tide of projections and aiding the nurse thereby). The therapist in turn can be helped to understand that his need to interpret the nurse's defences (or use of her countertransference) derives from the threat it represents to himself in his work, and not to a rational and useful wish to help the nurse thereby. The nurse can be helped by the recognition that the patient's projections are indeed massive, and her anxieties may be allayed. If nurse psychopathology is indeed the cause of a problem, then her countertransference can receive tactful attention, but from the appropriate persons for the right reasons: not from the therapist in acts of self-defence, but from the responsible nursing and/or consultant supervisors.

In short, those aspects of the nurse/therapist dyad requiring supervision are not the case material as such, but are questions as to

(a) the extent to which the therapist is able to understand his need to project onto or interpret the nurse's countertransference;
(b) the degree to which the nurse is being forced to defend herself from patient projections rather than to express her countertransference, and the degree to which any defences are not taken up for this reason (i.e. they may be expressions of her psychopathology);
(c) the extent to which the therapist is taking up the patient's projections to the nurse (thereby freeing her to countertransfer and induce object-usage) in the sessions.

The principal object of conversation for the nurse/therapist dyad's meeting would be the relating to, and using of, the nurse by the patient, in order to enable the therapist to intervene in this relationship (by investigating it with the patient in sessions) *so that the patient's progress from relating to, to using, to transitional using of the nurse countertransference is facilitated.*

Note that this formulation requires regular nurse/therapist meetings, and regular supervision of this relationship of a detailed and very specific kind. It is also new, it outmodes the 'therapist treats, the nurse cares' model, and replaces it with almost its opposite: 'the patient's change is increasingly realized as the treatment proceeds, in his relationship to the nurse, and the therapist exists primarily to facilitate this change'.

Perhaps this account is too one-sided in that it mainly concentrates on the problems which the nurse presents for the therapist by her *modus operandi.* It should be added that the nurse, by staying herself, helps the patient to a state of security in which he is able to tolerate therapy. Furthermore, in the N-T relation, the therapist's *modus operandi* is as much of a threat to the nurse's, as the reverse. Hence, the nurse will have to be aware of a wish to make the therapist work in the same way as her and to guard against hostility towards his more analytical ways. It might be said that the potential conflict between N and T reflects several differences which in this author's view are fundamental between the intellectualizing therapist (man) and the more down to earth nurse (woman); between a tendency to use words (therapist) and to use things (nurse); and between different trainings, authority, and rates of pay between the two. These make for inherent and inevitable conflicts which must be contained and accepted rather than acted out, if the patient's interests are to be served.

Further formulation of mutative processes in relation to nurse and therapist

The Cassel regards itself as being the proponent of a psychoanalytic orientation to mental hospital treatment. A psychoanalytic view, stripped to its bare bones, sees the adult's characteristic patterns of acting, feeling and thinking as being significantly affected by his infantile and early childhood experience. Where these patterns are disturbed, the psychoanalyst attempts to support the remaining undisturbed patterns whilst also helping the patient to understand the relation of both types to their early origins. However, what is involved here is not simply the recollection or re-enactment of these early experiences. The crucial problem lies in the way the patient experiences or *construes* his past. The objective of the treatment is to bring about a *reconstruction* of the past by the patient in such a way that he is ultimately able to carry on this work without analytic help.

The work of reconstruction does not change what actually happened to the patient in his childhood, but it aims to change the way these past events and patterns are experienced by the patient in the present: he develops a new relation to his past-in-his-present self, and this can render his past inert where before it was poisoning his present because of the way he was construing it.

This process can be described as being composed of three interacting psychical processes. These do not occur in any particular sequence, and the patient may fluctuate between all of them in periods of 30 seconds, 2 days, 3 months, and so forth. They are the registration or recognition of patterns of disturbance. There may follow interpretation or attempts to defend against such recognition and to defend against the third process, that of reconstruction, in which the relation between present patterns and those of the past is construed and experienced *anew*.

Since patients differ in their capacities to use different media of representation, they will vary in the extent to which recognition, interpretation and reconstruction are possible for them in verbal or non-verbal media. Their preferences for different sizes of social entity will also vary. Indeed, André Green (1979) has suggested that the patient's preference for some media over others (e.g. psychosomatizing as against the spoken word, written word, or action) may itself be regarded as a form of information about him, and a form or symptom of disturbance.

What, then, is the role of the nurse and the community in these processes? In the first instance, the nurse may attempt reconstruction, probably without verbalizing it, of her own and the patient's past. This is a means of helping herself to understand and withstand the patient's projections and transferences to her.

However, the nurse is also instrumental in helping the patient re-experience the dramas of the past *in a new way*: to reconstrue it as opposed to re-enacting it. For example, a patient may have repeatedly experienced his mother as instrusive, and may transfer this characteristic to his nurse repeatedly and in a pattern which takes no account of the extent to which the nurse actually is so. If the nurse 'stays herself', she may in reality be intrusive sometimes, generous at others, and plain niggardly at others. In attempting to re-enact his past drama, the patient will have difficulty (if the nurse sticks to her affective guns) in his role as director, in getting the nurse to play her part 'properly', that is, to accept the role of intruder. A new drama will unfold, with the nurse insisting on changes to the personality. Rather than being a re-enactment of a long gone experience, this will be a fresh, novel, *dramatic* one for the patient, whose performance is in itself a reconstruction of a tired and outmoded play. If the patient is able to get involved in this new play, he will have an experience of playing which will help to render the old script inert and obsolete. He will cease to experience 'mother' as an unreal, wholly intrusive figure, but as intrusive sometimes, detached and disinterested at others and so forth. This is a use of the nurse to obtain an experience of the diversity of the reality of self and other, based on an authentic separateness between imagined wishes and the reality and their interactive nature. Fantasy can become imagination, and the self's imagination can be enriched by that of others (if one can only accept their separate existence) in acts of playfulness and dramatic enterprise.

From such experiences the patient may be able to leave the hospital with some new, internalized object relations which are capable of withstanding the frustrations of there being an outside world. This formulation finally destroys the 'the therapist treats, the nurse cares' division: both treat, using different media of communication, with different utilizations of the self and the other's topographic striation of consciousness, but promoting the flow between registration, reconstruction and interpretation of defences against these processes. The notion that the nurse is merely 'the eyes and ears' of the therapist, 'spying' on the patient in between sessions and helping him to survive until the next, recedes into obscurity when confronted with the formulations described above.

Conclusion

The meticulous scrutiny of the patient's relations with, and use of the media of communication of, the social entities of the community is necessary if in-patient status is to be used effectively for therapeutic ends. The nurse and therapist play the key role in this scrutiny, and it is vital that their relationship, in turn, is the object of a well-focussed supervision.

Under these circumstances, there is no need for a 'separation system' (Ployé,1977). The free emergence of the patient's conflicts, and of their reconstruction, will be facilitated. Splitting of nurse and therapist (Main, 1946) should prove difficult and the tendency of each to impede the work of the other will be reduced to a minimum.

Our analysis, using Winnicott's concepts of using and relating to objects, has led us to make two principal claims:

1. That psychotherapy in the in-patient setting should take as its primary task the facilitation of the patient/nurse relationship. It is in this relationship, and not in the briefer and more structured one with the therapist, that the experience of a new and 'good' object relation occurs and is manifest. It is with this new object relation internalized that the patient leaves the hospital.
2. To make this possible, the therapist's tendency to invade the nurse's work with interpretations must be monitored and controlled through a well-focussed supervision of the relationship, and the therapist must be persuaded to regard the patient/nurse relation as a key consideration whilst in the consulting room.

Active communication between nurse and therapist is advocated if the patient's relation to the community is to be exploited for therapeutic gains. However, reasons are advanced for supposing that this relationship is inherently problematic, and requires careful structuring and supervision, if anti-therapeutic distortions are to be avoided.

[5]

Nurse Therapist Supervision

Lydia Tischler

THIS PAPER DESCRIBES a particular technique for monitoring the nurse/therapist relationship. It pays special attention to the feelings in the countertransference which patients inevitably evoke in their treaters, and the effect these feelings have on their work.

The need to monitor the nurse/therapist relationship was identified in the course of a research project undertaken by the hospital with the Brunel Institute of Organizational and Social Studies (BIOSS)in 1980-2. It forms part of a continuous process of refining the hospital's treatment practices and is rooted in the pioneering work of Tom Main and the late Doreen Weddell (the former matron of the hospital and a psychoanalyst). They initiated a process which drastically altered in-patient treatment. It grew out of the inter-related development of applying psychoanalytic principles and devising new techniques of nursing. Firstly and most importantly, it reappraised the view of the patient from a passive recipient to an active participant of his or her treatment, whose co-operation came to be regarded as essential for recovery. It altered not only the role of the patient vis-à-vis his treaters but the treaters too had to relinquish their customary roles vis-à-vis each other and their patients. The patient could no longer be seen as the helpless infantilized individual whose improvement depended on the treatment prescribed by the doctor and carried out with the assistance of the nurse; a change which was not always welcome, or at best greeted with ambivalence.

The nurse was freed to become an autonomous professional, to develop new skills and to take responsibility for her nursing decisions, being accountable to senior nursing colleagues. In her relationship to the patient the nurse now, instead of thinking for and doing things for the patient, addressed the healthy functioning part of the patient's ego and worked with him or her.

While during this first phase a number of settings existed to link the work of nursing and therapy, the emphasis was on the separate and distinct roles of the two, and on adequate communication between them. Questions of what constituted adequate communications were bound to arise; for example, what did therapist and nurse need to know from each other? How much should each know? What did the therapist need to select from his or her work with the patient? What did the therapist need or want to know about the behaviour, daily activities, moods and feelings of the patient as perceived and experienced by the nurses? How did the nurse select and judge what the therapist needed to know? Furthermore, how important was it for the therapist to know how other people in the community experienced the patient? What did the therapist need to know about the reality of the patient's life in the hospital, not only as experienced and related by the patient? How did nurse and therapist deal with communications from the patient about each other?

The application of psychoanalytic principles to an in-patient setting brought its own problems, not least how to combine psychosocial nursing and individual psychotherapy within a community dimension. Based on the foundation of Main and Weddell, generations of practitioners have contributed new insights whether in small or large measure. These have become incorporated in a corpus of knowledge (see Brian Muir's paper, p. 64). Nevertheless, every new member of staff has to find ways of reconciling the private nature of analytic psychotherapy with the more public life of the community. The analytic model is based on the primacy of the patient's transference to the therapist, and the interpretations made in the transference are seen as the important mutative agent. The contract between patient and therapist should be based on the rule of confidentiality; yet this has to be reconciled with the need for open communication amongst staff, and especially between the patient's nurse and therapist. It also has to be reconciled with the proliferation of the transference to the institution, not only the transference of the patient, but also the countertransference of the staff to patients and to each other.

While for the therapist the dilemma is deciding what aspects of the patient's inner world to communicate to nursing and other colleagues, the dilemma for the nurse is of a different nature. The nurse's observations, because they deal with the everyday, are often felt to be so ordinary and mundane as not to be worth mentioning. Hartnup (p. 129) observes 'there is no intrinsic reason why a nurse and therapist who are skilled at work with their patients should be skilled at working together or making use of each other's observations'. Nevertheless, the dynamic interplay between members of staff is crucial to the treatment of patients and was noted by Stanton and Schwartz in their classic work *The Mental Hospital* (1954). They draw attention to the dangers for the patient in a situation where the staff concerned with that patient are not communicating with each other, and how at times patients can be driven mad when different staff give contradictory instructions concerning the same patient. Such problems persist, as the following example shows.

A fairly new therapist told his very disturbed adolescent patient that he would be available at any time if the patient felt he needed him. During the night, the patient began to demand that he wanted to see his therapist. The nurse became very alarmed by the persistence of this demand, as she naturally assumed that it was an expression of a serious regression in the patient. She was nonplussed when she heard the following day in a staff meeting that not only had the therapist made the offer, he had also omitted to mention it to the nurse.

In his paper 'The ailment'(1946), Main shows how nurses and therapists ignore each other's communication at their peril and to the detriment of the patient. He highlights the dangers to the patient's treatment when critical feelings between members of staff and powerful feelings towards patients are suppressed or go unrecognized.

The dynamic forces which bring this about, i.e. the neurotic individual's need to evoke powerful feelings in those who treat him and consciously or unconsciously to create or exploit already existing staff splits, are as operative today as they were when Main drew attention to them. It is inherent in the treatment process that staff will daily be faced with pressures from transference and countertransference feelings, and projections and distortions from patients. It is the task of the nurse/therapist supervision to turn these to therapeutic use.

It may not be too fanciful to draw an analogy between the mental health worker and those who work with radioactive material, in that both are at risk from fallout of different kinds. The mental health worker is exposed to the emotional fallout of the regressed patient's primitive wishes and feelings, for which he still seeks gratification, and to the patient's unworked-through relationships to objects experienced as unsatisfactory. However, there is an important difference between the way the mental health worker needs to protect himself from the anxiety such patients can arouse, in order to maintain the capacity to function, and that of the nuclear power worker. Unlike workers with radioactive material, the mental health worker's protective devices (defences) must not be so impermeable that the 'fallout' fails to impinge; on the otherhand, they need to be robust enough to safeguard the worker's emotional health.

The promotion and maintenance of effective staff functioning is an essential aspect of the hospital's work, and a number of different settings and structures exist for this purpose. On the Family and Adolescent Unit, the nursing officer and principal child therapist or consultant have 2 weekly supervisions lasting 45 minutes; one with the nurse and therapist of a particular adolescent and the other with nurse and therapist or therapists of a family. Thus a family or adolescent is discussed about every 6 weeks in this particular supervision.

Nurse/therapist supervision is the latest in this line of development and, as has already been mentioned, arose from the study with BIOSS. As a result, new structures were set up in which the network of professional relationships of the different disciplines, (nurses, therapists, child therapists, social workers and teachers with their diverse training, skills and varying levels of experience and seniority) could be integrated. These differences as well as the distinct work settings in which therapists, nurses and teachers work, while extending the therapeutic potential, also add to the possibility of confusion, misunderstanding and misinterpretation.

To highlight only some of these areas: the nurse works in the public area of the hospital where her or his work and especially the interaction with patients is open to observation by colleagues and other patients. Except when they are in meetings together, the contact between nurse and patient is less structured, so that nurse and patients actively need to seek each other out or perhaps at times to avoid each other. Their time and activities together can be encroached upon by other patients and staff. In contrast, the therapist has regular times set aside for a patient; his or her work is carried out in the privacy of the consulting room. Although the differences described above relate to the settings and not to the content of the work, the setting does dictate how the work can be accomplished.

Hartnup, (p. 128), speaks of a need for a translation and synthesizing service to make the disparate observations meaningful. I would add that this depends on the degree to which the experiences with patients can first of all be processed by the workers concerned. Often these are highly charged, and need to be, as it were, 'decontaminated' (to continue with the analogy) by being subjected to reality testing.

When the experiences can be processed by linking feelings with thoughts, they can be represented in more usable form to the patient. This is a somewhat circuitous way of saying that it is more therapeutic for the patient if the worker can respond rather than react to a patient's communication.

While the details of the study with BIOSS can be found elsewhere in this volume (see Chapters 4 and 19) it is necessary briefly to summarize some of the findings here. The study highlights, amongst other things, how inequalities on many different levels (of status, pay, and so on) between nurse and therapist leads to a distorted view, adhered to consciously and unconsciously by both nurses and therapists, of the relative importance of their work.

This is a view which holds that the important work is carried on in the therapist's consulting room, while the nurse carries out the subordinate task of providing a 24-hour caring environment so that psychotherapy can take place. The model is one in which the therapist 'treats' and the nurse 'cares'. This has serious implications not only for the patient's treatment but for the way in which the patient may treat the nurse. The study with BIOSS led to an important reappraisal of the nurse/therapist/patient relationship and to a new formulation that both therapist *and* nurse treat, though they use different modalities, techniques and skills. These different techniques and skills *together* comprise the therapeutic process which facilitates change in the patient.

Elements of what James calls 'mutative process' (see Chapter 4) which he lists as 'holding and containment, actual care', are more often provided by the nurse; 'registering and interpreting distorted or inappropriate relating' are quite properly the work of the therapist, though the former functions would in different ways merit comment from nurse or therapist. James makes use of Winnicott's concepts of 'relating', 'usage' and 'transitional relating' as stages in the development of object relationships, terminology which on first reading is somewhat confusing, especially as in Winnicott's schema 'relating' precedes 'usage'(Winnicott 1972).

Nevertheless, this way of looking at nursing has provided a useful index for registering the changes as they occur in patients, viz. their altered perception of the nurse. The patients' disturbed relationships, both to their external and internalized objects are soon reflected in their relationship to their nurses, especially in their inability to see the nurses as useful people who are interested in their welfare. More often than not, the patient in the early stages of his or her stay will develop a hostile dependency which will leave the nurse feeling exploited or denigrated. The nurse may, on the other hand, be treated with defensive aloofness, which will make him or her feel useless and devalued.

When families are admitted they bring with them not only their own internalized problems, but the disturbed family dynamics. Admission is often if not invariably sought with the conscious or unconscious intention to force some member of the family to change. Quite often, an apparently healthy husband wishes his ill wife to be cured, while the ill wife demands a better, more understanding, devoted husband. Children, too, are usually caught up in particular roles to fit in with family pathology.

Similar projective mechanisms operating in the families will be employed by the patients in their relationship with the staff. How the nurse and the therapist will be able to deal with and make therapeutic use of the patient's projections depends on a number of factors, including the level of experience of the nurse and therapist. Over-identification with the plight of the patient can be one of the mechanisms whereby therapist or nurse, and particularly the less experienced ones, will deal with patients who render their work impotent or useless. When this happens to the therapist, he or she may embark on a campaign to change the nurse, or her way of nursing, apparently in the interests of the patient's treatment. There are many subtle ways in which the therapist, in the service of defensive denial, can exert these pressures, often resorting to interpretations of the nurse's conflicts, so that the patient's problems and difficulties, which he or she is fending off, end up being called the nurse's problems. The nurses, too, have their own defensive manoeuvres against feelings of being useless and inadequate engendered by the patient. They also have ways of putting pressure on the therapist to make more effective interpretations which they hope will make the patient more bearable.

These feelings can be especially powerful if the patient senses that the therapist unconsciously colludes with his attacks on the nurse, or vice versa. Let us go back to the example cited earlier about the patient who demanded to see his therapist in the middle of the night. The therapist's consciously good intentions and concern for the patient nevertheless resulted in reinforcing the patient's primitive needy demands and made him almost unnursable for that night.

We came to recognize the pressures for better nursing and more effective therapy as being in inverse ratio to a patient's treatability. In other words, the less the patient was able or willing to participate actively in his or her treatment, the more effort nurse and therapist wished that the other would exert. In nurse/therapist supervision, nurse and therapist would then exhort each other in the nicest possible way to improve their techniques, as a way of dealing with the guilt feelings that staff can experience when their patients are not improving. It would seem, then, that the patient successfully transmitted his or her problem to the nurse and therapist, who then experienced it as their problem. In the nurse/therapist supervision, the aim is to reconvert this into the patient's problem, where it belongs. At the same time, it is important to recognize that this process is one of the paths whereby we can get an understanding of the patient's pathology.

Nurse/therapist supervision, as a means of monitoring the working relationship, was a fairly recent innovation, and a way of working needed to be devised. The particular technique described in this paper owes much to the contribution of Ann Heymans, the then Nursing Officer of the Families and Adolescent Unit, with whom this work was jointly undertaken. The technique evolved gradually during the course of conducting supervisions on the Families and Adolescent Unit. While embracing the principles and rationale arrived at in the BIOSS study, it developed along somewhat different lines from those outlined in James' paper. In listening to therapists and nurses talking to each other, we became aware of the frequent misconceptions and distorted feelings therapists and nurses had about each other's work, and how this obstructed the work they could do. We came to recognize these as the conscious mutual fantasies they had about each other's work and how these were transmitted by both conscious and unconscious communications of their patients. In the nurse/therapist supervision we set ourselves the task of teasing out these distortions and confronting them with the reality. The emphasis was always to highlight the part the patient played in these distortions, and to help to free the workers from them, so that they could then be fed back appropriately to the patient by the nurse and therapist in their respective areas of work.

To subject one's work to the scrutiny of others in a mixed professional setting is never easy, especially at times when the treaters feel unsure of their competence. However, for the exercise to be useful, weaknesses, vulnerabilities and mutual feelings of mistrust must be exposed. It therefore requires considerable skill and tact on the part of the supervisors to allow the supervision to become a learning experience, rather than being experienced as only a criticizing one.

Description is bound to simplify what is essentially a complex process. It is important to find the right open-ended questions which promote reflection and discussion. It is very important not to have ready answers and solutions. Such simple-sounding questions as, 'When did you, nurse and therapist, last speak to each other?' can lead to the important discovery for the nurse and therapist that a whole week may have gone by when there was no communication between them outside the usual meeting structure. This may eventually lead to examining the dynamics operating between patients and staff that have brought this about.

For example, the following concerns were raised regarding the supervision of a family which consisted of mother, father, and two children, a boy and girl. Both parents had individual therapy; in addition the 4-year-old boy was being seen by the child therapist. Three therapists and the family's nurse were present. No one could recollect what happened in the previous supervision.

The father's therapist began by saying that she felt isolated from the nurses and other therapists. She had picked up some very inhuman qualities in the father and she needed contact in order to test the reality of her perceptions. The nurse responded by saying that she felt warmly towards the family, especially the mother, and she commented that she found them approachable. The mother's therapist felt that he was working in parallel but had no idea what was happening in the nursing, and he didn't think the nurse had much idea of what was happening in the therapy. I couldn't help feeling that these comments were presented in a phoney way. I said that this discussion sounded insincere, and reflected the family's attempt to present themselves as 'nice'. The boy's therapist then responded by describing his experiences with his patient, where the therapist was constantly left feeling that he didn't know what anything meant.

Eventually the more critical feelings between members of staff began to emerge and could be seen to reflect the covert feelings of the members of the family. For example, eating was a particular problem in this family; the father was a strict vegetarian and the mother surreptitiously let the children eat meat. Teatime was a specially difficult time for the family; their dissatisfactions were projected on to the nurse, who was blamed for whatever went wrong. In this supervision it transpired that the father's therapist had identified with his feelings towards the nurse. We eventually pinpointed what lay behind the defensive 'niceness', namely a fear that the exploration of critical feelings could lead to a dangerous explosion in the family.

Another example from a particular supervision concerned Family A. Their first nurse was, unusually for our hospital, transferred with very little notice to another unit where a staffing crisis had developed. Mrs A had individual therapy. No regular therapy had been set up for Mr A but there was a therapist available for him. The arrangement was that Mr A could request to see the therapist, but the therapist could also request to see Mr A if staff felt it was necessary. This arrangement had been arrived at in their assessment meeting and was known to all those who worked with the family. In the nurse/therapist supervision, which occurred shortly after a new nurse had been allocated, we became aware during the meeting that father's therapist had not turned up. He had not forgotten, but did not feel himself to be part of the treatment team and, therefore, did not think his presence was required. The parallel with the father's feelings of his position in the family was striking. The nursing aims formulated during review meetings had been passed on from one nurse to the other, but we heard from the new nurse that the family was not working with him. On the contrary, they made him feel very useless, and gradually it began to emerge that he was fed up. He saw no point in investing his energies in working with this family, in beginning to establish a relationship with them, (something quite unusual for this particular nurse), as the family were leaving in a month's time anyway. His frustration and dissatisfaction with this family and their treatment of him had given rise to a considerable degree of resentment, especially as he assumed quite erroneously, that a leaving date had been arranged with the therapist, and that he had been excluded from this decision-making. The leaving date, as it turned out, had been manufactured entirely by the patients, but somehow they managed to convey the feeling to the nurse that it had been a decision arrived at in a therapy session. The therapist, in her turn, became aware of her own feelings of anger and resentment that her working relationship with the A's first nurse had been disrupted, and that she was having to start with a new nurse, whom she felt was not interested in the family.

In another context, a formulation had been arrived at as to how the family used distancing as a defence against dependency, and the concomitant aggressive feelings this aroused. Here, we saw it reflected in staff attitudes towards each other, and enacted in their relationship. The nurse, because of the feeling it had engendered in him, had not gone to the therapist to check the patients' statements, nor had the therapist sought out the nurse for similar reasons. Both therapist and nurse felt relieved when we arrived at an understanding of the underlying dynamics. The nurse could use his understanding of how the family made him feel with the patients, while the therapist could use this material in her sessions to link it back to the original objects to whom these feelings belonged.

In another supervision, a newly-arrived therapist and a nurse who had just joined the unit met for a nurse/therapist supervision about a new family who had only recently been admitted. The nurse began by saying that there was really nothing to say as she had only just started with the family and didn't really know them yet. The therapist felt somewhat similarly. Furthermore, the family had so far presented no special nursing problem. In her therapy, the mother was also only just getting going. We noted a common theme of newness (it was also their first nurse/therapist supervision); to their surprise, feelings about that began to emerge both from the nurse and the therapist.

The nurse recalled how embarrassed and awkward she had felt when, on the day of admission, the therapeutic team met with the family. The little girl, finding her mother's lap occupied by her younger brother, went to sit on the nurse's lap. The nurse had felt awkward because of the potential rivalry which she felt the little girl had set up between the nurse and her mother. This led to other themes of rivalry within the staff group. These were all very pertinent issues in this family; in the end, the supervision time in this instance was felt to be too short.

Conclusion

Nurse/therapist supervision is one particular method which aims to further the work of the nurse and the therapist in their separate areas. It engages with the conscious fantasies, misperceptions, externalizations and projections which are an inevitable product of engaging *affectively* with patients. Anxiety, which staff are bound to feel, can be respected; by being subjected to reality testing, it is reduced. The focus must always be on the patient and the feelings he or she engenders in the treating couple or team, although at times, the supervision may be experienced as an attempt to treat the nurse and therapist.

Stressing the part the patient plays in these distortions is not to ignore any part the staff themselves may play in this. It is my contention, however, that it is not useful to use a setting primarily designed for work with patients for vicarious treatment of staff. However, if staff can make use of the insight gained for themselves, this is a useful by-product of the primary task. It was quite notable that the same treaters would at different times experience very diverse feelings about each other, depending on the family under discussion. This underlined the countertransference origin of these feelings. Although no systematic study was undertaken at the time, it was our impression that there had been a notable diminution in the defensive posturings often adopted by therapists where interpreting the nurse's treatment of their patient. There was also a greater readiness on the part of the nurses to accept the limitations of what the therapist could achieve through interpretations in the consulting room.

Part Two
Clinical Work

[6]

Regressive Distortions in a Psychotherapeutic Community

Richard Burman

On admission to the Cassel, patients may regress to modes of behaviour that have concrete qualities and in which action is prominent. I wish to describe this with clinical illustrations from work with families. I will also refer to some causes and consequences. The observations here are my own, although a number of these phenomena have been described by Dr Tom Main in 'The Ailment'(1946). Some of the basic mechanisms I have taken for granted are well-known from the writings of Wilfred Bion, Herbert Rosenfeld, Hanna Segal and Isobel Menzies Lyth.

The invitation to admittance to the Cassel leads in many instances to a worsening of the patient's functioning. In some cases their behaviour may become so bizarre, demanding or intolerable, that early discharge is resorted to. But even in most instances, in which the patient becomes engaged in the treatment and nursing culture, I see an inevitable concomitant of this engagement as including what in out-patients would be described as unhealthy regression and alarming acting-out. In some ways, regressive events seem to become a regular part of the patients' behaviour in the hospital, at least for a portion of their stay. The staff therefore need to embrace within their view of their task an appropriate sense of responsibility for what I think of as iatrogenic elements in this regressive disturbance, with the latter's primitive and concrete modes of expression. There are in every patient, of course, individual pathologies and distortions, but I am here describing what I see as more general behaviour consequent on coming into the hospital, although the intensities of this regression to concrete forms of functioning will vary.

A social organization such as a hospital cannot deal with more than it is designed to do, although there may be flexibility which depends on personal and interpersonal attributes and tolerances. In general, we are not able to cope with overt criminality, violence, or more than a small degree of out-of-touch bizarreness. Structure is composed of interpersonal and not physical or medicinal boundaries. Nor do we have facilities for coping with medical disease much beyond what would usually be handled in a medical or surgical out-patient. In this paper, I wish to describe behaviour that is difficult for the staff even within the limits of our social structure for tolerating regressive interpersonal behaviour.

I suppose that one of the reasons for this regression, whether it is within or beyond our capacities to bear, is to do with the inherent ambiguousness of an organization that aims to be sensitively accepting of any impulse at a psychic level, and which at the same time provides a range of actual material provisions (food, shelter, state moneys, etc.). Another aspect is the impression and, of course, the wish that the patient has on being admitted that responsibility for his or her welfare, treatment and future, rests entirely with the staff. These fundamental attitudes are projected onto the staff, because of the patient's impairment of self-responsibility. As I mentioned, much of this should be seen as inevitable, and its consequences a part of the daily interactional struggle.

One of the features of the regression is the concretization of expectations of the hospital. Later I wish to describe clinical manifestations of frank parasitic demands for provisions. Another feature is a distortion of behaviour that seems to me to be associated with a widening split, or a defusion between two things. On the one hand, there is the desiring side of impulse life, with its extreme consequent appearance of apparently unconflictual insatiability and, on the other, there is a severe persecutory fear of retaliation for the harm inevitably felt by the patient to be perpetrated on the staff and the institution. Because of the concretization of the behaviour, this harm is not only in the patient's imagination, but becomes felt by the staff in a very real interpersonal way.

Certain characteristic forms of behaviour tend to occur. The positive or desiring impulses may manifest as a holding on by the patient to insatiable demands for more time, attention and physical supplies, with indignation at the eventual discharge date even where this is arranged months ahead. It is not rare for windows to get broken as the discharge date approaches. The persecuted side, with its fear of realiation, can be manifested by repeated panicky urges, assertions, and actual moves to leave the hospital. The actual moves range from brief dashes out with the hope of being invited or fetched back by forgiving staff, through to more extended flights home, to permanent leaving which is unilaterally decided by the patient. Another well-known form of persecuted behaviour in in-patient situations, is self attacking acts; these no doubt also include intentions which are meant to punish staff by incurring feelings of remorse or loss in them; thus usually mixed motives apply in these instances.

The emphasis of the behaviour is, to a significant extent, on physical action in contrast to the verbal communications that one expects in out-patient treatment. This proclivity for action implies marked concrete thinking, and these actions may be examples of the primitive symbolic equations described by Segal. They also seem to consist, in condensed form, of repetitions of significant aspects of the patient's make-up. At times the patient's motivation appears so non-conflictual that one thinks of the description of the id in which all impulses exist together without contradiction, and in which highly condensed symbolizations occur. At times, one may feel amazed at an appearance of unconflicted wishfulness in the patient's attitude, as if the hospital is just as he or she wishes it to be. In such a situation, 'passive' may be converted en bloc into 'active', and various degrees of running away from the hospital, especially as the arranged discharge date approaches, can be an example of this.

For each patient, a mode of behaviour, or way of coping, tends to become idiosyncratic for him or her, a kind of shorthand combining the different aspects of the patient's make-up. These action-condensates contain products of disguised transference to individuals, but the regression becomes applied to the transference as well, resulting in an appearance of the transference being towards the hospital as a whole. In this way, the hospital can be wishfully perceived as a depersonalized provider of a service. Another distortion of such an apparently generalized transference in this id-like state of functioning, is that issues become important only with regard to their quantity. The patient, and the staff too, can become confused as to whether provisions, whether of emotions or of food, are too much or too little. This can extend to an extreme form in which the addiction to quantity becomes the conviction that more and more is better and better. Another general regressive tendency is that in which discriminative capacities tend to disappear and to be replaced, in patients as well as in staff, by rationalizations that particular external events, such as changes in the hospital or the staffing, are the main or sole cause of the disturbance in the patient. In such an atmosphere, the pressure has been for the patient's and staff's potentially individual and specific difficulties or perceptions to disappear. No doubt one of the motives for this tendency is its serving to avoid rivalry, it appearing to be safer to join in with uniform, standard beliefs.

These above forms of regressive behaviour with, (to the patient), their apparent advantage of avoiding conflict, necessitate severe ego defences. A typical ego defence in a helping institution such as this is for marked splitting of the personality and functioning to take place. There is projection by the patient of that aspect that would otherwise be in conflict into the staff. To the extent that staff support systems are not functioning adequately, the danger is that the most troublesome patient may be prematurely or precipitately discharged. Since one of the main pressures behind the projection of frightening impulses into the staff is the persecutory fear of having that impulse within oneself, the staff will become, in the patient's experience, persecutory and will tend to become attacked for this. I will mention later some characteristic forms of attack upon the hospital, the staff and its methods of working.

Some clinical examples

These examples are derived from a particular period of work in the in-patient Family Unit.

The parasitic exploitation of the hospital's provisions, in this first example, takes a very concrete form in which the hospital is treated as a limitless store of such provisions, or as a robot-like service facility. A 41-year-old divorced mother of a boy, her first child, aged six months at the time of their presentation to us, was admitted to the Cassel after she increasingly believed that certain neighbours were unmanageably 'hostile'. She behaved as if her child's excreta were dangerous, her referral being precipitated by, among other considerations, the increasing need of her local health visitor having to remove more and more of the baby's soiled nappies. She had, a few years before, been left by her husband. Not long before admission here she had been abandoned by the married father of her child. In the hospital, she increasingly demanded special food provisions, or money to buy these, for her child, whom she treated as specially precious and as if it were in continual danger from murderous other patients, or in danger from certain nurses whom she believed would steal the child's affections or loyalties from her. She did not readily verbalize these ideas; she always giving the indication that to do so might, as if by dangerous magic, bring about the very horrors that she feared. It soon looked as though she was able to treat the child as a prized object in this way as long as she had the hospital and the staff to criticize or abuse and demand from. She also believed, at times in the face of evidence to the contrary, that she herself was treated without warmth or consideration by the hospital, her therapist, or her nurse. She once imperiously threatened to report the hospital as failing to provide her with the food she said was necessary for her child. She provoked helpless indignation in other patients and nursing staff by not contributing to the housekeeping aspects and the cleaning tasks, or to the hospital community existence generally. At the same time she, on occasions at least, left debris which the nurses felt obliged to clean up for her; there was at least one period when the nurses felt helplessly unable to obtain her co-operation in keeping her room clean. The room became smelly and messy with leftover bits of food. There seemed to be no awareness in her of the efforts made on her behalf; rather, whatever helpful offer was made to her she would criticize as inadequate and demand more. If she was offered hospital money for travelling fares by bus, she said she needed taxi fares, and so on. She repeatedly expressed inexplicable symptoms of 'fear' in her sessions; it was either non-specific fear or else she would refuse to specify what it was. She expressed continual fear of other patients. She had, indeed, in her stay been struck violently on two occasions by two different patients, one male and the other female. She also feared that her child might be harmed or killed by other patients. In actual fact, the only dangers that befell her baby in the hospital were caused by repeated minor mistakes made by herself; for example, there was a period early on when, while changing her child's nappy, the child would somehow inexplicably fall off the bed onto the floor while she was, say, rolling up the nappy. On one occasion, both the present writer and the patient's nurse were in the patient's room, during the very early part of her stay. While the two of us watched with mounting alarm, the child rolled towards the edge of the bed, under the patient's nose, while she did nothing to stop it. (This I see as only one of the numerous examples in the hospital in which projective identification has scope for being enacted by the employment of actual interactions, as opposed to the verbal communications in out-patient psychotherapy). Another mistake made by this mother was when she wheeled her baby in its pushchair into a nearby supermarket; she forgot to tie the strap across the child so that he found himself tipped up onto the floor as she lifted the chair. As much as she could provoke indignation and frustration in some staff, so she could elicit great solicitude and anxiety, quite often on behalf of her child, in other staff members. (Of interest is the fact that so much of the interactions between staff and patients, at least certainly in such family situations as this one, consists of the potentially therapeutic understanding of, and management responses to, the way in which one person is used by another. In this woman, the key is the quality of her treatment of the staff members, or clearly, her child. This general point is dealt with in the paper presented by Alan Wilson (p. 54).) She asserted that she could not trust any of us. At the same time she made very little actual useful contribution to the running of the hospital. There is objective evidence that she was successful as a writer and researcher in a partnership with her husband, before their divorce. Her later motherhood, her regression in the hospital to severe non self-sufficiency and to demandingness, was a surprising contrast to her pre-admission successful sublimation. Her admission was not the exclusive reason, though, since her breakdown began in earnest during the time she was caring for her infant at home. She also had a history of out-patient psychiatric treatment. While the latter consisted of the prescription of psychotropic medication, her state then did not seem to include the kind of extreme regressive behaviour she settled into after admission to the Cassel. There are, of course, other points of relevance in her management which are not central to the purpose of this presentation, whose aim is mainly to describe some general behavioural phenomena in the in-patients. But for greater completeness of the main idea I should mention that, some weeks after her discharge from the hospital, following a stay of one and half years, she rushed her then two-year-old child to her local psychiatric casualty unit, saying that she feared the child had taken an overdose of some tablets of hers, (the nature of which not known to me at this point). However, this turned out to have been an obsessional panic. This would appear to be an illustration of how, following her discharge, she reacquired a degree, albeit an over-anxious degree, of self-responsibility that she had had more opportunity, while in the regression of the in-patient situation, to project into the staff.

A second clinical situation illustrates a concreteness of projection, by both index patient mother and her husband, of blameworthiness and dangerousness into the hospital. The mother was admitted to the Cassel with her husband and three young children, after in-patient psychiatric treatment elsewhere for very disturbed behaviour which included numerous instances of her running off into the night, running away from the previous hospital and an apparently dangerous attempt to hang herself while in the previous hospital. She had clearly felt deeply deprived all her life and she was chronically angry towards everyone around her. She gave an account of her own mother having gone into hospital for an unknown physical illness round about when she was four. Her mother died in hospital somewhere near the patient's seventh year. (The ages of her own three children on admission here just over a year ago were between three and six years). She never knew her father, to whom her mother was not married. Between her fifth and ninth year of age, she was in various homes, and briefly and intermittently cared for in private homes until she was finally fostered permanently at the age of nine by a sensitive and childless couple, her foster father being a church minister. She described feeling extreme and unwavering gratitude for their acceptance of her, though she also described having been legally adopted by that couple only at the age of 15 and then only after she herself had asked them to do so. She has described how, when she was still in a children's home, she used to be taken monthly for weekends to the family home of kind people, but she says she found her envy of the real and only daughter of that family so painful that she eventually refused that monthly outing. In the Cassel she would talk of her natural mother in rejecting tones as 'that woman who gave birth to me!'. In contrast, she talked of her adopting parents in idealized terms. She married a rather begrudging, usually disapproving, socially inflexible but apparently consistent and family-devoted man. They both depended on each other almost exclusively for adult company, rarely socializing outside the home. Before her admission to this hospital she was listed by her local social services department as a mother whose children were potentially at risk, although that department had anxiously avoided letting her know of their views because of their explicitly stated fear of her angry reaction. One, or both, of the younger restless and 'fractious' boys were accident-prone and demanded constant attention and vigilance due to anxiety about their physical actions. Indeed, one of them had, at home, made electrical contact at a safety wall plug by poking wires into it and giving himself a wide but evidently not deep burn on his face and hands. Immediately following admission, the mother adopted critical and blaming attitudes to the hospital for what she said were unmanageable dangers to her children, and she soon insisted that an extra stable-door be fitted to the end of the outside passageway of the Families Unit living quarters. She made sure that a couple of extra metal bannister palings were added to the short staircase just outside the Families annexe. Her husband had all along invariably tended to concur with his wife about her views of others. He had no psychiatric or admitted psychological disturbance in his history and he always spoke in a somewhat pedantically logical way, apparently untroubled by any self-doubts. His only problem was his wife's florid disturbance and, indeed, shortly after coming to the Unit she initially continued to make sudden sporadic dashes away from the hospital. Also, in the first half of her stay here she took two separate overdoses of analgesic tablets, one of them of a hundred tablets. Before admission, she used to complain of inability to cope with her children, for which she was receiving attempts at home help. She would convey to her husband that his going out to work left her with difficulties. She periodically telephoned him at work on his rounds via his radio telephone, so that he would have to return home to attend to her. Even in the previous psychiatric hospital, when she ran away, the staff there would telephone him. On one occasion at least it was he who actually found her hiding place. In this setting of an absence of any psychologically complained about symptoms in him he was, some months before they came to the hospital, admitted to a medical ward of their local hospital with what was diagnosed as an episode of 'unstable angina' lasting 48 hours, the organic basis having been substantiated on ECG and biochemical disturbance. The experienced psychiatrist who referred the couple to us told me that he feared that psychotherapeutic treatment might cause the husband to have another heart attack. The couple's overt appearance together was a rather grim and dour picture, each looking disconcertingly disapproving, she looking thunderingly critical and he wearing a near chronic frown of concern. Their characteristic way of talking to each other was with wary skirting around the subject, and with emotionless logicality; they were never openly or spontaneously angry towards each other, certainly as far as I was aware. In the absence of any emotional symptoms revealed by him, he, on one occasion in a conjoint session with his wife, gave a strange and unexpected reaction: without any stimulus apparent to either his wife or the writer, he suddenly took fright, got up from his chair and moved to another one across the room. He explained that he had heard a sound leading him to think that there might be a large water pipe in the wall behind him and he feared that it might suddenly burst over him. I should add that he had revealed a general secretiveness towards interested psychotherapeutic enquiries about personal matters such as his earnings, and also a persistent anxiousness not to talk about the nature of his technical work in case, he feared, of terrorist attacks on himself or his family. Not especially surprisingly, the woman referred to his sexual arousal towards her as being quickly over.

It is notable that with her description of a deprived childhood, this woman had married a man who appeared objectively to be affectively subdued and generally withholding of himself in treatment. Their togetherness was characterized by an absence of confrontations between each other; rather their emotional troubles seemed to be expressed, and experienced by them, mainly in a projected form outside of their relationship. It was the social services department which felt an anxious responsibility towards their children; it was others who felt horror at her suicidal behaviour. I should add here, that both she and he, following her large overdose in the Cassel, indicated that that action of hers should, in some way, have been prevented. They stated that she had warned the therapist in their previous conjoint session that she was suicidal, although the writer remains of the memory and belief that any such warning was actually nonexistent or that, if she had alluded to it, this warning was so disguised as to make it very likely that the therapist's attention to it, or responses to it, would amount to failure. The hospital was the place that was not satisfying her or curing her, or which repeatedly and indifferently took treatment time, in this or that form, away from her. The hospital was the source of danger to her children. Finally, it was always anger and not sadness which she expressed in reaction to these beliefs of hers. Her situation illustrates how the physical situation and organization of the hospital allowed her numerous opportunities apparently to justify her projection of blame, and failure, and dangerousness onto us.

The coalescing of, or displacement between, the impressions of two objects was reaction which another mother resorted to in a defensive attempt to evade a sense of loss of one of her objects. Her pre-admission behaviour consisted of flamboyant fights with her husband. She would scream at him in the home and in the street. During her stay here it appeared that episodes of increased shouting and attacking of her husband were associated not only with brief absences by him, but that these episodes tended to occur when an absence by her husband happened to coincide with her therapist's also being briefly away. Neither we, nor she, knew to whose separation from her she was reacting. It was as if dependency on one significant person was too much of a threat for her to face. She also demonstrated very vivid examples of turning the fear of being the passive and helpless victim of separation into its active form. She would persistently state that she wished to leave, or would threaten to leave, either her sessions or the hospital generally. This latter behaviour exemplifies another fact of general applicability here, namely that the most sensitive area of work becomes that associated with the acute and intense ambivalence around staying, as opposed to leaving, the hospital. The behaviour in this area frequently takes a literal, physical form, for example alternately leaving and returning. When adolescent patients decide to stay away, or to return late, this is usual adolescent rebelliousness and identity assertiveness, but the hospital seems also to provide an imagined transference-parent for some of the adult mothers I am describing.

The final clinical example I wish to mention is briefer, and is intended to lead on to the phenomenon of the severity of the attacks made upon the hospital once the bad, or the non-desiring, elements in impulse life have been projected into the staff. A mother of two small children had, in her pre-admission history, had in-patient treatment at another psychiatric hospital following a self-poisoning episode with sedative tablets. She had also been abusing barbiturate and other sedatives. In the Cassel Hospital, she soon began to boast frighteningly of her physically vicious urges. She related having thrown a brick at a boy's head while on a weekend home; she described with apparent relish her hardness and callousness, and she used to say that she only felt comfortable when hating someone. She made threats of bodily harm both to herself and to others. She carried these out on herself in the form of repeated burnings of her arms with cigarettes, and by a few smaller or larger overdoses of sedatives, as well as a more subtle form of sedative abuse. She once threw something at another patient causing wide bruising of the other's arm; but more often she would lash out at her husband, once kicking him viciously on the shin. (He appeared to take these things with a kind of stoical resignation as if this was his life's lot, but more worryingly he adopted strangely accepting attitudes when she took overdoses. He tended also to verbally justify the reasons or rationalizations she would give for her self-attacking, or other-attacking, actions.) One of the reasons for the family's referral was that they first presented elsewhere because of her seven-year-old son's nightmares. In the Cassel, concern soon developed in us and became a persistent area of management worry due to her verbalized feelings of impulsive hatred towards the boy and, indeed, her occasional impulsive beating of him when, she said, he was rejecting her. During her stay she broke a number of hospital windows. The breaking of windows or glass in the hospital, although by no means an everyday occurrence, appears to be a prominent physical form of attack on the hospital, most attacks being against interpersonal expectations or the community routine and, of course, the psychotherapeutic arrangements. It is evident that the totality of the living-in situation, plus the psychotherapy, allows of a variety of areas in which the acting out of hostility can manifest itself.

Attacks against the physical structure of the building are apparent as to their aim but are not a frequent form of behaviour, one obvious reason for this being that such blatant violence may be followed by rapid discharge of the patient. The projective processes involved in attacking behaviour are, no doubt, complex. In bodily self-attacks (self-poisoning and self-cutting) the patient may be enacting self-punishment for his or her wishes to render staff bad or useless. At the same time, the patient has projected feelings of regret at his or her self-destructiveness into the staff. The patient often appears to be amazingly unconcerned about the consequences of self-attacks to health, and behaves as if the responsibility and sorrow or regret remain in the staff. It is so often the staff who find themselves agonizing over a sense of blame and responsibility within and amongst themselves for such typical actions as overdoses or self-cutting. Self-attacks tend to run in epidemics in the hospital, which again has relevance to the view that individuals may try to hide their own problems and impulses by jumping on the bandwagon of a supposed community-wide justification for feeling aggrieved.

Attacks against the physical structure of the building, particularly windows, crockery, mirrors and table legs, lead one to suspect that the patient may be attacking the very brittleness or fragility which he unconsciously wishes to project into the hospital. Some of the obvious parasitic tendencies I have mentioned above, especially in the first clinical example, indicate the wish to view the hospital and the staff as mechanical and impersonal providers. One reason may be that the patient then feels he or she can remain free of remorse. But the more the staff are treated in this way, the greater the accumulation of persecuted feelings. The brittleness of the building, its glass and so on, is then attacked for at least three reasons: one is that it is paranoidly hated as being impersonal and indifferent and the patient believes, in this regressive institutional transference, that it is the original cause of his or her deprivation. Secondly, if some of the brittleness in the building has been projected into it by the patient as a result of his or her fear of owning it, he or she may attack it as if it is safely not his or her own brittleness. Thirdly, the denigration implied in a dehumanized view of the hospital may tempt the patient to concretize his or her denigration physically. The patient hates what he or she feels he or she has done to it. The patient will attack it further for its persecuting him or her with threats of guilt. Combinations of mechanisms must be operative here. Projective and introjective processes in this regressed community situation can be impossible to disentangle. One can only take up, in treatment, the aspects presenting as amenable for insightful intervention at that moment.

Behind these phenomena must lie a fear of helplessness in the face of emotional pain, and this needs psychotherapeutic enquiry. Further ideas about causation may be more discernible when the patient's behaviour is less physical and is more obviously an attack on the routine, especially when he tries to disturb in one way or another the co-ordinated staff management plan. I see the aim of the attacks here as being very much against the staff's implied actual and potential togetherness. The patient might envy this, and the staff's apparent overcoming of their own individual narcissistic self-interests in the service of their capacity for collaboration. For attacks in this area to succeed, I suspect that unconscious staff collusion with this envy is required; I see it as possible that a nurse or therapist might unconsciously join in an envious attack, in identification with the patient, on something perceived as a higher order method of functioning, namely collaborative work as opposed to grandiose individual aims.

Viewing it from a more acceptably conscious level, staff may find threatening demands by a patient for sudden changes in the existing treatment arrangements, or even demands for a particular staff member to go against the expected arrangements, simply too much to bear. It is difficult to resist the temptation to hope that by accepting some reasonable justification for the patient's requests, that things may become easier. Experience with at least one such patient has shown me that such a hope is fallacious. In the Family Unit, these attacks can be manifested by the patient's overt demand for, or even apparent need for, a changed psychotherapeutic treatment modality. Patients have sometimes succeeded in giving the impression that the treatment plan is incorrect by such actions as not attending individual sessions, coming very late for sessions, not returning after weekends, staying away from hospital or Unit meetings, or by impulsively leaving the hospital, and various other sorts of sudden behaviour. Where this is persistent, one can suspect that one or more staff members is covertly agreeing with the patient in the latter's interruptive actions against the collaborative plan. The patient will not be able to resist exploiting staff dissent, as Dr Main has described in 'The ailment'(1946). As soon as either a therapist or nurse, feels that *their* work is exclusively valuable, trouble develops. In 'The ailment', Dr Main related how one by one, a number of staff members came to discover that while each had believed that she was the only one to know of a particular patient's secret information, the others had all been entrusted in turn with the same secret, and each had accepted that prized status.

The physically vicious patient I described earlier succeeded, by using extortive threats and demands, in getting her treatment setting changed from conjoint sessions to individual sessions, then back again. Her demands for these changes became almost innumerable and ever more desperate. She interfered with ongoing treatment in a number of ways, such as leaving the hospital and drugging herself, which merged into potentially dangerous overdoses, and physical threats, while her overt reasons appeared to contain desperately positive appeals and need.

Over and above individual rivalries, I suspect that the very pride that a whole staff group can take in believing themselves to be flexible and adaptable in their choice of treatment modalities, obscures a deeper envious attack against the structure which they are ostensibly identified with and working together in. At a fundamental dynamic level, it is an attack on a slow, painful, depressive position process, and the attacks on this process appear in concrete form as being aginst the treatment structure.

In our setting, management can probably only function when it is based on treatment units that, at their minimum, contain two people, this frequently being the therapist and the nurse, under consultation and nursing officer supervision, though various other professional role combinations might also be relevant at specific points or for particular periods.

[7]

Psychotherapy or Placement for the Troubled Adolescent Expectations and Limitations

Trevor Hartnup

This paper arose from the experience of in-patient psychotherapy at the Cassel Hospital, where the adolescents referred and treated are both troubled in themselves and often so troublesome to parents or residential social workers that the question of placement is under considerable. The main aim of the paper is to explore some of the emotional issues involved in the breakdown of family or placement, and their role in the adolescent's development and treatment. In particular, it examines how the expectations of psychotherapists and social workers and their sense of their own and each other's limitations can be aroused by painful developmental tasks which the adolescent is, or feels, unable to face. The paper suggests that the establishment of an appropriate working relationship between social workers and psychotherapists is difficult to achieve but is itself important to the adolescent's development and treatment.

Most of our adolescent patients could be described as borderline or in the process of establishing personality disorders. Usually they have dropped out of school and work, and their relationships with their families and sometimes with the referring agencies have broken down or are in danger of doing so. Most of them have made some kind of suicide attempt, some have shown violent behaviour, and psychosomatic illness is not uncommon.

The facilities are not appropriate for the treatment and management of gross psychoses.

For admission to the hospital to be useful, it is necessary for the patient and parents to have *some* notion of the adolescent as 'ill', unhappy or depressed. Parents or parental substitutes are asked to continue to hold parental authority and responsibility, which includes having the adolescent home at weekends. The parents are asked to attend a weekly meeting in the evening which is also attended by the adolescents and is staffed by nurses and a social worker.

Professionals in disagreement

Experience has led many of us to the conclusion that these adolescents and their families inevitably produce tensions in and between the professionals working with them, and that these tensions reflect the adolescent's and family's avoidance of, or defence against, some pain or anxiety.

As well as representing a danger, this offers us an opportunity to study staff interactions about patients in an attempt to discover the patient's influence upon them, which can then be fed back to the adolescent in digestible doses. But as the adolescent's behaviour is *constantly* producing tensions between parents, nurses, psychotherapist and referrer, it requires an *ongoing* relationship between the workers and parents to process the strain. This clearly requires considerable time and energy, and resources are scarce. But it is arguable that the quantity and quality of contact between workers determines the extent to which open disagreements and covert criticisms between professionals produce usable understanding or impede the work on all sides.

Part of the work to be done between workers is that of translation and synthesis of their different points of view. A psychotherapist in the Cassel will see a patient for up to two hours per week in the consulting room. The patients are in the nursing setting for 120 hours per week or more. The psychotherapist is trained and experienced in listening to a patient's account of his experience and relating it to the patient's unconscious conflicting wishes, to his internalized parents (who are not identical with the real ones). The nursing task is partly to assist individual patients to function in the external day-to-day reality of the group setting, and to observe the ways in which the patients are and are not able to do so: in cooking the evening meal for the community, cleaning, and changing bedlinen for example.

Both the psychotherapist and the nurse are subject to projections and transference but work with them in different ways. In the following account, we hear nurse and therapist speaking their own languages, but unable to communicate immediately with each other.

Jane, aged 17, goes to her psychotherapy session on Tuesday afternoon, grumbles about a crying baby who kept her awake in the night, and says that she does not feel like doing anything today. The therapist regards this as a communication about the transference to him and points out that she does not tell him about her own distress because she is afraid that he will be angry with the crying baby in her. Later, the nurse tells the therapist that after the session Jane goes to bed and does not turn up in the patients' kitchen where she was expected to help prepare the evening meal. When the nurse approaches her, the patient yells, 'Piss off! I'm tired!' The therapist says that at the moment the patient is feeling vulnerable and in need of looking after. The nurse says, 'Yes, but the patients had to have a cold meal last night because she and another patient failed to join the cooking team'. Nurse and therapist both feel that the other does not understand. It takes an outsider to take the overview and to synthesize the two perspectives by wondering if the patient is creating dissension between the staff as she does between her parents. To facilitate this understanding, the senior nurse and consultant psychotherapist try to find time to offer a joint supervision of nurse and therapist.

There is no intrinsic reason why a nurse and a therapist who are skilled at work with patients should be skilled at working together or making use of each other's observations. Without the development of a translation and synthesizing service, the observations which each offers the other could remain quite unusable.

What is the relevance of this to the relationship between psychotherapy and placement? The title suggests that they may be viewed as alternatives. Certainly that is often how the problem presents itself. 'This adolescent will be unable to make use of a hostel or foster home,' says the social worker, 'until he has come to terms with his inner problems, his past, his depression.' The psychotherapist replies 'He will be unable to use in-patient psychotherapy unless he has a home to go to.' Both feel that their own resources are inadequate to the task, but far from feeling that they have something in common, each is tempted to blame the other for his or her so-called 'unrealistic expectations'. It is at this point, when the two workers are about to give up on each other, that it is important to ask, 'What part does the adolescent play in all this?'

The developmental view

Adolescent breakdown which necessitates placement or hospitalization can rarely be pinned down to either internal processes or external influences alone. Usually one has a sense of both playing their part. From the adolescent's point of view, both psychotherapist and social worker are external influences and neither worker can be *absolutely* sure what effect their interventions will have on the adolescent's internal world.

From the point of view of the internal world, adolescent difficulties stem from the processes of physical and emotional development. Physical growth and the maturing of the sexual functions upset the established order within the child as represented by his or her capacity for frustration, tolerance, and self control, for example. This is an established order which provides the basis for the child's relationship to the physical and human environment in terms of family, school and social life, learning, hobbies, sport, the capacity for concentration, co-ordination, and so on. Stormy relationships at home, disruption of school work, taking risks on the road, law-breaking, and experimentation with sex and drugs, are all signs of this fundamental change taking place within the individual which affects the whole of his or her relationship to the environment. However mild or extreme the behavioural manifestations, the breakdown of the old order in the internal world is essential to the developmental task of adolescence, namely the assumption of responsibility for him or herself and independence in preparation for adulthood.

It is often pointed out that our society has confused expectations of adolescents which make matters worse, and that in other cultures adolescents seem to pass through initiation rites without crisis. My own reading suggests to me that initiation rites replace identity crises in precisely those societies where social role is highly developed and where the sense of self and individuality have relatively little place. It may even be that survival depends upon this kind of social organization in such cultures. From this point of view adolescent crises might be seen as the price we pay for the development of the individual adult personality.

The adolescent blames reality

The adolescent himself, however, frequently sees the problems *solely* in terms of environmental failure. Particularly in the early months of treatment in the Cassel, adolescents often explain their presence there in that way. 'I had no choice.' 'My parents put me here.' '*They* should be having treatment.' 'I didn't like it at home.' 'I wanted to get away.' We can readily see that these statements place the problem firmly outside the context of the adolescent's own behaviour and the internal (as opposed to external) factors which govern it. Those who are in close touch with adolescents are familiar with the feeling of 'not being able to get anything right', a product of how the adolescent treats them. We are constantly pushed by such adolescents to examine ourselves and environmental provisions *instead of* (not *as well as*) paying attention to the adolescent's own contribution to the situation.

We have observed that patients tend to recreate in the hospital the conditions in which they had been living outside. Often these conditions turn out to have an important unconscious emotional motivation – namely that they represent the avoidance of a painful situation and a painful experience. If this avoidance had been successful, then clearly there would have been no occasion for hospitalization. Similarly, if it becomes successful in the hospital, then the adolescent is relieved of the necessity for facing, tolerating and understanding his or her own pain or anxiety, and a treatment opportunity is diminished. In this context, the statement 'I am in hospital because of my parents' may well represent an idea that being in hospital is a way of 'getting better parents' or 'having a break'. Similarly, the physical separation from home may be conceived by the adolescent concretely as the achievement of emotional independence – i.e. a way of avoiding the painful, difficult business of growing up. Sometimes this pattern is repeated when, having formed similarly ambivalent attachments to staff and patients in the hospital, the adolescent, threatened once more by his or her own feelings of dependency, will decide to go home because 'I'm better now'. On both occasions, physical separation masquerades as a real capacity for emotional independence.

So how do we know what is a real capacity for independence and what is not? One clear indication may emerge from ordinary humdrum questions asked in a spirit of enquiry. These might include 'Where are you going?'; 'What are you going to do?'; 'Where is the money coming from?' and so on. These questions are an expression of reality testing, and the adolescent's reality testing is one of the important psychological functions which is disrupted in the developmental crisis. When their reality testing is inevitably shaken by changes in body, emotional state and social standing, the adolescents discover what kind of reality testing exists in the adults around them and whether the adults are able to hang on to their own judgement about what makes sense.

Feelings of cruelty and persecution

If one asks adolescents these humdrum practical questions they often feel persecuted, furious and belittled. The relatively healthy adolescents can nevertheless, with much protest and ingratitude, make use of such interventions. It is as if the adult's reality testing had brought their own into play. However, adolescent clients and patients often find reality intolerable and at times it may be experienced as an attack on their whole being by a cruel, insensitive adult. The main thrust of the adolescents' efforts may be towards creating a reality around them which corresponds as nearly as possible to their wishes, as opposed to managing their own feelings and impulses in such a way as to make a life *for themselves* in the real world.

Carol, for instance, had withdrawn from college aged 16. An intensely shy and taciturn girl, she nevertheless frightened her parents with a number of suicidal gestures. After a period of work in the Day Unit, she became an in-patient. It seemed that at home there was little sense of privacy and boundary in a small house which they had converted to open plan. In the hospital, Carol seemed to welcome a space for herself but continued to worry her parents at weekends and to give them cause to criticize the hospital's treatment. We drifted into a situation in which Carol was not at school, nor at work, nor on a regular sickness certificate. To all intents and purposes, the world outside family and hospital did not exist for her. Her nurse felt strongly that, by now aged 17½, Carol was not ready to face these issues. However, we could also see that Carol was using the hospital as a cocoon, a hiding place from the troublesome intensity of family relationships, a hiding place which also revealed by implication her criticism of her parents. As the therapist, I felt that the nurse should be tougher about bringing reality to bear, but for a long while I hesitated to push the point too hard for fear of upsetting the nurse. It was some time before I found a way of confronting the patient's concealed destructiveness effectively myself.

I am now touching upon the adolescent's part in producing a

situation in which a social worker and psychotherapist might view each other as 'unrealistic', 'soft', 'unfeeling', and so on. There are various forces at work. Firstly, it is a common experience for parents that the very empathy which involves the recall of their own adolescence may ensnare them, so that they identify with their offspring to the extent of suspending their own parental authority. This may happen to professional workers too. Secondly, the capacity for empathy and sensitivity to the client's or patient's feelings which one might expect to find in social worker and psychotherapist alike, may make them particularly vulnerable to having their own sense of reality overwhelmed by the troubled adolescent, through processes of transference, countertransference and projection.

Making up for the past

There are times when it seems to the workers that the adolescents have an overwhelming case. Their reality does seem to be a cruel one. They have had a harsh life with few opportunities and there is a strong wish that somehow everything could be put right by providing in the present what was missing in the past. In some circumstances finding the right place, the right person, the right interpretation for the adolescent may become the over-riding preoccupation of psychotherapist or social worker, whilst in the client or patient, anger about the past and the compulsion to repeat experiences can lead to a rejection of the new opportunities.

A young man referred to the hospital from a voluntary hostel some distance away, came for a consultation accompanied by the head of the home. In a one-and-a-half hour interview we heard about the boy's *past,* a history of separations and failed attempts to move out into alternative protected accommodation. There was no adult in his present life who had known him for more than 18 months. The head of the home stressed his own wish to find somewhere where the boy's 'needs' would be met because his own establishment did not have the 'right' resources. It proved impossible during the consultation to locate the boy's anger or suffering, or the head's exasperation with him. Both seemed to agree that it was a question of finding the 'right' place, rather than locating and working on the *present* difficulties. The head felt badly let down by the hospital when no place was offered. Two days later we heard that the boy had been told to leave the hostel. From all points of view it was a distressing episode. In the context of this paper it illustrates an attempt to avoid the boy's 'unwantability' by means of a new placement rather than to face it in a way which might enable the boy to become aware of his part in it. Had it been feasible, an ongoing relationship between the professionals would have provided conditions more favourable to the gradual emergence of the notion of in-patient psychotherapy, as distinct from that of accommodation and substitute parenting.

THE WORKERS HAVE A PROBLEM

The examples I have given show social workers and psychotherapists attempting to protect adolescents from a reality which is perceived as cruel. Sometimes the cruelty is perceived as lying elsewhere, in the police, the magistrates, the parents, the local authority, the psychiatrist, and so on. This can become a matter for particular anger when it is felt that the adolescent is so delicately poised that the 'wrong' move will spoil everything or lead to a suicide attempt.

Now here are some interesting paradoxes. The title refers to the troubled adolescent, but here the subject is a troubled adult: the parent, social worker, or psychotherapist. The adolescent is seen as the victim of circumstances, helpless in the hands of cruel fate, but the workers find themselves suffering, feeling that they have no choice, little room for manoeuvre, with the threat of anger, persecution, guilt and despair hanging over them. This offers us the opportunity to understand the adolescent's difficulty in facing the cruel, bullying, guilty and despairing aspects of himself, which he attributes to us. However, we often find ourselves regarding other workers as the cruel ones or the soft ones and, in this way, join the adolescent in his denials and projections. It is easy to see from this that unless the social worker and psychotherapist can create a safe setting for their meeting, it could merely serve to confirm their prejudices about each other.

Issues of autonomy, authority and control

For adolescents whose sense of their own boundaries is distorted and confused, the maintenance of clear roles by the workers is as important as co-operation. Patients of the Cassel hospital are regarded as responsible for their own behaviour; staff are responsible for the hospital; a visiting social worker has his or her own area of responsibility. To organize a visit to a client who was also a patient here, a social worker could maintain the boundaries by making an appointment directly with the client *and* with the staff in whose building the appointment would take place. To avoid misunderstanding I would stress that, whilst elsewhere this might be considered a matter of courtesy, here it is a matter of professional service to the adolescent.

The in-patient setting is one where confusions between care and treatment, between parental and professional authority frequently arise, and can sometimes be usefully elaborated. In the case of adolescents we hold the view that this distinction can only be made if the adolescent has an identified parent, or substitute parent figures, and an identified home outside the hospital. When the hospital becomes *like* home this can be explored. When it becomes home, then the patient's efforts may be directed towards leaving it or staying in it, at the expense of working in it. Psychotherapy sessions can become, in the patient's eyes, a condition of staying there – a way of paying the rent. At such a point, the fundamental task of the hospital is perverted. For the patient it has become a placement, and even if the patient remains in hospital, treatment is unlikely to take place. Furthermore, a legitimate placement is delayed.

The maintenance of these differences enables us to address with greater clarity troublesome questions such as 'Whose is the responsibility for success and failure of placement or treatment?'

'Can you do a "good job" without a "good" patient or client?' 'Are we dependent upon our clients and patients "getting better" or "not causing trouble" for our own sense of professional worth?'. Such questions touch upon our capacity to tolerate the adolescent's existence as a separate person who can have his *own* failures. The failures that I have in mind are, for instance:

1. The failure of expectations to correspond to what is the best available, evoking anger, disillusionment and depression which inevitably accompany the process of coming to terms with reality.
2. The failure of omnipotence, i.e. the devastating realization that one actually has to work at things to develop skills, a fact which may threaten the adolescent's false sence of specialness.
3. Failure due to destructiveness, i.e. the painful realization that one has spoiled things for oneself.

Thus the workers' capacity to maintain a sense of separateness can provide favourable circumstances for feeding back to the adolescent, in tolerable doses, his projection of feelings of failure on to the social worker or psychotherapist.

Conclusion

What I have tried to do is to look at the troubled adolescent's attitude to psychotherapy and placement and its effect upon parents, social workers, nurses and psychotherapists. I have also considered what kinds of external conditions are in my view favourable to the adolescent's development and psychotherapy. I have suggested that it is important for parents and workers to have a clear idea of their own areas of responsibility and authority, but that the overview can easily become lost. We are faced with the twin dangers of confusion and fragmentation. When social workers and psychotherapists meet to discuss the question of psychotherapy and/or placement, it is important for them to clarify their individual powers, responsibilities and areas of work in order to find ways of working together. If this proves possible then, in my view, it provides favourable circumstances for the adolescent to develop the capacity to deal with his or her own feelings of confusion and fragmentation. However, the experience of the Cassel Hospital (in relation to psychotherapists and nurses) suggests that sometimes this working partnership cannot be easily achieved without the assistance and co-operation of senior practitioners in the two professions, who can help the social worker and psychotherapist to develop their skills in working together.

[8]

An Adolescent Patient's Relationship with her Nurse as a Focus for Treatment

John Woods

This discussion of the roles of nurse and therapist is illustrated by clinical material that highlights the significance of their working relationship. The supervision of that relationship is seen to be an essential part of individual treatment in an in-patient setting.

'There is no intrinsic reason,' writes Trevor Hartnup (p. 129), 'why the therapist and nurse who are skilled at work with patients should be skilled at working together or making use of each other's observations.' Their roles are not only different but, as Oliver James (p. 78) describes in detail, they are in some ways antithetical. The use each makes of countertransference experience is an example. If the therapist's aim is to develop understanding in the patient of his or her internal world, then it is important for the therapist to resist impulses to take actions that would be in accordance with the patient's projections. Abstaining from activity creates space for inroads into unconscious elements. The nurse does act, and intervenes in accordance with nursing aims and plans for the patient. Feelings aroused by the patient are expressed and may be brought into the interaction with the patient. Making interpretations about unconscious motivation would militate against this. When the nurse and the therapist meet, therefore, each will have been doing what the other needs to resist, and it is quite possible that each will feel their work threatened or invalidated by the other. The contention of this paper is that a creative tension arising out of such differences may, under certain conditions, help meet the therapeutic needs of the patient.

The provision of nurse and therapist creates a dual perspective in that therapeutic attention can be directed to both the internal and external reality of the patient. People who require in-patient treatment will have shown such borderline psychopathology that their relation to external reality is seriously impaired. Elements of the internal world and unresolved infantile conflicts have invaded, so to speak, their external reality, producing distorted social relationships and inhibited individual development. The origins of these distortions in infantile experience are split off and disowned, resulting typically in blaming the world, the family or 'life' for being malevolent and always injurious. Out-patient treatment is inadequate for the needs of this patient group and may have already been unsuccessfully attempted before admission. This is not to say that the in-patient does not require a capacity to tolerate the stress of disruption in the status quo between inner and outer worlds. The greater the degree of splitting and projective identification, the more painful will be the process of integration. The two workers need to make considerable efforts of mind to create a partnership that holds the patient in both inner and outer worlds; if this is achievable it may be beneficial to an otherwise untreatable patient. How does this partnership work?

Roger Kennedy (1984) has pointed out that psychoanalytic treatment tests the capacity of the analysand to experience a duality in the relationship to the analyst. The analyst must become perceived as both the recipient of projections and as different from them. The patient who fails to make use of out-patient analytic psychotherapy has been unable to make this separation and so has remained with the perception of the therapist as a persecuting or abandoning parent, a replica of some element of their internal world. A working alliance with the therapist as an external and separate person responds to the therapist's holding, within which a negative transference can be explored. Treatment in this frame of reference is broken off because of the inability of the patient to allow the therapist a separate existence, as someone who is there both for the patient and for something different, the analytic work. This essential duality of psychoanalytic psychotherapy is provided for in the in-patient setting by the two primary workers for a patient.

It would be an oversimplification to think of one worker providing the holding via a positive transference so that the other may more vigorously pursue (or be pursued by) the negative transference. Such an apparently rational division would in reality be no better than the situation created by patients who continue to blame the world for their miseries; they reject external reality in the form of the nurse in the wish for an idealized relationship with the therapist. As in the analogy with the dual function of the analyst, the two workers need to integrate their functions into a unified whole, to synthesize what is projection and what is external reality in relation to therapeutic aims.

Treatment commences when the therapist and nurse share the staff group's formulation of the focus for a particular patient. During the course of treatment, the interaction between nurse and therapist is monitored so that each may inform the other whilst retaining their characteristic identity. Structures provided by senior staff exist to regulate this working relationship. The nature of contact with the patient by nurse and therapist differs considerably and distinct relationships are thereby created. Just as internal and external reality have distinct characteristics and the invasion by one of the other produces an impoverished and ineffective personality, so the two aspects of the patient's treatment need to be connected but not indistinguishable.

A patient's experience of the Cassel Hospital is like that of a drama, an enactment of the internal world on the screen of external reality using real people, things and events. The drama will include many people and situations over which the patient has no control, but there is a drive to repeat earlier and unresolved conflicts. This is partly to obviate the need to change and partly because these conflicts need resolution. The drama is thus a creation, or a created world, in which the patient may perceive characteristics of him or herself. Nurse and therapist constitute with the patient a triangular relationship which comes to be created in the likeness of similar relationships in the patient's internal world. This provides a medium for the patient to discover changes which may be possible in the quality of those relationships and thus for internal changes to become a possibility.

Intolerance of anxiety by the borderline patient may militate against nurse and therapist working together. Anxiety may be produced by projections being challenged, since the distortion of external reality already achieved by the patient serves the purpose of defending against primitive threats which are felt as externally real. The greater the threat that exists for the patient in integrating inner and outer reality, the greater will be the patient's attempts to divide nurse and therapist and set them against each other. It is important therefore that the therapist's technique should not limit itself to transference interpretations toward the therapist alone. As it becomes clear to the patient that there is a working relationship between nurse and therapist that exists despite efforts to split, the split in the patient's psyche may become modified into a normal level of ambivalence, (normal in the sense that it may be utilized to inform ongoing work).

Some adolescents admitted to hospital may be seen as having broken down in the context of separation from parents or parent substitutes. Hospital admission produces a physical separation from the family, and the hospital takes on to some extent the possibility of working through any unstable family dynamic that led to breakdown. Since patients are normally required to return home at the weekends and parents are expected to attend a weekly meeting where current issues are discussed, a certain amount of the family conflicts are brought into the field of therapeutic attention, and it is here that the nurse relates directly to the hospital social worker. Thus a chain is formed, from the therapist who seeks to make contact with the patient's internal world, to the nurse in touch with what a patient needs to learn in the community, to the social worker who is in contact with the conflict within the patient's family. Good communications between these workers will prevent the relative separation of the adolescent from the family, from becoming a 'removal' in Katan's sense, which leads to repetition of the original conflicts in relation to new external objects, (Anna Freud, 1958).

Admission to the hospital offers the opportunity for a certain level of acting out or 'behavioural free association' (Muir, p. 67) but a minimum level of symbolization must remain. The hospital may become *like* home for the adolescent. Nurse and therapist may be treated as though they were the infant's parents, but if they are seen as nothing but the replicas of an archaic object world then treatment has no chance of promoting change. If, for example, the therapist is seen only as the castrated and powerless father, and the nurse as an intrusive phallic mother, then the adolescent has no choice but to escape. This kind of situation may be created by the borderline patient with a defective capacity for symbolization, and where each worker is feeling he or she is making no progress. Communication between workers may then be affected by frustration, anger and blame. Each worker's role will come under attack; nurse and social worker may feel the therapist is colluding with the patient's regressive or destructive needs, and the therapist that the others do not understand the patient sufficiently well. The therapist, to compensate for feelings of helplessness, may take on management functions; the nurse may begin to make interpretations about therapist and patient. Given the strength of projections particularly in cases of adolescent breakdown, it is clear that the quality of the nurse/therapist partnership will play a crucial role in transforming the 'acting out' of the patient into interpretable material and thence into constructive behaviour.

The above account is based on the analysis of an extreme type of therapeutic dysfunction described by Main in 'The Ailment'(1946). It is in a more attenuated form that the following case description illuminates some of these difficulties in a residential individual treatment. The borderline pathology of the patient described brought her workers close to the point of breakdown in their working partnership on more than one occasion. Processing our differences proved constructive to the patient's treatment and can be seen as informative of the nature of the patient's internal world. It is not intended to discount the importance of other aspects of treatment, viz. the hospital community as a therapeutic social environment which continually fed back to the patient the quality of her relationships, nor of the educational resources of the Day Unit, of which she made good use; nor of the nursing work with the adolescent group; nor of the work with other family members, which is to some extent brought in to the picture presented here. The spearhead of change, however, seems to have been the efficacy of the nurse/therapist partnership. A reduction in the otherwise implacably destructive qualities of this patient's internal objects seems to have been facilitated by changes in the nature of the working partnership of her two closest workers, the nurse and the therapist.

Referral

It was on her mother's birthday that Joan A, aged 14, took a serious overdose of painkillers. After a period of intensive care the hospital referred her to a child psychiatry department. Joan was at that point unable to attend school or face any situation unaccompanied by her mother. The child psychiatrist recommended in-patient treatment at the Cassel Hospital and Joan refused. However, she accepted the offer of regular therapy sessions with the psychiatrist, together with anti-depressant medication. The psychiatrist, reported that work was undermined constantly by Joan's hostile dependence on her mother. After about 18 months, Joan's older brother was due to go to military college. He had always been the 'successful' one. Joan at this point, aged 16, stated that she would like in-patient treatment in order, she said, 'to live a normal life again'.

Family

Joan had always been the 'difficult' child of this family, but the background of the parents showed that there had been other problems. Mrs A's own mother had killed herself shortly before Joan's birth. A depressive breakdown ensued for Mrs A which she described as having been 'cured' by taking on voluntary work with handicapped children. As treatment progressed we learned of Mrs A's need to have a suicidal daughter. She would speak of Joan fatalistically and even as though she were already dead. Any moves towards Joan's independence horrified Mrs A. She would care for Joan's physical needs and have long intimate talks with her sharing their sense of hopelessness. Mr A was excluded from this intimacy. He had remained all his career in a low paid clerical job and seemed obsessed with money management; most of his leisure time was spent in a secluded room with his stamp collection. He expressed the intolerability of the stormy scenes between mother and daughter and their resulting depressive phases. His opinion was that Joan required hospitalization as a more permanent psychiatric patient. His own childhood was never spoken of but seems to have been one of bleak unhappiness. Mr and Mrs A's hopes and ambitions seemed all to have been put into Joan's older brother. He was supposed to know nothing of Joan's problems and there was little communication between brother and sister.

Childhood and adolescence

Mrs A fell whilst pregnant with Joan and thought for a time the foetus was dead. She described Joan's babyhood as unbearable, the baby not sleeping or eating properly, but screaming constantly. By 18 months, Joan had developed asthma which became life-endangering and required several hospitalizations. At 6 years old she was referred to a child guidance unit for aggressive and disruptive behaviour; there are no details of treatment as such but it does seem that her obsessional patterns date from that point. In sessions in the four-week in-patient assessment period, she recalled her mother denying her any freedom to play with children, particularly boys, and never being allowed to get dirty in any way. She was forbidden to touch animals. On one occasion when she did so, she was told by her mother that she would catch a tapeworm and that, after some years, it would eat her up and kill her. She became convinced that she would die by the age of 14. She felt as though she was surrounded constantly by cameras and microphones, and that God was judging her and seeing her badness. Her bad actions resulted in bad things happening to others. If she did exactly what God wanted her to do, particularly in matters of small detail, for example, the precise way that she would put an object down, or which foot stepped first onto the bus, then evil or illness could be prevented from falling onto others. God left her shortly before her suicide attempt and the Devil took his place, whom she had constantly to fight. She feared that others would discover the evil in her and her evil intentions towards them. She was entirely dominated at the time of admission by a perpetual process of rumination over the details of her interaction with others. Constant self-assurance was necessary to her, so that others would not discover her hatred and fear of them. She had, however, become a tyrant in her own home through what she could and could not tolerate or by how depressed she was feeling. Obsessional behaviour and cleaning rituals dominated the household. The touch, sound, sight and smell of her father was strenuously avoided. Everything she touched would have to be cleaned first in case he had touched it. Then, everything in the house had to be repeatedly cleaned; she could never eat or be with her family but silently communicated her resentment of them. She had no contact with people her own age, schooling having been abandoned in favour of joining in her mother's voluntary work. At the age of 16, she was small, pretty, neat, rather too well-groomed and somewhat asexual in appearance. There was periodic loss of appetite and other psychosomatic symptoms, all of which emerged during treatment as an expression of hatred of her sexual body.

Assessment for psychotherapy

Joan used her vulnerability paradoxically to maintain a rigid control on everyone around her. Basic expectations made by her nurse about attendance at meeting, mealtimes, bedtimes and the consumption of alcohol produced a cold rage that she controlled but expressed in her tight-lipped, compliant behaviour. Opportunities taken by her nurse to discuss issues such as her income and expenses were felt as ruthless invasions of her privacy. Deeply suspicious and guarded with the therapist, she showed a false self organized round the notion of illness. The enjoyment of suffering seemed based on an identification with her mother but it barely concealed a more deeply suicidal wish to destroy her world in order to protect a highly vulnerable 'true' self that could not be allowed to live in the cruel world. The symbiotic tie with her mother in which this vulnerable self resided is demonstrated in the circumstances of her suicide attempt: Joan was due the next day to sit an exam for which her mother had done all the course work.

The offer of treatment, it was thought, would reduce Joan's paranoia. There were signs, in her giving up of medication, taking part in community activities, and in her relief in being away from home, that sufficient motivation might exist for treatment. Positive contact with other patients, particularly mothers in the Families Unit, provided holding in the community. However, the relationship with the nurse seemed so uncertain that it was decided to make this the central focus of treatment. Our assessment of Mrs A's capacity to tolerate the separation of her daughter was such that this could not be worked with directly.

Nursing aims were, therefore, a crucial element in treatment and, in collaboration with the patient required periodic reformulation and revival. They began in three areas of symptomatology: poor relationships with others, food, and occupation. The overall aim was to provide tangible gains in Joan's capacity for independent action and thought. Given Joan's ambivalence about this aim, the continued focus was always upon the working relationship between patient and nurse.

Treatment

Signing on: the establishment of a working relationship with the nurse

The efforts of Sister Munford, Joan's nurse, to work with Joan on the above areas aroused a more overt expression of hostility after the assessment period. In therapy sessions, Joan protested that her nurse was so unloving that she felt in despair. My lack of support for that depiction of the nurse as 'horrible' and 'cruel' made her feel so angry that she felt she could not stand it and that she would have to take herself off to die. Further rage was provoked when I pointed out how hostile she was in fact being towards the nurse. I put it that when she was made so anxious and to feel such a helpless child by her own difficulties in working towards our agreed goals, then she began to see her nurse as though she were a sort of mother who simply wanted to humiliate and destroy her. It was preferable to blame her nurse than to become aware of her own limitations in the achievement of practical goals. More manageable feelings of anger towards me were then expressed for my always siding with the staff, for letting her down, for being cold and hard, and so on. These seemed to assist her albeit resentful attempts to meet the challenges presented to her in the community.

A preoccupation from the initial period of treatment, whilst she was as yet speaking fairly freely to me, was the question of what was real and what was false. She felt forbidden to show her 'real' feelings of aggression and depression; co-operation and activity seemed based on falseness since they were expected by her nurse. Exceptions were at moments when she could sustain an illusion that only she was the object of her nurse's attention, to the exclusion not only of others but of the aims and purpose of her treatment. Consequently the relationship with the therapist was also not a 'real' one. She came to view nurse and therapist as conspiring to mould her into a 'made-up' person, someone who had nothing to do with her own reality; thus her own reality would then be lost forever. I put it that her 'reality' was simply what she controlled, and this was made clear after a weekend when her nurse had sufficient concern, after some shared worry about how Joan would be with her mother, to telephone her at home. On Monday she came in in a fury about this 'intrusion'. Since she had not ordained this action of the nurse it was inevitably felt as an attack irrespective of the motives or the purpose of the nurse's work with her.

Positive responses to the nurse were at the expense of working with the therapist. It seemed she could only communicate to me when feeling hatred towards the nurse. Working with the nurse (and slowly but surely this became a dependent relationship) seemed to mean that she had to cut herself off from the therapist. Whether this was fear of my envy or her greed or her hatred of the nurse and therapist's alliance it was never easy to say, but a profoundly negative transference full of distrust, fear and revulsion took hold from about the third month of treatment. Verbal communication shut down but for an occasional barbed comment about her reason for not being able to work with me. Sometimes these comments consisted of a personal attack, although at later stages of the treatment there was a more depressive tone, more of an admission of her own failure to use my help. For a good while, however, in the first six or eight months the reasons centred on the fact that I was male. There was a sense of outrage that she should 'have to speak to a man'. Her problems were such that I 'as a man, could never understand'. Without a woman therapist she could never get well. She hinted at a sexual attraction for her nurse and wept that I could never understand. There were rules, she said, of what she could and could not say in the session. The sessions came to have a pattern, beginning with her anxious silence and a heightened defensiveness after my attempts to verbalize her anxiety perhaps connected with some events that I knew about external to the session. This would be followed by her tears of helpless rage that her needs could not be met. She would sink further into an isolated depression until, as she put it, she was 'kicked out at the end of the session'.

The announcement of her nurse leaving her post at the hospital seemed to lift the ban on communication, if not the strength of negative feeling. In the last few weeks of her nurse's availability Joan worked to overcome her difficulties about signing on for part time work and for unemployment benefit. Each of the steps involved in this fairly complex procedure aroused paranoid anxiety and fears of exposure and humiliation. She ranted and bitterly complained that neither I, nor 'the rest of them' understood her fears and her pain, that we were callous, indifferent, inhuman, and so on. Any reference to the progress she was making outside of the therapy room was taken as an effort to steal her achievements and claim them as my own.

I wondered about this 'stealing', and conjectured that it could be that she felt she was stealing some achievement from the nurse. She said that what she was doing was not really her own, it was all really her nurse's and that is how it was in this hospital; that she never got any credit, but was always criticized for her failures. The destructiveness towards her progress was not, however, acted out outside of the sessions. This was due, I think, to the positive relationship with the nurse at that time, perhaps based on projective identification. The nurse was leaving to further her own education and career. Joan's envy was such that she needed to deny the separation and to take on some comparable activity as though she were being herself the nurse.

Identification by stealing the nurse's abilities and identity was Joan's way of coping with being separate; this also produced a fear and rejection towards the new nurse. Sister Chappell, the new nurse, was, however, involved in a transitional period with the work of signing on and with the provision of an educational programme in the Day Unit. Joan seemed to feel that she would be able to make use of these facilities. In a brief moment of communication, she told me that now she was going to make her life work. I asked whether it really had to be on her own. In fact it was against fierce resistance from Joan that her new nurse attempted to engage with her over other areas that needed attention viz. her difficulty in sleeping, in having a balanced diet and eating with others, and over her obsessional rituals. Hard work as it was, her nurse was able to construct specific nursing plans around these areas which provided a framework that Joan could fight against and finally return to. In each case it was the plan, the concrete reality of the nurse's expectations, that the two of them could relate to, each in their own way. With the therapist, however, there was no middle ground, no work, but an overwhelming feeling of failure, emptiness and despair.

A change of room

Joan had been sharing a room with a young adult coming to the end of her long stay in the hospital, who had made little contact with Joan. When her room mate did leave about six months after Joan's admission, it was recommended by her nurse that Joan move into a room with two other adolescent girls. Joan had been quite comfortable with her rooming arrangment, however. To come into contact with two people of her own age, one of whom was also my patient, provoked such feelings of jealous rage of not being special enough to have her own little niche, that she refused in the most outright fashion. Her defences of isolation, obsessional behaviour, and illusions of symbiotic self-sufficiency were threatened. The nurse's efforts to put the rooming change into effect aroused such primitive anxieties that the nurse became for Joan the hostile and destructive witch-mother of Joan's earliest fantasy. There were threats of precipitate leaving and suicidal impulses if she were not permitted to remain in her 'own room'.

The rest of the staff group put it that the change of room was a requirement made by the staff as a whole and in fact reflected a hospital policy about the sharing of living space. Despite the fact that I had included myself in this process and had taken up Joan's avoidance of the issue as an expression of her resistance to treatment, Joan managed effectively to convey to the nurse an impression of neutrality and permissiveness on my part so that she could hide behind my non-committal attitude. She refused to discuss the matter with her nurse, saying that it was something she was talking about with her therapist; and the days dragged on with no movement forward. The intention was not only to make the nurse feel useless and a nag, but also to make her feel helplessly excluded from Joan's supposedly more important therapeutic relationship. The nurse began to express the feeling that Joan was using her sessions defensively and that perhaps her therapist was colluding in this.

The reality of Joan's therapy sessions was of course quite different from the comfortable intimacy suggested by Joan to the nurse. Joan froze into a silent rage that was ostensibly not much different from what had gone before, but the feelings that were generated for me in the room were of quite a new order. She was dressed entirely in black, always concealed her face, and was so motionless as to appear dead. There seemed to be something about the way she sat that meant that she was not there. I translated the destructiveness towards her treatment into a suicidal urge in the context of her relationship with mother; changing rooms, becoming a separate person, seemed to be impossible for her. She had difficulty breathing, straining and choking, whether with tears of rage I could not be sure. The tightness with which she held herself I took to be a means of warding off primitive fears of disintegration. I related these communications to what I knew of her early childhood – to the inconsolable screaming and asthmatic attacks. Her hatred of nurse and therapist seemed to stem from our being like the parents who could not console her. These links, however, produced no change until something happened between nurse and therapist; and things were also happening in relation to her mother.

The conflict was taken back to her mother, who became alarmed at Joan's depression and overt threats of suicide. Joan's provocation of her mother took the form of a crushing depression on the weekends at home, regressing into a dependent and semi-invalid relation to her mother and verbalizing such depressive feelings that her mother became convinced that Joan was on the verge of suicide. Mrs A began to claim that the treatment was killing her daughter and sought to withdraw her from the hospital. Joan evoked a strong protective urge from some of the mothers of families on the Unit who came to brand Mrs A as a destructive woman. The conflict came to a head in a violent scene where Joan was being physically pulled back into the hospital by patients away from her mother. It should be acknowledged here how much the hospital social worker in conjunction with the nursing staff helped family and hospital weather the storm produced by Joan at this point in her treatment. Hard work was involved in taking up the mother's part in Joan's depressive wallowing on weekends.

The turmoil with Joan's mother could be related in therapy sessions to the history of suicide in the family. I put it to Joan that she remained suicidal out of some revenge on her mother, to work on Mrs A's guilt about her own mother's death. The idea of the tapeworm baby eating away into the inside of mother's body was a reflection of Joan's own wishes to destroy her mother. In destroying the internal mother she had to destroy herself. This formulation seemed to give some faint relief to Joan who then informed me further about the self-infliction of small cuts, fantasies of overdosing and of seeing how people would react after her death. Suddenly, and to my surprise, she reported that having been for a time in the grip of suicidal feeling, she took a decision that she would not 'do that' to her nurse. She was afraid her nurse would blame herself for Joan's death. These were, however, only brief glimmers in an overwhelming gloom of death. Quickly she would revert to her determination to give her mother a dead daughter above all else. Nurse and therapist were seen as equally 'irrelevant'. She broke her silence only to tell me that she had told me nothing because I could give her nothing to take away her despair. In retrospect, I can see now that the brief contacts she made had the effect of further holding me hostage to her suicidal threat. At the time, I was too aware of the very real possibility of her suicide.

Preoccupied as I was with her murderous and suicidal rage and with my attempts to think my way around it, it was easy for a mirror image to develop of the nurse's doubts about the therapy sessions. Could it be that I stood accused of being too 'understanding' because the nurse did not sufficiently understand the internal obstacles for this patient to fulfil the nursing aim?

The dangerous split between the two workers was examined in the setting of a nurse/therapist supervision. Once the mutual projections were shared and when contained with the assistance of senior staff, we saw how we had replicated the family pathology as a direct result of the patient's projections. The therapist had become like an impotent father who passively provoked mother's rage that the rivalrous daughter could wind him around her little finger (the phobic treatment of me by Joan bore this out). The nurse had become, in Joan's eyes, the hated and vindictive mother who drove her daughter to suicide by denying her right to a separate existence. Joan herself had become the tapeworm baby eating away at the nurse/therapist couple to destroy their creative power. As these fantasies were discussed and their production traced back to our specific experiences of the patient, they could be more clearly identified as projections; the workers were able to get some distance in their view of each other's work. Therapist and nurse could then re-affirm the common goal that the patient be able to live with other people. I made interpretations to the patient, not simply about how she was treating the nurse or was seeing me, but how she reacted to the fact of nurse and therapist working together. The nurse was supported by the knowledge that therapist and patient had not made a secret alliance against her. Joan moved rooms.

Leaving

A more positive relation developed to the nurse whilst the intensity of negative transference remained with the therapist. Developments in Joan's sexual maturity were shared with her nurse, inhibitions about work and education were being managed and she was able to keep to nursing plans about drinking alcohol and sleeping. These gains would have been impossible had the nurse remained the intrusive witch-mother of Joan's fantasy world. Of course it was not so one-sided and the nurse reported how hostile Joan could be when she felt she had to share the nurse's attention, being for example, quite insulting in group meetings. The ambivalence of the patient, however, was not blocking her treatment. With the therapist, the working alliance was much less in evidence. In fits and starts, she communicated her anxieties around the things she worked on with her nurse. On each occasion, the contact aroused fears of the therapist as an intrusive mother who would take her over. Sharing her thoughts and feelings seemed inevitably to evoke her regressed 'ill' state in which she was 'looked after' by mother. A degree of separation from the nurse, however, and consequent use of her help, was facilitated by the holding in the therapy sessions of this much more primitive and destructive aspect of Joan's internal world.

The precariousness of this holding was something which came out over the issue of ending Joan's treatment. Despite previous experience, nurse and therapist found this issue to be a severe test of our working relationship. It was in the context of the very sporadic working alliance with the therapist that Joan first brought her sense of panic and alarm at the thought of leaving. She had been at the hospital a year at that point and was aware that an adolescent patient's stay is somewhere between a year and eighteen months. She was terrified at the thought that all her gains depended solely on being at the hospital and that she would break down if she tried to be self-sufficient. Interpretations of her conflict about dependence towards nurse and therapist were ineffective in reducing her demand to know when she would be leaving. She needed this, she said, in order to make adequate preparation for accommodation, work and to continue her education. I stepped out of my role of interpreting to discuss how much preparation she could make if, say, she were to leave in about three months. And then she was satisfied.

Nurse and therapist, however, were not satisfied with each other; the nurse pointed out that it was premature to even discuss a leaving date since there were so many areas of continued underfunctioning which would not then receive attention. It was, in addition, likely that this patient, being still quite a young 17, would require quite an extended stay. After some heated discussion, it became clear that over the months there had developed in a concealed way quite different attitudes which had now become polarized. In a sense, it was an opposite version of what had happened over the change of room. The exclusion of the therapist from the working alliance between patient and nurse provided the temptation to overstep the boundary of the therapist's role. Joan meanwhile had caught onto the effects of her pressure on the therapist and began to persecute the nurse for not complying with what had by then become a dictum from the therapist. With the therapist there was a triumphant contempt that her nurse's hostility had at last been exposed. The therapist was himself regarded as impotent since she predicted that my 'leaving date' would be countermanded by the 'stronger personality' of the nurse.

This bitter triumph was shortlived when it was made clear that there was no leaving date as such but that I had spoken in a very different sense of a possible period of time that she would have before the end of the treatment. The patient's response was to plunge into suicidal despair. A positive move towards her therapist arose out of this when I verbalized, in the face of her deafening silence, a suicide plan that I felt she was concealing. In the next session she said that she no longer had the compulsion to kill herself since it was not now her secret but something I knew about. Her wishes then to tell me more about the hated mother and the 'difficult' nurse seemed based on an idealised oedipal transference in which I had become the father who rescued her from the murderous rival mother. Outside of the sessions her hostility and contempt were making her virtually unnurseable.

The split between nurse and therapist continued to work away. I had begun to feel that the nurse was denying Joan the freedom and ability to leave and was thus provoking a possibly precipitate and suicidal end to the treatment. It was at a nurse/therapist supervision that I learnt how the nurse felt I had ruined the good work she had been engaged in by offering in effect an easy way out for Joan to avoid all her difficulties. With the senior staff at that meeting we saw how nurse and therapist were enacting elements of Joan's unconscious conflict about leaving. The nurse had come to represent a dependent and regressive urge towards a 'symbiotic' state that Joan could then reject and destroy whilst the therapist was used to build up a narcissistic over-valuation of herself as having no need of treatment. This pattern gave rise to the paranoid rejection of all attempts to engage with her in the therapeutic community.

It was in our attitude towards each other that nurse and therapist had allowed the invasion of these hostile projections into the treatment setting. The difficult feelings towards each other's work had to be shared before reconsidering the question of a leaving date. In fact, when we looked in detail at what Joan needed to be able to do in order to leave treatment and broke these tasks down into manageable short-term goals, the concrete question of a leaving date disappeared. Nurse and therapist met with the patient to put these specific plans related to the acquiring of skills necessary to leave, and in so doing we were putting the responsibility of leaving and the power to work towards leaving firmly back into the patient's hands. With the primacy of the nursing aims re-established the patient's attacks diminished and work was resumed.

Separation continued to be an issue fraught with anxiety, defensiveness and hostility. After the experience described, nurse and therapist were in a much better position to work with the patient. Her leaving, when it came, was stormy and difficult. However, at the time of writing, three months later, it seems that Joan has acquired some independence and ability to manage her life. She is working and living away from home, has sat some examinations and is preparing to further her education and career.

Discussion

The original focus of the nurse/patient relationship was in recognition of the extent of Joan's separation difficulty with mother.

Our assessment also was that Mrs A lacked the capacity to work directly with the separation of her daughter in a constructive way. In the assessment period Joan showed an intense ambivalence towards the nurse which had some correspondence with that towards the mother. If treatment were to work this would have to be the main focus. The task for the therapist was to uncover the conflicts within that relationship to the nurse, and to withstand the patient's efforts to make the therapist a participant in the drama that was being enacted. That task was made difficult by the paranoid character of the patient's pathology and her low tolerance of anxiety. The technical problem of what should pass between therapist and nurse with regard to session material disappeared when the object of transference was seen to be neither nurse nor therapist as separate workers but to be their relationship. This does not contradict the primacy of nursing work because nursing aims are formulated and carried through with the therapist's interpretations in mind. The nurse/therapist couple and their working together evoked a primitive envy in the patient of a combined parental object; as this emerged and was contained by the two workers, Joan ceased to convey the inconsolably screaming infant of her early childhood and moved away from the later childhood false self based on illness and martyrdom.

A comparison between the two extracts from treatment shows a move from pre-oedipal to oedipal conflicts. In the change of room, the split between nurse and therapist was promoted to deal with extreme and early fears of separation from a symbiotic internal mother. Both nurse and therapist were required to take on libidinal and aggressive elements between them. Father is important at this point only insofar as he can be used to attack that mother. Six months later, over the leaving issue, the therapist becomes the focus of a more discernible father transference as an alternative choice of object from mother. The dependence on mother was less regressive by this point and the urge to separate seemed at an oedipal level and in a more appropriately adolescent form. There has not been space to go into material (or the lack of it) concerning drives and psychic structure since the focus has been on the use of objects; it has to be said though, that the treatment was limited by strong resistance due to paranoid defences against bisexual conflicts and that ego structure continued to be weak and subject to a very punitive super-ego. There remained for these reasons even towards the end of treatment a dependence on primitive forms of projection and projective identification.

This case description shows the value of maintaining both the distinction and the connection between nurse and therapist in the course of treatment. Each role contains a recognition of the other. Blurring of boundaries occurs when feelings of failure are induced in the workers who then begin to view each other with envy. Certain patients are especially sensitive to feelings of envy and rivalry among others. Joan's sensitivity to such feelings in staff arose out of her own tendency to identify with an object by a form of psychic theft. Staff conflicts were exploited in order to perpetuate a pathological attachment to internal parents who were in a mutually envious and destructive relationship. In this way Joan sought to maintain her role of being a victim to her parents' failures. Alterations in the nature of the nurse/therapist relationship expressed and exposed the patient's inner conflicts. Through the workers' efforts to process the equivalent feelings of murderous rage and envy, those forces in Joan's internal world were modified.

There is a parallel here to the work done by the analyst in the more traditional treatment setting. Nurse and therapist together perform the task undertaken by the analyst, that is the measuring of what the analyst is being 'made to feel' by the patient's projections against the analyst's own reality, which is external and different to the patient's emotional reality. For the therapist, the nurse provides an essential link to external reality and a means of helping the patient discover where and how the developmental breakdown is occurring. The nurse then should be assisted in the formulation of what external conditions would prepare the way for internal changes to take place.

[9]

Nurse/Therapist Supervision as an Impetus to Change

George Leach

In his paper, Oliver James (p. 80) states: 'We argue that the patient's personal and social structural relation to the occupants of the roles and the social entities of the community *is diagnostic of the vicissitudes of particular aspects of his psychodynamic functioning, and is the medium for changes in these aspects*'. The following is a descriptive account of nursing work with an in-patient family which illustrates the above contention, and points to the value of joint nurse/therapist supervision for both diagnosis and change.

I had never worked in a therapeutic community before, so it was as an enthusiastic newcomer to the Cassel hospital that I was assigned a caseload within the Families Unit. One of my cases was the A family, admitted three months earlier as an emergency. I was to be their third successive nurse within that span of time, which was unusual, as in most cases families suffer few changes to the personnel working with them during the entire period of treatment. In a clinical setting where the relationship with the nurse is a key area of work, such a focus benefits from continuity. My seniors at the Cassel expressed doubts about the feasibility of a family continuing to derive benefit from treatment after a second change of nurse. I was sure they were being unduly pessimistic. After all, in other hospital settings I had become used to nursing a rapidly shifting population of patients. I did not see why nursing work in a therapeutic community should be so very different. However, upon meeting the family I began to have reservations of my own which felt quite separate from these concerns.

Initially, I was greeted by a mixture of indifference and cynicism. The family clearly had doubts about my likely span of work with them. 'I expect they will be dragging people in off the streets to nurse us soon,' sighed Mrs A. Mr A said little. As I began to discover more about this family, my naive enthusiasm was dampened further. Although they had been admitted so recently, Mrs A having had a diagnosis of puerperal depression at the time, the air of emergency around their admission had dissipated. It seemed that their problems had all but disappeared and that there was little with which I could legitimately involve myself. It is always difficult to establish oneself in a new place of work and the A family were doing little to ease my sense of uselessness. There was a marked contrast to some of the other families on the Unit who existed in an almost constant state of crisis and incident. The A family were giving me a clear message that the hospital was being not so much a help to them as a source of additional burdens. Mrs A, particularly, expressed dissatisfaction with the standard of the living accommodation and the way she felt that the hospital's structure, timetable and expectations made caring for her two young daughters almost impossible. The other patients were an additional source of strain to her. After witnessing some of the insolence and disorder of other children on the Unit, I could well imagine how she felt.

Often the A family were early to depart for their weekends at home and late to return. They reported few difficulties as occurring during their times at home and it became hard to challenge the idea that they were in some way better off there. Indeed, they frequently expressed a wish to be discharged. They saw themselves as functioning better than the other families, whose company was making things worse than they needed to be anyway. Of course they were under no compulsion to stay, but it was difficult for me to remain aware of a true sense of their ambivalence in the face of such a torrent of complaint.

I felt no real relationship with Mr A, whose remoteness was only partly explicable by his full-time job which took him out of the hospital a good deal. Even when he was present, he was uninvolved with hospital life and seemed all but invisible. I wondered if the hospital stay might be putting something of a strain on their marriage. Perhaps the puerperal depression had indeed lifted during their three month stay, and they simply needed to be allowed to get on with their own lives. It is significant that I made little attempt to discover whether these suspicions of mine were borne out by the therapists' experience of the family. Privately, I wondered if the therapists could really have this family's best interests at heart.

My faltering sense of engagement was not helped by the fact that Mr and Mrs A were members of the caring professions themselves. It was hard to perceive them as patients, and tempting to collude with their attempts to distance themselves from patient status.

The final blow to any sincere wish to nurse this family came when I heard from Mrs A that her therapist agreed that the family should leave in about a month's time. It did not cross my mind to question Mrs A's contention that this was the case. I did not attempt to check with the therapist herself. My resentment grew as I felt left out of a decision about the family's future. I felt demoralized by the prospect of investing energy in work with the As.

It was roughly at this time that I attended my first nurse/therapist supervision. Looking back at previous ones, it seemed that a sense of deadness prevailed which had made it difficult for nurse and therapist alike to think about their work with this family. Although I had a theoretical understanding of the concepts of transference and countertransference, I was unconvinced that this deadness represented anything other than the inappropriateness of having the As in treatment at the Cassel. And now, of course, it seemed that the therapist had come to the same conclusion.

It came as quite a shock to discover that this was not the case, and that no such leaving date had been suggested. Mrs A's idea that one had been considered could now be seen as an expression of her ambivalence about treatment, and on some level it had also served to undermine my relationship with the therapist. On reflection, it seemed that a split indeed existed between nurse and therapist. We could remember very few times when we had spoken together about this family. It was clear that in my short time with them, I had been exposed to the family's principal defence mechanisms of distancing and denial, which were primarily employed around feelings of anger and dependence. Hearing that these themes had emerged in therapy, I was able to re-interpret much of my experience. It was difficult but useful for me to become aware of ways in which I had been recruited into this family's defensive stance. I was also able to re-experience my relationship with the therapist as reflecting something of the internal dynamics of the family, rather than being a purely professional difficulty.

In other work settings, my experience of differences of opinion between medical and nursing staff was that they would be resolved by one view prevailing over the other. This often seemed to lead to feelings of resentment and inadequacy for the party that 'got it wrong'. By contrast, as a result of the nurse and therapist being able to express their mutual perspectives on the family and on each other's work in a supervised setting, it was possible to accurately locate the major source of difficulty in the family pathology. This supervision allowed the therapist to raise issues that had distorted the nurse/patient relationship. In my nursing work with the family, I became better able to dissociate myself from their denial of the true problem and to be alert to future misrepresentations of what might be happening in therapy.

This marked a turning point in the treatment of the A family. The joint supervision was rapidly followed by a case review. When the main points of this review were fed back to the family I began to experience a true sense of engagement with them. We expressed concern to Mrs A about her real ability to cope at home with the mothering of her daughters, and commented on Mr A's unhelpful lack of involvement with hospital life. As the weeks went by, we began to hear about marital arguments that took place during the previously idealized weekends. Indeed, these arguments became frequent within the hospital itself. The couple began to express the idea themselves that they might not be able to cope at home as a family if they were discharged. The atmosphere within the Families Unit became increasingly tense as Mrs A became more openly critical of the parenting within other families and seemingly less able to cope with the demands of her own children. She began to place more demands on my time and increasingly attempted to recruit me to support her in battles against husband, fellow patients and the therapists, who she frequently criticized for being cold and unhelpful. She presented me with such a barrage of needs that it was difficult to hang on to my own idea of what would constitute an appropriate nursing response.

Oliver James suggests that when a nurse is subjected to constant projections, there is a danger that these will either be introjected and accepted as real, or defended against either by a rigid adherence to impersonal professionalism or by collapsing into an uncritical niceness. The A family had, in some sense, projected their own sense of uselessness into the nurse and the institution itself. As the nurse involved, I had taken this projection on board by the time of the nurse/therapist supervision. An element of collapse was also there in my failure to challenge the A's perception of their status as 'non-patient'. Now that the family seemed more committed to treatment and some of their defensiveness was replaced by dependence, the pressure to cave in and supply what they felt they needed was intense.

An example of this followed shortly after the review and arose around the provision of food. In the light of concerns about Mrs A having sufficient maternal resources for her children, it is interesting that she expressed intense dissatisfaction about the hospital's catering arrangements. The substance of her complaint was that the wrong food was being provided at the wrong times. Mrs A was feeding her youngest daughter on reconstituted dried food at an age when the child would have tolerated mashed-up hospital food. In addition, it seemed impossible for Mrs A to structure sleeping and eating times for her baby in such a way as to allow for a sufficiency of both and for some participation in the life of the community. Lunch times (which are communal and shared by nurses) were particularly fraught. Mrs A found it difficult to tolerate her baby's messy experiments with self-feeding, but if she took over and fed the baby, she would have to cope with tantrums from her three year old. This all left Mrs A too exhausted and distressed to manage a proper meal for herself.

My offers of practical help were rebuffed amid complaints that it was the hospital that was making things difficult by not providing enough time for all of them. Mrs A went on to ask me if her family could begin lunch ten minutes before the others. Amid all her other complaints about the hospital, it was difficult not to respond in some way by giving her something she appeared to want – and this was it. I helped her to effect the change and the special meal times began. Lunch did indeed become a little calmer, but at the cost of resentment from the other families who felt that they had special needs too.

Subsequently my 'helpfulness' was questioned by the therapist, who was able to link Mrs A's concrete attempts to restructure the hospital's provision with her difficulty in having time for both her children. In other words, as the nurse, I was under pressure to provide something that was lacking in the mothering but in an inappropriate and concrete way. This again became clear in a subsequent supervision, and enabled me to encourage a return to normal meal times. Mrs A was helped to be less concerned about her baby's messy eating habits, her other daughter was consequently less rivalrous for attention, and Mrs A herself was able to eat. The lessening of distress at mealtimes freed the family to focus on other issues and gave Mrs A particularly a sense of how she could be helped by nursing work.

I feel that my work with the A family was facilitated and perhaps only made possible by the perspectives gained in nurse/therapist supervisions. The ability of the nurse to hold on to a sense of the value of nursing work can only be enhanced by the opportunity to understand its context. This in turn makes it possible for the patient or family to face issues that were previously avoided.

[10]

Working with an Adolescent Boy in a Therapeutic Community

A Nursing Care Study

Mary-Ann Munford

This brief account describes how one young person, John, and his family engaged in the therapeutic programme at the Cassel, and my part in nursing them over an 18-month period. John's behaviour during his in-patient stay occasioned a series of crises for himself, his family and the hospital community, and this report shows how they were dealt with in ways which enabled him to be contained and encouraged to find more productive ways of self-expression.

John left with many unresolved difficulties, and our relations with his family were never satisfactory. Nevertheless, he made considerable progress and many positive changes.

John and his family

At the age of 15, John had been considered by his teachers and parents to be an intelligent, keen scholar with a successful academic career ahead of him. However, while studying for his mock 'O'level examinations he became increasingly withdrawn, depressed, and inconsistent in his work. Eventually, a suicide attempt led to his admission to the local psychiatric hospital, where he was treated for depression and borderline psychosis with anti-depressants and, at times, major tranquillizing drugs. For the next two years, John's life fluctuated between home and hospital. Although medication helped reduce his symptoms he was unable to return to his studies or resume an active life consistent with that of an adolescent boy. When he was 17, John's psychiatrist referred him to the Cassel hospital in the hope that he might respond to a very different treatment approach.

At an initial consultation where he and his family met with a therapist, social worker, and the medical manager of the Adolescent Unit, it was agreed that John might benefit from in-patient psychotherapy and nursing. A routine nursing assessment through a home visit was crucial before an admission date could be agreed, and as the nurse allocated to work with John, I visited him at home with another patient, an adolescent girl. The aim was to meet him and his parents on their home ground, to understand a little more about his home environment, and to give the family an opportunity to ask questions about the hospital. The family consisted of mother and father, both in their mid 40s, John aged 17, who had been adopted at a few months old, and their natural son, a year younger.

The visit provided some valuable observations. John hardly spoke throughout. His mother answered for him on most issues; his father joined us late, having had a previous appointment. I observed that John had taken on an invalid role in the family. His mother seemed overprotective and overindulgent. She clearly had few realistic expectations of John. She did all his washing, cooked all his meals, and had become used to the fact that he spent most of his time listening to loud music in his room. Both parents were keen that John should resume his studies and impressed upon me that a place had been offered him at the local technical college for the next school year. John was able to say he wanted to get well and was terrified at the thought of spending the rest of his life as a mental patient. Before we left, John showed us to the shops and became quite chatty and animated while describing some interesting local history. Notably, this change of manner happened in the absence of his parents, and there was a hint of showing off to the young girl who accompanied me on the visit.

John was offered admission to the Cassel for an assessment

period of one month, during which time the hospital staff, John, and his parents, could decide whether a period of treatment would be useful. His mother and father were asked to support his treatment by coming to weekly group meetings attended by the adolescent in-patients and their parents, and to have John home for weekends.

Early days in the hospital community

John's first month in hospital revealed many of his difficulties, and also those of his parents. From his arrival, his mother and father seemed to want to hand over all responsibility for him to me. For example, John arrived with no medication, despite the fact that the family had been told to bring his usual drugs, which he would have to take before having the amount gradually decreased during assessment. I was left to scurry round to find a doctor to write the necessary new prescription within an hour of their arrival.

The assessment period was characterized by John's dependence on patients and nurses to get him to the right place at the right time for therapy sessions, group meetings and meals. A younger girl took John under her wing for a while and made it her business to know where he was most of the time. John presented as a silent, passive boy who slouched around with a hangdog look. He had greasy hair and a shuffling gait with his hands held stiffly at his sides. In group meetings he spoke only when spoken to, and replied in monosyllables. He looked tense and shaky, and usually covered his face with his hands. On one occasion he stayed away from a group meeting after being told by his room mate to 'get off your backside and do some work'. John felt so hurt by this remark that he spent the morning hiding under a tree in the garden until I found him and brought him back into the hospital. This incident was to be the first of many where John turned his back on confrontations with patients or staff, leaving us feeling anxious and guilty for having challenged him.

My observations of John's behaviour in the community, and

his therapist's experience of him during his individual sessions three times a week, led us to an early formulation of the dynamics of John's behaviour. It seemed that he did not feel looked after by the community, or kept in mind by people. We wondered if this related back to his early years when he was first adopted. There had been a sense of unpreparednesss around John's admission to hospital: his lack of medication on the first day, his failure to attend his psychotherapy sessions on time, the constant need to chase him up, all despite the fact that we had talked over the anticipated problems of admission many times. This might have reflected John's parents' sense of unpreparedness when he was first adopted; his mother had not had nine months of pregnancy in which to prepare herself for his arrival. This formulation led me to include in my nursing care plans arrangements with other nurses and patients to help John remember times of psychotherapy sessions, medications, and a clear timetable of the day's activities.

John worried continually about his appearance. He described himself as ugly, moronic and physically deformed. His poor self-image was unshakeable despite my efforts to point out that none of this was true and had the quality of a fixed delusion. He revealed homosexual anxieties too, telling me in confidence that he thought he was effeminate and that he might be attracted to men. This became a frequent issue in psychotherapy sessions, where John asked his therapist for 'advice' on homosexuality.

In our assessment of John's first month in hospital, his therapist and I felt pessimistic about his capacity to make use of treatment within the community. He had responded poorly to our expectations of attending meetings, meal times, and generally being in the right place at the right time. He remained isolated from his peers and frequently worried or frightened them. Other nurses, like myself, found him awkward to approach, to challenge, or to make reasonable plans with. His therapist felt uncertain as to whether psychotherapy could help John gain insight into his problems. However, there was something very likeable about John. He was obviously highly intelligent, and there was a strong wish on our part to help him. A number of patients had voiced the opinion that John should stay in hospital, particularly one of the mothers who seemed to be able to talk with him and who was ready to challenge him over bedtimes and his infrequent appearances in group meetings.

We also noted that after two weeks of slowly reducing medications, John managed to do without drugs and had experienced no ill effects. However, we feared that John's suicidal behaviour might re-appear. This is a common phenomenon when antidepressant drugs are curtailed. We reminded ourselves of the seriousness of his illness which had led doctors in the past to prescribe major tranquillizing drugs on a long term basis.

As a staff group, we concluded that John should be offered treatment with the proviso that alternative arrangements could be made for him if he became impossible for us to manage with our particular style of work. John's local general practitioner was informed of our assessment and agreed to take him back into his care should it become necessary. It was agreed that John's progress would be continually assessed for the next six months.

Our conclusions were explained to John and his parents in a family meeting. His parents agreed to support his treatment by attending the weekly parents and adolescents group and helping to plan his weekends at home. However, this expressed willingness to co-operate soon waned, and the parents began to show ambivalence about their son's treatment, and feelings of guilt around his illness. Battling to keep the parents' allegiance with staff over John's treatment became one of the main focuses of the nursing work.

Crises and containment

During one of his first weekends at home John took a small overdose of anti-depressant tablets. He was admitted to a general hospital for 24 hours and then returned to the Cassel. This incident was significant in a number of ways: Firstly, having swallowed the tablets, John immediately phoned a patient at the Cassel who alerted the duty nurse to phone John's parents. He had clearly engaged at some level with us and had asked for help, albeit in a self-destructive way. Secondly, the parents wanted this incident to be kept secret from the other patients and their parents because they felt guilty and embarrassed that this should happen to their son in their own home. While we respected the parents' feelings, we also realized that this might have been one of many painful secrets that they wanted to keep out of John's treatment. Thus we decided to try to discuss the incident openly in the parents and adolescents group meeting. The result was an hysterical outburst from John's mother; this led to her and John leaving the group for a while. Later, however, one of the other adolescents expressed his fear that John might have other tablets hidden in the hospital, and that one day he might find John dead in bed. John reassured his fellow patients and staff that would not act in this way again, but would try to let people know when he was feeling despairing and destructive. This incident set a precedent in working with the family; we demonstrated our expectations that difficult situations should be openly explored, along with accompanying feelings of anger and guilt.

Despite my anxiety that John might repeat his behaviour, I continued to expect him to join in all the day-to-day activities of the community. He was interested in going camping with a group of patients, myself and two other nurses. I was pleased at his interest in a potentially enjoyable, active event, and with permission from his parents he joined the group preparing for the trip. This work emphasized his inability to tolerate frustration and to look after himself adequately. He 'adopted' an older female patient who 'mothered' him through the preparations, getting him to the right meetings, helping him to think about packing, and generally keeping him in mind. I felt anxious about the responsibility of taking him along, but felt well supported by other patients and staff in deciding we could manage him. We made it clear that John must not wander off on his own, drink alcohol, or bring pills with him, and that he should join in with the chores. Our main concern was that John might become frustrated and angry and that his self-destructive behaviour would ruin the camping trip. He was, in fact, provocatively lazy about doing his chores, and difficult to challenge, but with the help of another patient he was able to stick with the group's activities.

John's worries about his body and facial expressions were challenged during this camping holiday by the sea in hot sunshine and living in close proximity with a small group of people. For the first two days, John refused to change into cooler clothes or even to take his shoes and socks off. He hid his face if anyone took a photograph, and often threatened to destroy the film in the camera when he was caught unawares. Slowly, however, the group's patience with him paid off; we stopped nagging him to sunbathe or swim and left him to his own devices. On the third day we noticed he had taken off his shirt on the beach and was contentedly sunbathing. Later that day he even borrowed someone's shorts to go paddling in the sea. The rest of the group had the presence of mind not to comment until our return to the hospital.

It was only on our return, however, that John revealed to his therapist that one afternoon he had turned on a gas cylinder inside his tent in the hope that he might gas himself. He had been interrupted by myself and another nurse insisting that he help cook supper, but we had no idea of his intentions. The incident revealed the aggression inherent in John's suicidal gestures, and his therapist and I discussed this with him, pointing out how he caused others to worry about him continually but failed to communicate any worries he had about himself.

John's capacity to tolerate or express difficult feelings was very limited. He bottled up his anger and frustration and frequently acted them out by getting very drunk, bolting from rooms without explanation, kicking doors, and in one extreme case, taking a serious overdose of aspirin tablets. This occurred one Friday a few hours before he was due to go home for the weekend. Earlier in the day John had been silent and unapproachable, leaving people concerned and trying to understand what had upset him by guesswork. He did not turn up for lunch that day and by teatime it was clear that he had left the hospital. Patients are required to write details of the times they leave the hospital, their destination, and what time they expect to return. John had written '1 p.m. – ?', with no destination. I was the night nurse, and arrived at 6.30 p.m. to find that John was missing. He had not been in contact with his parents, and our anxiety about him was high. After consultation with the duty team, including a doctor and a nursing officer, I informed the local police. Just as I had finished doing this, John arrived at the hospital, soaked to the skin in the pouring rain. While other patients and I relieved him of his wet clothes he told us he had swallowed 60 aspirin tablets and washed them down with alcohol. I rushed John off to the casualty department of the local hospital in an ambulance, hoping it was not too late for a stomach pump. My intense anger that he should cause such anxiety to nurses and patients alike, helped me to understand a little more about his parents' feelings when John overdosed: guilty for not having prevented it, frightened that he might die, and furious for his lack of consideration for others.

John spent three days under close observation in an intensive care unit. His parents did not visit him but kept in contact with the general hospital staff and ourselves. After much consideration, John's therapist and I decided that we could not re-admit him until he and his family had met with the manager of the Adolescent Unit and myself to re-state the terms and conditions of his treatment. These were:

1. That patients were expected to make efforts to communicate feelings of despair, anger or frustration by putting them into words and sharing them, not by self-destructive or violent behaviour.
2. That John must agree to try and comply with his nursing care plan, which would be revised to provide more structure to his day.
3. That John might be expressing a need for a more structured environment than we could provide, and perhaps drug therapy. If so, did John's parents want him to continue treatment with us and did they still feel able to support the staff's work?

These statements of conditions of treatment represented our decision to take a tough line with John, and to give him the experience of authority figures taking his behaviour very seriously. By this time, his therapist and I had realized how powerful and aggressively controlling John's behaviour was, and how difficult he made it for anyone to get cross with him or to have an argument with him. I was frightened to challenge him in case he should overdose again or become violent. This same fear prevented his parents making reasonable demands on their son or getting cross with him. The hospital staff therefore decided to set a model of confrontation and confident authority, and to help his parents try this alternative approach to fear and timorousness. In practice, this would mean saying 'no' to John's demands when necessary, thus providing an arena for him to be more openly and verbally angry and rebellious.

John recovered quickly from his overdose, and the following week he and his parents came to this proposed meeting. John was re-admitted to the hospital with plans for a formal re-assessment of his progress at the end of two months; his parents were made to understand that the risk of another serious overdose was always present. The other patients had mixed reactions to his return. They did not want to have the anxiety he caused, yet they liked him and felt relieved that he had recovered from the overdose, so that he had another chance. It became clear that John's staying depended heavily on other patients' degree of toleration of him and their willingness to lend active support to my revised nursing plan, which was as follows:

1. John may only leave the hospital if he
   a) is accompanied by another patient, member of staff, or parent
   b) has informed the duty nurse of his intentions and time of return.
2. John is asked not to drink alcohol while a patient in hospital.
3. Patients and nursing staff openly challenge John's passivity in group meetings and activities with the hope of mobilizing the anger and hostility on which it is based.

I explained to John the reason for this unusually rigid plan. He had shown many times that he was not in control of his own behaviour, and out of touch with his feelings, and that at that moment he needed another authority outside himself to contain him. Very soon, John began complaining about being treated like a child: 'I'm old enough to go out by myself!' he would say. Other statements also indicated his ability to rebel verbally against the firm limits we had set.

John's behaviour changed over the next two months. Both in psychotherapy and in the day-to-day life of the community, he became more approachable, chatty, spontaneous, and involved with other patients. He was a little more real as a person. He spent time with the young children on the unit, being playful and responsible with them; he responded constructively when asked to help out with other patients who were going through difficult times, and spoke for himself in groups. I asked him on one occasion to think of ways of helping another adolescent girl while she was feeling depressed and suicidal, and he managed to get her to play snooker all evening, and go off to bed at a reasonable hour. He accompanied me on a home visit and had some useful comments to make about the visit. He was quite good company on the long drive and showed his skills as a map reader. He also composed a song about the 'madness inside him' and asked another patient to set it to music.

There were, on the other hand, two violent episodes when John smashed a window and damaged his bedroom door by kicking at it. While I felt relieved that his aggression was becoming more openly visible, I worried during this time that he might lose control and become physically dangerous. I realized I was picking up his own fear that he would lose control once his anger and frustration came to the surface, and this insight led John's therapist and I to make a clear statement to him that any physical violence would lead to us calling the police. Similarly, if he became violent outside the hospital, a member of the public or his family might need to contact the police. The rationale behind this was to present John with a realistic response to his behaviour, and our statement did seem to have the containing effect we had hoped for.

By now, John had been in hospital for five months and I felt generally optimistic that we could go on working with him. I felt less optimistic about our faltering alliance with his parents. From the beginning they had, (while professing the opposite), demonstrated distrust, scepticism and rivalry towards the professional staff. John's father had regularly attended the parents and adolescents group, but had colluded with John's passivity and defended him against criticism or confrontation with others in the group. His mother's attendance had declined after her hysterical outburst over John's overdose at the beginning of his treatment, and also because of her own hospitalization for a routine though major surgical operation. John's father colluded with John's reluctance to make plans for weekends, to manage his money, or to participate in decisions, and protected his wife from hearing anything 'bad' about her son. John's parents' unspoken wish was for us to 'adopt' their son, which his therapist and I saw as a re-enactment of John's adoption in infancy.

The social worker and I felt uncertain about life in the family's home at weekends and uneasy about not hearing his mother's point of view. We decided we needed a full family meeting in order to make a satisfactory re-assessment of John's progress. We thus arranged to visit the family in their own home. We used the meeting to impress upon the parents that the hospital had not taken over responsibility for their son and that we could only continue working with him if we had their full support. I described the expectations we had of John in the community and the restrictions put on him for his own safety, and tried to help the parents think of how they could apply similar principles at weekends. I also suggested that he needed to be challenged over how he spent his time at home, even though this might lead to family arguments.

Soon after this meeting, John spent ten days at home over the Christmas holidays. It proved a useful time in that he had a fierce row with his mother, the first openly angry confrontation with her for many years. The row hurt his mother greatly because he accused her of not noticing his illness earlier or doing anything about his problems before they became so entrenched. However, for John, this expression of anger without violent loss of control enabled him to be more lively and argumentative in other situations. He became openly angry with his father in the next parents and adolescents group, and though he rushed out of the hospital to the pub at the end of the meeting, he soon returned of his own accord. I acknowledged with him the next day that he was capable of controlling himself and acting responsibly, especially after emotional upsets with other people.

This period was a turning point in my approach to nursing John. I had constantly felt the need to be rigid and authoritarian in response to his failures to comply with my nursing care plans. Every time something went wrong I felt furious and resentful, and often wanted to wash my hands of John and all his struggles. Through discussions with John's therapist and the unit nursing officer and consultant, we realized that John reacted to me as if I were like his adoptive mother, expecting me to behave in the same cold, resentful way that she did. John's therapist wrote a useful summary of the dynamic hypothesis underlying their struggle:

> I suspect that John's mother looked after him out of a sense of duty and was probably, from the beginning, unable to enter a symbiotic relationship with John which would have enabled some integration within his own affective life. I suspect that driven by her own conscience, John's mother may have treated John as if he were her own conscience. This may have led him to develop a self-image in which he had a threatening and omnipotent control over his mother. It seems as if these primitive destructive impulses remain within John, unmodified by the more positive relationships which might have softened them.

I needed to find a balance between offering John containment of his feelings and a sense of safety, and at the same time encouraging him in taking responsibility for himself. I decided to modify my nursing care plan to lift some of the restrictions on him and allow him more self-reliance. This coincided with his requests to be allowed out on his own, and continual reminders to me that he was now 18 years old and should not be so restrained by adults. We agreed that he could now come and go freely with the condition that he used the signing-out book correctly and that the duty nurse would be able to challenge him about it as she would any patient. It became much easier to elicit a reasonable response when these challenges were made, and John responded quite well to this increased responsibility.

One further incident provoked a dramatic change in John. As mentioned earlier, he had many worries about his sexuality. We had observed that his relationships with female patients often took the form of infatuation and dependence, usually with women many years older than himself. A new adolescent girl joined the unit, two years younger than John and openly sexually provocative towards men. She and John soon paired up and on one occasion ran off to a nearby park and had sexual intercourse together. The girl, Liz, came to me full of worries about being pregnant. John insisted on being present at our meetings, and for the first time I saw him as caring and frightened, able to consider the consequences of his actions both for himself and for Liz. I informed Liz's father of the incident and John accompanied Liz to the family planning clinic for a pregnancy test.

John's therapist and I managed the incident by allowing John space to have feelings about what had happened, without condemning him. John told his therapist that it was the first time he had had full intercourse with a girl. He had felt 'free' and taken out of himself. My job was to help John with the realities of the incident. I pointed out three things: firstly, that if he was going to have intercourse he needed to think about getting contraceptive advice; secondly, that the hospital rules prohibit sexual intercourse between patients in the hospital building; and thirdly, that both he and Liz were in hospital because of severe difficulties they had in making relationships, consequently the hospital was not the best setting for their relationship to develop and might add to Liz's already very worrying problems. John surprised me in his grown-up attitude, for though contemptuous of my questioning his relationship with Liz, he did take an active part in caring for her through her fears of pregnancy, which proved to be unfounded. His therapist explored what thoughts and fantasies this incident may have stirred up for John about his own birth, adoption, his early wonderings about who his real parents were and why they 'gave him away'.

During this eventful time in John's stay, our communications with his parents were faltering again. John's mother continued to absent herself from meetings with the parents and adolescents, and family meetings with the social worker. John's father reacted ambivalently to his son's behaviour. Sometimes he was critical of the hospital for not supervising John adequately; sometimes he was pleased that John had 'sown his wild oats'. Particularly at this time, John acted towards me as if I was like his mother – a useless, nagging, persecuting figure. His therapist supported me in understanding this transference phenomenon, which enabled me to retain some much-needed objectivity.

Progress at ten months

By the time John had been in hospital for ten months he had a number of important jobs in the community with other patients and nurses. It was clear from their comments that it was now much easier to talk with John and expect him to take responsibility for his actions – in other words, to treat him like a real person. His progress was demonstrated in other ways, too. For instance, he took on the responsibility of looking after the sports equipment in the hospital. This required him to make an inventory of all the items and report to the activities committee. We finally managed to work together on this and he was able to listen to my suggestions and to contribute many of his own. He presented the results of his work with confidence to the 15 or so people present at the activities committee – a marked contrast to the catering meeting six months before, when he could not bear to read out a menu and feared people were staring because he was ugly, deformed and 'insane'. Also, he had taken it upon himself to apply to the local college to sit 'O'level examinations. After completing the application form with help from his father he was offered an interview and was accepted for part-time study. He was assigned a personal tutor who took a helpful interest in his progress.

John's appearance had altered. He was walking taller, looking people in the eye, had his hair cut very short in a modern style, and wore a new pair of tight black jeans. He had a good sense of humour, and his intellectual abilities, demonstrated in games of chess and scrabble, were much admired by others.

John leaves in his own way

Six months later, John still had a long way to go. He had made some dramatic strides within the containing environment of the therapeutic community but had only just begun to make use of psychotherapy and daily community activities. His home life remained fraught, and our alliance with his parents remained tenuous. John's mother agreed to attend monthly meetings but was still reluctant to openly face the battles with her son.

At this point, I saw the next step to be John's discharge to an appropriate place. I thought that a young people's hostel, one familiar with problems of rehabilitation yet allowing a fair degree of independence, would be a logical move. However, these ideas did not come to fruition. At this time, John became less and less available to me and to his therapist, and seemed to close down the shutters on the community. Patients' and staff's toleration of his stubborn and at times delinquent behaviour diminished. He began to abscond from the hospital, to return late from weekends, and he threatened to discharge himself. The change in his behaviour was related to two main issues. Firstly, John's therapist had gone away for three weeks' holiday two months before. John was unable to acknowledge what this meant for him, and chose to go home rather than explore what resources were available to him in the community. Secondly, his attendance at college, which had been a major focus of my work with him over the last six months, had put him in a position where he was again in competition with his peers over academic abilities. He truanted frequently from lessons despite sympathetic encouragement from his teachers and from the college counsellor.

Finally, John left hospital after an 18 month stay. We decided to accept his decision to discharge himself, having invited his parents for a final family meeting where they agreed on his leaving, provided he either enrol at their local college or find a job. At least they had some realistic expectations of him now. I was left with many unresolved feelings, in particular, great sadness that John had been unable to say goodbye or acknowledge any feelings about separation. Four months later, John wrote to his therapist. He apologized for his 'despicable behaviour' during his stay at the Cassel, and told us that he had been given a place at college to study mathematics, but had not yet turned up for class. He also said he had joined a chess club and had played two games for the local league, both of which he had lost! It was hard to evaluate from this letter how well he was functioning, but certain points made me optimistic: Firstly, he had written from home and was apparently managing to have some life of his own – in contrast to two years ago, when he played loud music alone in his room for weeks on end. Secondly, he was still following some of the plans which had begun at the Cassel, in going to college, even though he was still finding it difficult to turn up; and lastly, his chess club membership suggested that he was continuing to make social contacts through his intellectual abilities as he had done at the Cassel, was risking competition, and coping with failure.

Conclusion

Despite the fact that John left in an unsatisfactory and worrying way, his stay at the Cassel, with all its attendant difficulties, had enabled him to grow through some important crises. The Cassel had provided a safe environment in which to challenge and contain his self-destructive behaviour, and in which to begin to take responsibility for himself and others. The patient community played a great part in supporting him through his stay, and my colleagues' support was invaluable in helping me recognize and respond to the psychodynamic and managerial issues as they arose.

[11]

A New Look at the Vulnerability of Puerperal Mothers

A Clinical Study of Two In-patient Families at the Cassel Hospital

Anne Zachary

THE PUERPERIUM IS ordinarily a time when women in general are especially vulnerable. Primitive anxieties are stirred up at a moment when it is essential to be adult. There is a complex interplay of elements from different levels in the mind – pre-oedipal, oedipal, sexual; these have to be held together. Where breakdown occurs, it can be at one particular level or all of them at once. Thus childbirth and the puerperium, as well as being a pleasurable experience, can be traumatic both for the baby and for the mother whilst this unique and specific developmental stage is negotiated in a way that will lead to improvements or to permanent setbacks.

Lomas (1960a) likens the baby to a psychotherapist, breaking through its mother's defence mechanisms and establishing her as a new person more in touch with her real life. Where this process is harsh and untimely, the unfortunate mother breaks down. There are also some mothers whose own characters and backgrounds make this more likely. For them, psychotic anxiety is stirred up and their vulnerability increases to an extent which arouses concern both for them and for their babies, who are at risk either from neglect or abuse, depending on the degree and nature of the mother's incapacity. The Cassel Hospital is viewed as an environment in which such babies can thrive because their mothers' needs and difficulties are recognized, and because their mothers are provided with a structured setting in which uncertainties can be tolerated.

The main task for a new mother is the re-negotiation of the mothering which she herself had. If this was successful, she can tend her baby and fulfil its needs. If this cannot happen, usually because there were flaws in her own mothering, breakdown occurs. Universally, women turn to their mothers in the puerperium. This represents a psychic turning to the internal mother again, having turned away towards father in the oedipal situation. If there were problems in her own early mothering, why should she turn back? Instead she turns to the baby, identifying with it and its needs, regressing and becoming unable to mother, in her need to be mothered.

There has been a considerable amount written already about the particular approach by the Cassel towards puerperal mothers in difficulty, (Lomas, 1959, 1960 a,b) based on psychoanalytic understanding. In 'A Fragment on Mothering' (1958) Dr Tom Main describes very clearly and beautifully the way in which this identification with the baby occurs based on the fact that every mother was once a baby herself.

But there are other important factors involved. He describes how, because the child wishes for its mother to be at the centre of its universe, a mother is not primarily a sexual woman; and how the father is thereby stripped of sexual joy. Psychoanalysis views this childish refusal to countenance sexuality in parents to be one of the central human defences against pain – the envy, anger, contempt, blame, denigration, murderous fantasies and jealousy of the oedipal situation. Crushing guilt and anxiety about femininity and sexual enjoyment arise when maternity tests the whole system of hidden rivalries and guilts of the oedipal situation. Can the new mother allow herself this baby which affirms her own sexuality which she believes her mother hates as much as she hates her mother's? Can she allow herself to enjoy her baby which represents a phallic triumph over her father? Psychotic anxiety abounds, retaliation is expected and masochism is the only way out when breakdown occurs. This takes the form most often of a depression; this must be understood in terms of loss. There is failure to mourn a lost object which in this case is the pregnant body (see Freud 1917). As the baby grows in the womb, the mother feels filled up and fulfilled. At birth, she is emptied. Where her internal mother is weak, her resources are low and she becomes depressed. Melanie Klein would say that this depression re-awakens the problems of the depressive position, where loss must be acknowledged and survived.

Dr Peter Lomas in a series of papers (1959-60) describes various aspects of the psychodynamics of puerperal breakdown, quoting from earlier works such as those of Helene Deutsch writing in America in the 1930-40s. First, he describes the typical husband / wife relationship in which breakdown occurs. A dominant, masculine woman, masked by an overtly masochistic attitude, 'mothers' her passive husband. Understandably the advent of a child disturbs this liaison. Having felt masculine, superior and maternally giving, she now feels dependent on him but unable to receive support from him. She is made anxious by being surrounded by the baby's tremendous insatiable demands which she cannot satisfy. She identifies with the baby, but then this produces a reaction of punishment from the super-ego because of the intense primitive desires stirred up by such an identification. Fears of greed and sadism are also then projected on to the baby, as they are disowned by the mother. Guilt arises especially from the unconscious masculine success of producing a boy.

Next, he describes a rigid defensive organization whose aim is concerned to control and conceal hatred and anxiety. In puerperal breakdown, the defensive organization is overwhelmed, unlike the usual gradual development of undefendedness which Winnicott called 'primary maternal preoccupation' (1956). Moral masochism and denial give way to a breakthrough of primitive impulses related to sexuality and aggression. This leads to projection by the mother of the feared badness onto the baby. There is shame and anxiety about the baby's displaying aggression. Alternatively, there is fear and guilt about pride at the baby's success, and about having pleasure in the baby. This mobilizes a need for punishment. The appearance of the baby in the external world may symbolize not only the mother's concealed primitive aggressiveness, but also her buried hopes, pleasures and ambitions which in turn evoke anticipation of the envy and jealousy of others.

In a paper devoted to this dread of envy where the baby is idealized, Lomas (1960 b) describes mothers who cannot turn to their own mothers because of feelings of hate and envy. They have had poor relationships with their mothers in childhood and absent or ineffectual fathers. They fear their own mothers' envy of their creative achievement and do not turn to the natural provider of a protective environment in this time of regression whilst close to their babies' instinctual urges. Masochistic defence against this dread of envy may itself be sufficiently powerful to destroy these mothers' maternal capacity or even to reduce them to states of psychiatric illness.

In reviewing these classic papers, I am struck by the way in which recent patients at the Cassel stand out as easily recognizable in the theories and clinical examples of several decades ago. I am going to describe aspects of our work with two patients admitted with their families, concentrating in particular on their vulnerability in the puerperium. In doing this, I hope to be able to replicate features of the important earlier work at the Cassel and to illustrate some of the techniques used now by those findings in working with these particular patients.

The family unit

When the previous work was in progress, only the mother and baby were admitted to the Unit, though husbands were encouraged to visit and spend as much time as possible with them. Now, the husband and any other children are also admitted and are involved in the active treatment plan to varying degrees. This enables the mother's plight to be viewed not only as a problem of her own or between her and the baby, but also as one related to her environment. Admitting the whole family allows them to bring their pathology and living space into the hospital and to recreate a piece of their reality there. They repeat their breakdown where it can be monitored and used to elicit change in their functioning as a family.

The admissions procedure is usually a carefully planned elective one spanning some weeks, when we investigate suitability and test the motivation of patients. However, in the case of puerperal mothers, this procedure is often waived in view of the particular vulnerability of both mother and new baby and the need for swift action to prevent lasting damage. Both mothers I will describe were admitted with their families following urgent domiciliary visits when the situation at home had become desperate.

The two mothers were actually both from the same profession. Prior to marriage and childbirth they had been fairly ambitious and reasonably successful. However, especially for Mrs B there were signs easily picked out from her history to suggest character weakness or a potential for breakdown.

Mrs A and her family were admitted to the Cassel shortly after the birth of the second child, a second daughter in the space of two years. They were living in crowded conditions trying to buy a house in place of their one-bedroomed flat. Mrs A had become increasingly depressed and withdrawn, complaining of feelings of wanting to lash out at the furniture or at the children. She worried about not having enough space of her own. She was increasingly dependent on her husband, who was having more and more time off work. The referrer, the family GP, had indicated that this was an increasingly desperate situation.

There was a strong resistance to being admitted to the hospital following the domiciliary visit, especially on the part of Mrs A, who believed that as soon as she was with someone supportive, things would quickly get better. It was plain to see that through her rigid defence of denial she was struggling to conceal her anxiety. But as soon as she was next alone with the children, she decided upon admission, to the obvious relief of Mr A. Once the family had been admitted, he quietly got back to work though he continued in his supportive motherly role, taking a large part in the care of the children whenever he could.

Here is an excerpt from the nurse's notes on Mrs A one week after her admission:

> Mrs A seems very fragile, is slow and tearful, and only brightens up at the mention of her elder child. She seems to want to be in control and a perfect mother, maybe denying feelings of not wanting to be a mother and any negative feelings she has for the children. This is especially apparent around mealtimes. She gets very anxious then, and finds it difficult to control the elder child and to meet the baby's demands. She feels panicky almost at screaming point, then has to sit down quietly for a while to calm down.

Having observed this anxiety around mealtimes, the nurse set us a rota at lunchtimes when Mr A was at work so that Mrs A always had the support of a nurse and another patient whilst she was feeding the children.

Another aspect to this family was recorded in the nurse's notes soon after admission: 'Mr A finds it difficult to cope with his wife's demands and her inability to cope. He gets fed up and angry but doesn't express it, just goes quiet. He makes his wife feel hurt, angry and even more guilty.'

A theme quickly became evident, namely the way in which this family functioned in order to control their aggression: by distancing themselves from it. Mr A remained quiet and passively compliant, unable in meetings or in his weekly therapeutic sessions to display any negative feelings. Concern was expressed among the staff about the strangeness of the little girl aged two, who rarely spoke and who seemed precociously independent and oblivious to any need for adult company, wandering away from her mother or babysitter without anxiety.

Mrs A was in more intensive therapy than her husband. I was her therapist. Mrs A found it hard to leave her professional role aside and to come to terms with the humiliation she felt at being a patient. More often than not, the family would return to the hospital late after their routine weekends at home or after holiday breaks. She was continually trying to convince us that they were almost ready to be discharged; she set herself limits to her stay a few weeks ahead. A great step forward was taken when we were able to convert the leaving date they so much wanted, into a 'staying' date.

Mrs A's difficulty in engaging masked an extreme degree of dependence most noticeable at the end of sessions. She found it hard to leave and occasionally indicated a wish to be cuddled, becoming very angry when this was not granted. She felt this need of her total abandonment. Separation for her was an enormous test, in the manner of someone who has never properly engaged, so that we began to suspect an inadequacy in the mothering she had received. She complained incessantly that she found the practical arrangements for her family at the hospital wanting, that nothing was quite right, that she did not receive enough in terms of time, and that what was available was not the kind of support that she needed. She was often an unpopular patient in the community. It seemed she continually set out to prove to herself that she was bound to fail, to be scapegoated, to have to cope with enormous unfairness and discrimination, acting out an unconscious belief that she was so bad that no-one cared about her or could give her what she needed. In this way, she illustrated a moral, masochistic attitude to life.

Her own history bore out some of these transference elements. She was the middle child of three, traumatically displaced at the age of four by the birth of the only son. Her father demanded high achievement and was mockingly punitive. Her mother was described as passive, dependent and inadequate. The parents had a violent relationship in which ill-treatment of the mother by the father was often witnessed. The mother especially was dependent on alcohol. A picture emerged, again experienced in the transference, of a distant impervious mother whom no amount of attention-seeking could hope to engage in meaningful communication. It was as if Mrs A had been perpetually banging her head against a brick wall.

In the early days of therapy, Mrs A's baby was tiny and was brought to the sessions by her. This offered an opportunity to observe a strong identification with the baby. The mother could switch in and out of the infantile role, appearing desperately needy, dependent and helpless. She was only rescued from this by the real baby needing attention. This she provided, using professional skills and a practical efficiency from which she seemed cut off emotionally.

There are various features of the treatment programme at the Cassel which are specifically designed to cut down unhealthy regression and dependence. It is important that the families have a home address. They are encouraged to return there at weekends. There is only one nurse on night duty, so that the patient community is relied upon to find support within itself. Patients are responsible for cooking breakfast and supper for themselves as a community, on a rota basis. A recent development is that they have taken on planning and ordering for these meals also, in a structure known as 'the patients' pantry'. It is essential in this setting that patients who are extremely regressed, as was Mrs A on admission, can find support within the community and the nursing to contain their anxiety and needs between therapy sessions (which are only one aspect of the treatment plan). By having the baby present at the therapy, its own needs had to be recognized by the mother. This served as a rescue from profound regression or total psychosis which would be unmanageable within the Cassel structure. At the same time, it could be pointed out to the mother how much of a burden it was on the baby to be in the position of having to rescue its mother from her own vulnerability and having to carry her projections.

This point was illustrated also by the projection apparent in these early sessions. If the baby cried, it often seemed to be at a point when it served well as a channel for the depressed mother to express her hate and aggression. A very interesting phenomenon related to this mother's difficulty in receiving anything good again projected into the baby. On many occasions the baby, having been drinking from its bottle throughout the session, would vomit messily on the carpet or on the chair just prior to leaving. This signified that something potentially good given by her was rejected by the baby. Extending this, it also signified that the mother had received nothing good in the session; thus she could continue with her fantasy that she was deprived of anything good.

Projection was used in another way, in that this baby was particularly bonny, healthy and attractive although she did begin to look rather overfed, since the mother in view of her own inadequacy continually fed the baby as a form of anxious reassurance destined to fail. By contrast, the mother herself was thin, frail and neglected in appearance. Depressed and lifeless, she dragged herself about the hospital but seemed to carry her larger-than-life, smiling baby held up in front of her. She herself would hardly be noticed whilst the baby was greeted by everyone. She would be referred to as 'baby A's mother' rather than by her own name. The baby therefore not only served as a channel for the expression of all the negative feelings the mother could not own, but also contained all that was alive and of value projected by her guilty, depressed mother.

There were covert suicidal wishes and even intention, which came to light in therapy soon after admission. This theme of not wanting or feeling able to live continued until it was suddenly intensified by an unexpected and tragic event in which Mrs A's own mother died in a fire. Identification with this dead mother was profound and appeared in both waking and dream life. Some particularly poignant dreams were described around the time of the inquest. First, she dreamed that

> her mother's coffin was divided into three portions. One portion was only partially buried, one portion was in the sea, and the third portion was swinging on the tide.

Of course, Mrs A's mother had had three children and Mrs A was preoccupied with the effect of the sudden death of them all. The dream indicated a lack of peace and also a concrete identification. On the second occasion, the patient dreamed that

> she saw her mother in the dream, half buried, with her face only partially covered with earth. A six-year-old boy, the child of another in-patient family, was kicking more earth over the face. As she watched, the face changed into her own.

The dreams illustrate the strain of the half-finished mourning process resulting from the need for an inquest several months after the death. They also illustrate how this suicidal patient was identifying concretely with her own mother. Again, the baby played into the dynamics. Whilst the second dream was being described tearfully and with total preoccupation by Mrs A. The baby, now six months old, played on the floor with her toys and pulled the plastic carrier bag used to transport them right over her head.

At this time, Mrs A was functioning in a psychotic manner. She could not differentiate between being a mother and being inside the mother. She could not differentiate having a baby from being a baby herself. This could clearly be seen in the interplay of generations with its identifications. These signified the various levels of Mrs A's mind that she was struggling frantically to hold together and to keep under control.

Throughout these months, there was a deadness about staff discussions around this family. The deadness within the family was being mirrored by the deadness in staff communication. Communication between staff is an important tool in the Cassel's way of working and attempting to understand patients in order to be able to help a family change. Nurse and therapist work closely together and make use of such observations. It was interesting that Mrs A managed to create quite large splits between the nurse and the therapist as often as she could. It was viewed as Mrs A's way of avoiding her own anger. This was particularly striking at a time when her nurse was changing Units, which meant that she was to have a new nurse. Her anger in relation to the separation perhaps required her to attempt to split nurse and therapist who had to work especially hard to maintain communication so as to avoid mirroring the family's way of avoiding confrontation.

Mrs A tended to overfeed her baby, but there were problems relating to mealtimes and food which had much wider implications. She had great difficulty in providing for both children at once. This was the basis of one split between the staff when she negotiated longer mealtimes with her nurse, thus losing a valuable opportunity for interpretation in her therapy. She had trouble with her own intake, often feeling sick and developing a routine whilst in hospital of not eating anything till mid-afternoon. She had complex vegetarian and health food ideals and at times began to look anorectic. This was paralleled in her therapy where, as I have said before, she could take nothing in, despite tremendous needs. This leads on to discussion of her sexuality.

In Tom Main's 'A Fragment on Mothering', he describes how human beings deal with guilt by suffering severely in order to placate the rage of the internalized forbidding mother. A woman may be unable to enjoy and advance in feminine achievement as a sexual being; and motherhood becomes for her a matter for shame and suffering, drudgery and depression. She may wreck her relationship with the father of her child, renouncing the pleasures of adulthood and retreating back to a childlike state of innocence and obedience. Another aspect may be the woman's masculine wishes. In extreme forms, bitter rivalry prevents her from pursuing a relationship with a man. In minor forms, she may choose a less than truly masculine man for her partner, a weak man who can be mothered, who can prevent her from feeling small and who averts the terror associated with passive surrender to feminine passion.

Mrs A illustrates these characteristics well. Whilst in treatment she had the appearance of a little boy. She was too thin, and dressed (albeit in the current fashion) in various versions of long shorts. More often than not she went barefoot. She had married Mr A whilst abroad and had been attracted to him because he did not try to dominate her. This led to problems, in that he was particularly indecisive, but a marriage was made in which she did not feel too threatened. It was not entirely planned, but developed as a result of a quick succession of pregnancies. The first of these was aborted and remained in Mrs A's mind as the son she needed. Breakdown occurred after her second daughter was born, when house, mothering capacity and family life had become unbearable. She had suffered to an extreme to combat her guilt about sexual achievement, and felt unconsciously unworthy of her husband and her healthy children. For some time, she kept secret an overwhelming passion for a former lover who was from a different cultural background. It transpired that she still spoke to him at length on the telephone and entertained wild fantasies about their life together. When the reality of his plan to return to his own country came home to her, she disclosed her fantasy world.

Her fantasies about 'the black lover' represented masturbation fantasies as a defence against anxiety. She basked in her wanting of him rather than recognizing fully that she felt that she did not deserve her chosen partner. To avoid the full extent of her suffering in order to manage her guilt about sexual achievement, she turned to a sadistic attack on her objects – on her husband and on the primary object, her mother. Feeling attacked by her mother, who is impervious and unavailable and so alive in the transference, she turned this round and attacked her mother. Her destruction thus went hand in hand with her distraction, as she put her marriage and her children's wellbeing in jeopardy by her attempts to find gratification in fantasy.

As this family approached the time when they would have been a year in treatment, we began to work with them towards a leaving date. They had successfully moved into a larger house shortly before this decision. The thought of discharge raised enormous anxieties in Mrs A. Having been ambivalent to treatment throughout, when its withdrawal was in sight she began to protest that just when she was beginning to benefit, her supports were being taken away from her. She persistently demanded reconsideration of the leaving date and began to write letters to me between sessions in order to cram as much material as possible into the last few weeks. These letters were rambling and without start or finish, impressing upon me her insatiable need. A dream presented in this way and illustrated, a year after delivery, continuing identification with the baby:

> She was pregnant with chinchilla babies, a breed with which she was familiar in childhood. Her father was trying to get them out but had to take her to the vet. By the time they arrived it had turned into her baby daughter's problem and she felt vexed because the baby was too young to have an internal examination.

A final task was to interpret her fantasy that I was stopping her treatment because she had exhausted and damaged me. I think she was able to leave hospital with some sense of preservation of a good object which was alive. Her guilt and feeling of responsibility for her mother's death were beginning to subside. She was aware that there were still psychological difficulties to be worked on, but she was much more in touch with the realities of her situation. She was able to play with her children and to respond to them in a way which was unrecognizable in comparison to her incapacity on admission.

This family can be regarded as a success in that they benefitted considerably from treatment. My second example illustrates how a treatment plan can break down when a family does not have enough of a working alliance to enable us or anybody else to work effectively with them. This second mother was more severely psychotic in her mental functioning but, again, she illustrates well some of the previous observations about failing motherhood. In describing where treatment broke down it is possible to outline some of the working structures made use of at the Cassel, and to shed some light on how they operate. However, it must be said that even though we viewed the treatment of this particular family as a failure in our more usual terms, there did seem to be an enormous paradox in operation, related to Mrs

B's mental functioning, which resulted in there being some gain for the family after all.

Mr and Mrs B first became known to us as a family with a two-month-old baby girl, in difficulties because Mrs B had developed a severe obsessional neurosis in the puerperium. This had arisen in most tragic circumstances. They had previously had a son with brain damage from birth, who had eventually died aged ten months, when Mrs B was already five months pregnant with her daughter. The obsessional symptom had arisen around Mrs B's preoccupation with the germs which had afflicted her son in his recurrent chest infections from which he had died. Gradually, it seemed to her that her hand washing and ritualistic cleaning was not adequate for the house to be a safe place for her daughter.

Before proceeding, a little should be said about our understanding of Mrs B's symptoms and their use as an effective method of avoiding the pain of loss, since we viewed the situation as one in which there had been a failure to mourn. The second pregnancy had been an unconscious attempt to find a substitute for the dying baby. The birth had followed the death after only a few months, leaving little time for the parents to come to terms with the loss. Though the second baby was healthy, she could not replace her brother, and the guilt and remorse in the parents was such that unconsciously they were not able to allow the new baby to thrive normally.

Our first introduction to the family was via enormous anxiety in the various agencies responsible for them in the community, because the baby was felt to be at risk from neglect and had actually sustained a minor, though worrying injury. The intensity of this anxiety was a clue to the powers of projection that were in operation, since the family seemed to arrange things such that everyone around them was anxious and uncomfortable whilst they remained free of troubles. (This was a focus of hot dispute with Mrs B later in treatment, when interpreted, but one felt that she had confused the effort and pain in achieving a trouble-free life with the real pain she was so desperate to avoid.) Thus, on our emergency domiciliary visit to their home we discovered that they had ceased to live there and had been staying uninvited and disruptively with one of Mrs B's sisters, only to return briefly to meet us at their own house.

The anxiety in the referral agencies transferred to us, resulting in an offer of immediate admission. This was seized upon by the couple. But it was not to be straightforward; the arrival of each parent separately, the baby arriving with mother, set the scene for a most stormy eight months' admission. We had heard about and soon experienced the violent rows which occurred between the couple. Mr B had to be reminded that physical violence towards his wife was not compatible with remaining at the hospital. Other patients were disturbed at night by the rows. The baby was witness to these interminable scenes, and whilst subjected to obsessional rituals as part of her practical management, was suffering severely from emotional neglect. She was thin and lifeless and behind in her development.

The rows caused anxiety and discomfort all round. Patients were alarmed and staff were uncomfortable. The staff working closely with the family held regular family meetings with them. We were surprised to find that contrary to the usual valuable disagreements between nurse and therapist which form the backbone of the way in which we work, where movement forward becomes possible based on understanding of these, as regards this family we were almost totally united. We were stuck fast as it were, feeling thrown together in the face of the barrage of abuse, insults and threats meted out constantly by the couple. Communication between us became excessive, firstly day by day, increasing to hour by hour, until it was not possible to be at a routine meeting either about patients in general or specifically, in short to work and function normally without an interruption due to concerns around the B family. Here is an excerpt from the nursing notes:

> A crisis period is in progress which is stretching the nursing, community resources and therapy to the limit, leaving us

> wondering whether we can actually treat the family here. The arguments have reached full scale and Mrs B is also arguing bitterly with some of the other mothers here. It is almost unbearable to nurse them individually and efforts to plan constructive daily routines are continually rejected. Mr and Mrs B are able to irritate each other sufficiently to thwart any offer of support from other patients, who are calling a nurse immediately a row begins. Massive nursing input is being required but only to be rejected and criticised by the couple.

When this stage was reached, the powerful mechanism of the large group showed its effect and complaints from staff of other Units at the weekly meeting of all clinical staff influenced our management. How could this family detract from and jeopardise the treatment of other patients so radically? How could they be allowed to encroach upon staff's working arrangements and freedom to such an extent? With the insight we have available as a result of Main's 'The ailment' (1946) it was imperative to examine these factors. It came to light that various members of staff had gone to enormous lengths around this family, attending meetings on their days off, and thinking excessively about them whilst off duty. It was even possible that one staff member's decision to leave was in part due to the B family who, amidst this situation of dire discomfort all round, reigned supreme whilst devaluing every resource in sight. It was a true example of projective identification, and on a massive scale. But, examining the facts and weighing up the pros and cons, it was felt that Mrs B's only chance of success in treatment would be if she could come to terms with her feelings of inadequacy as a mother who had produced a damaged baby, and who now could not allow a healthy baby to develop normally. And it was realized that she would only be able to begin to do this if she could make people understand how devalued she felt. That was why it was necessary for the staff to experience it first hand by means of projective identification: what it felt like to feel totally inadequate and devalued.

But Mrs B remained for the most part oblivious to the mechanisms involved and continued her constant projection of all that was painful, almost entirely unconsciously.

In parallel with the unease I have described, certain practical arrangements were gradually instituted as an attempt to create a viable treatment setting whilst the struggle to engage the couple constructively continued. When the only outcome looked to be transfer of Mrs B and her baby to a psychiatric hospital whilst discharging Mr B, they requested separate rooms. This was almost unprecedented for a couple being treated as a family, but the rows were so intense and Mrs B's control over Mr B so irrational, (he was not allowed to wear certain clothes, or to put his things in certain places, and was involved in endless rituals after they had settled for the night requiring him to get up numerous times), that the request was granted. This led to the complex situation in which the couple could not remain together, but found it difficult to be apart. Tension rose to a pitch when Mr B impulsively walked out for a period of several days. Mrs B spent most of that time in conversation with him on the telephone. A second arrangement was for the family to remain in the hospital at weekends. This was largely due to concern for the baby but also to do with the mother's complete phobia about their house. It came to represent her whole pathology. There was a powerful split between all that was bad which was bound up in the house and all that was good which was bound up in the two-person relationship between Mrs B and her baby. She cooed and fussed around her in a most caricatured and exhibitionistic way whilst her world, seemingly unnoticed by her, continued to collapse around the families. The couple were heavily in debt, trapped in the hospital, and alienated from each other and everyone else. Albeit with a struggle, we had given up the idea for the time being of supporting this family in getting to their house.

The nurse who accompanied them on a visit in the early days of their admission reported:

The relationship between the couple is very stormy and it is

> difficult to be with the two of them when they start to argue, particularly on a journey with them by car. The home visit became more difficult the nearer we got to their house and once inside the argument developed in full flood. Meanwhile, Mrs B was continually going upstairs and washing her hands whilst ordering Mr B to remain confined to certain parts of the house.

When the loss and the fears were successfully held at bay there would be periods in the hospital of relative calm, when people took a breath and where information about the B family was remarkable in its absence from staff meetings. It was possible to deny the enormous parasitic drain on our resources for a time, but at our peril in terms of personal integrity and moral values around the use of NHS hospital facilities. There was no denying that this family's plight was tragic, and this account is not meant to portray a lack of feeling about this. Space and time were given to them albeit on the wrong terms, but sooner or later they had to be encouraged to come to terms with the pathology.

The B family's admission had averted a referral to social services which was being considered in view of concern about the baby. When it became clear that the family were not engaging in treatment and the baby remained at risk, we decided to proceed with this referral and to work closely with social services, who held ultimate responsibility for the wellbeing of the child whether or not she was a patient in hospital.

Mr and Mrs B were threatened and made angry by this referral. They could not accept the terms on which it had been made and for what purpose. They could only view it as an attempt to take the baby away from them, and they introduced the idea themselves of the possibility of a care order. This might be interpreted as an unconscious wish to be rid of the responsibility for the baby, following on from their difficulty in accepting a healthy baby. The conflict experienced by the couple around our insistence on working with social services never resolved and they tried hard to forge a split. Having been totally against the referral, from time to time when their hostility towards the Cassel was at its most intense, they tried to engage in secret meetings with their allotted social worker, idealizing him and his potential to help them avoid their loss by being rehoused, (although they were not in danger of losing their house).

Now to focus on the couple's sexual relationship, which will help to illustrate just why they rowed and fought with each other so vehemently. They had had a stormy, rivalrous and bitterly resentful relationship from the beginning, long before they had children. Mr B was impulsive and immature and Mrs B envious and competitive. During her first pregnancy, they had been preoccupied with the idea that intercourse was possibly harmful to the baby, focussing the violence in their personalities and their relationship on their sexual activities. When Mrs B had an antepartum haemorrhage, their worst fears were to them confirmed. Their guilt was such that though the professional workers involved might have humanely accepted that the baby would die quite soon after birth, Mrs B with her husband's support struggled with unceasing effort to keep him alive. It was only when she was pregnant again that she could finally accept that death was the only human outcome for her first baby, and relinquish her excessive efforts.

With this as a background to their present situation, Mrs B was now attempting as every new mother does to adjust to life with a healthy baby. The whole frightening situation of the new three-person relationship so well described by Dr Main in 'A Fragment on Mothering' needed negotiating. How could she allow herself the indulgence of sexual intercourse? The internal mother controlled, punished and restricted her as a way of protecting the baby from the painful knowledge that mother is not just mother, but also the sexual object of its potential rival in father.

Thus, though Mr B had a separate room, the couple from time to time came together and resumed their own adult relationship. But a pattern developed which reverberated around the hospital for days after the Bs had been reported to spend a night together. Mrs B's obsessions increased and intensified. Mr B was controlled by her until he could no longer contain his anger and he began to act impulsively. The violence within the relationship, accentuated by the internal restrictions operating as a result of childbirth, was felt in the disruption of the hospital's daily routine which followed the Bs spending a night together. Much effort was required to continue to work with this couple as a couple, because their behaviour did not lead to a peaceful existence.

Mrs B was not entirely closed to a psychotherapeutic relationship. Working with me as her therapist, though I experienced for the most part the hurled abuse of projection, occasionally there was a possibility to get through her brick wall facade. Interestingly enough, it was usually at a time when her husband was little in evidence and she could convince herself that she and her baby existed alone with me.

In the beginning, whilst her second child was still only a few weeks old, it was possible to reach at times the suicidal, hopeless core inside this apparently ruthlessly defended mother.

Many weeks later Mrs B was making some efforts to organize the chaotic realities of her life. Though heavily in debt, she had still not claimed any benefits owing. Her healthy daughter, now more than six months old, had not received any child benefit to date. Mrs B explained tearfully and with feeling how applying for it meant stating on forms and verbally the details and whereabouts of previous children and benefits claimed for them. It was obvious to me and also to her that since she had failed to mourn her first child, her second child was not being allowed to live healthily and normally with the full benefits and resources which were her due. This basic anomaly provided the framework in which a pale, dull child was being deprived of emotional stimulation and the vigour of life. No wonder she was still cradled like a newborn (or a brain-damaged) child, her head protected carefully as she was put down on a rug at an age when she should have been experimenting with trying to sit up and with crawling. No wonder she nearly choked as her mother over-vigorously winded her, and cleared her mouth out at the slightest hiccup. In the mother's mind the two babies were completely confused. The healthy child in the present was confused with the brain-damaged backward child in the past. The mother's unconscious efforts to help the present child survive were, uncannily, subjecting her to risks of ending up like the first. Perhaps this was not only related to guilt and a failure to mourn but also to the mother's need for a brain-damaged child; she was feeling unworthy of achieving the rewards of raising a healthy one. Possibly the confusion between her two babies related also to the fact that she herself was a twin.

But in the end, after waves of unrest and disruption, interspersed with periods of relative calm, yet stalemate, a decision was taken to discharge the family. Anxiety in the community services ran high. How could this family so trapped by their pathology and their differences, possibly be able to survive anywhere but the hospital? We held an emergency meeting with social services to anticipate events. But when the mother had convinced everyone that the situation was impossible, that she was completely phobic about her house, that she and her husband could not exist in harmony together, it was possible to move forward. She arranged for her parents to come to take her and the baby home from the hospital, to the outlawed house where they would remain with the family for a month. To the end, the staff at the Cassel were left with high anxiety and unease. The father left for work planning to return home at the end of the day. The mother rowed with her parents about the travelling conditions in their car – too much luggage, not enough room for the baby, and she left with the baby on the bus. An anxious few hours ensued in which fantasies about suicide ran rife, despite no rational fear of this for some months. The learned interjection of a senior member of staff that this woman had enough of a psychopathic side to her personality to enable her to stay with a friend in the way she had stayed at the Cassel, calmed us. We learned by phone within a few hours that she was at home, too busy feeding the baby to ring to register their safe arrival.

That, of course, was only the first hurdle. We are not in a position to be responsible for or involved in the future outcome. Responsibility was handed back to the GP and social services. It was only for us to wonder at the 'impossible' task Mrs B had accomplished so that she had actually been 'treated' by discharge. Only time will tell whether treatment had been successful as was beyond doubt in my first example. Whilst they were patients they could only be considered as a worrying failure.

Of note was that for months after their discharge their battered old car remained in the hospital car park. Eventually we had to ask the council to tow it away. It symbolized a damaged and damaging penis; it contained all the germs of the obsessions. We heard later that the family had moved into bed and breakfast accommodation and then that they were rehoused, but to a new district and social services department.

It is interesting to compare these two families and their response to treatment by in-patient psychotherapy. In many respects their situation in life and their pathology were similar. Each family was negotiating the arrival of their second child. Whilst the B family had the added trauma of what had happened to the first, Mrs A was also affected profoundly by her abortion. The two mothers had many personality features in common. Both were ambitious and humiliated and treated their husbands to a barrage of nagging and control in order to defend themselves from their pain of unfulfilled masculine wishes. Both struggled to provide their babies with adequate mothering whilst feeling the lack of this themselves based on their deficient earlier experiences. Both found the task of furthering their female sexuality enormously threatening and difficult, handicapped by their internal persecuting objects. Mrs A resorted to neurotic measures involving control of her food intake and physical development. Mrs B presented with a severe obsessional neurosis to avoid the loss she could not mourn. In this aspect they demonstrated different symptoms but it can be put forward that the underlying pathology in the psychological make-up of the mothers was very similar. In the shifting and stressful period of the puerperium, both exhibited evidence of psychotic mental functioning.

Also in the families, the mechanisms leading to breakdown and the symptoms arising were strikingly similar. Renegotiation of a husband / wife relationship whose covert problems had been unmasked by the demands of childcare had led to breakdown in the ordinary day-to-day functioning of family life and the usually automatic tasks of organizing a household; eating, washing and so on. These tasks were then brought to the fore, requiring focus and attention because they had failed. Outside agencies in each case were anxious about the wellbeing of the children as a result.

If, as I argue, these families presented with very similar problems and pathology, it is interesting to ask why one benefitted from treatment whilst the other did not. It would appear to depend on the working alliance, which was a struggle to reach with the A family but which was eventually possible. Both Mr and Mrs A had enough strength, despite Mrs A's disturbance of mental functioning, to eventually accept the tasks involved in treatment and to overcome enough of their resistance in order to benefit from it. The B family, however, never managed to engage in a successful working alliance. Mrs B would have found it too painful to stop projecting all her unbearable feelings into others, and Mr B was too paranoid and hostile to form a trusting treatment alliance either in support of his wife and child or for himself. We would suggest that it was this failure to form a working alliance which led to treatment not succeeding, rather than it being due to the pathology as such.

These two examples, I hope, serve to illustrate the psychotherapeutic in-patient treatment of puerperal mothers at the Cassel today. The mothers are treated as part of a family with understanding of their own psychopathology and the dynamics of childbirth and the puerperium, but with reference to the relationship with their husbands and the conversion of a two-person to a three-person relationship. My paper has concentrated on the specific problems which arise in pregnancy, around childbirth, and in the puerperium, seeing childbirth as a life event as a result of which things can either be improved or set back permanently. It is not just a situation in which a baby is born but leads to a fundamental change in the mother, who enters a new developmental phase. Early anxieties are stirred up in her by the presence and needs of the baby and she has to renegotiate the specific and unique re-emergence of both pre-oedipal and oedipal anxieties. These are 'psychotic' anxieties stirred up by the realities of the baby's needs, the presence of the father, (often shadowy and difficult to allow into the foreground), and the capacity to renegotiate with her own mother. The mother finds it difficult to hold both her love for her husband or lover and her love for her baby together in her mind. When breakdown occurs, the mother is desperately seeking to negotiate this new developmental phase and, failing, turns inappropriately to the baby to provide the answers.

Summary

This paper reviews some previous writings by Dr Tom Main and Dr Peter Lomas about the work of the Cassel hospital with puerperal mothers. It goes on to describe the case histories and treatment of two patients recently treated with their families. The emphasis is on actual material produced in therapy, but with reference to other aspects of the much wider treatment structures employed by the Cassel, for example the role of the nursing and the community. Important aspects focussed upon include the essential experience of good mothering in becoming a mother, how closeness to the infantile impulses and urges of a real baby can lead to profound measures of identification and projection, and the effects of motherhood on femininity and sexuality.

[12]

The Child's View of the Hospital

An Examination of the Child's Experience of an In-patient Setting

Denis Flynn

THIS CHAPTER EXAMINES the rationale of focussing on work with the children within the in-patient Cassel Hospital setting. I believe it will become apparent that the child does not simply *accompany* the parent who may primarily seek treatment, nor conversely does the parent simply accompany the child for whom they may seek treatment, but they enter together into a unique kind of *setting*, which provides opportunities to examine relationships from a number of points of view. Just as within the psychoanalytic hour the patient will express views about the analyst or his setting, his arrangements for times, the room, and any personal details he may be aware of, so within the in-patient hospital setting, the patient, adult or child, will express views and demonstrate within their everyday life their reaction to or awareness of that setting, and their contribution to any needed changes. Such reactions and feelings can be examined in various community meetings and in psychoanalytic therapy times, and may provide insights not simply into that outer life, but into the patient's inner emotional life.

The child's view can be especially valuable. Typically, children betray themselves, and adults, especially their parents. But in reality, this is not because all children are bound by secrets which they unwittingly divulge, although some children undoubtedly are, but because the child's perception is frequently simple and unequivocal. Children express their own views and sometimes those of others, notably their parents. When the child does express views for others, important insights can be gained into parent/child relationships, family dynamics, the impact of events within the therapeutic community, and the changing life of the community.

Here are two examples from family consultations prior to admission, of how the child's view of the hospital provides understanding about the child's emotional life and his or her place with the family.

In the first instance, the mother, a single parent and a twin, could only consider in-patient treatment for her family if her daughter, aged five, could describe for her what the hospital was like and how it worked. While the mother sat talking to my colleague, unsure about what to do and incapable of making any decision, the child engaged me separately, asking me a number of intelligent and apposite questions about what people did in this hospital. In particular she wanted to know details about how they could get in and out, and asked, 'Is the fire escape safe?' At this point, it seemed that the child was doing decision-making work for her mother. After this first consultation, just before admission, her mother was again delaying. This time, the mother was worrying about a medical appointment for an eye defect her daughter apparently had. A most significant piece of work was needed by the nursing staff to persuade the mother that the family admission and the child's appointment about her eyes need not conflict with each other. The issue of her daughter's eyesight was symptomatic, for the mother's reliance on her daughter was such that the family could only go ahead with the admission, if the daughter could see for her mother.

In the second instance, an eleven-year-old boy showed in his random associations about the hospital on his first visit, his acute capacity to get to know us on the inside. This illustrated a complementary process in his relationship with his mother, whom he 'got inside'. Again, it was a single parent family and the main presenting difficulty was the irritation the boy was felt by his mother to cause her. As we made our way through a series of corridors to the consulting room, he chatted about how the building looked like 'mum's work' and the garden was 'like my uncle's which has 24 acres'! His mother was irritated with him and rebuked him, correcting him on details and saying that he was being inconsistent. I felt, however, that he was relating to the hospital and to the grounds, and telling us how it fitted with his previous experience. He had picked up that his mother wanted to be the professional with us, like at her work, and identified me as an uncle figure. But what was striking was how quickly this boy made himself at home in the hospital and in his contact with me. I now began to see why his mother got so irritated with him. He accurately pointed out the direction of nearby important buildings, even without the compass he said he wished he had brought. He produced an interesting drawing of a fire engine which had come out of a 'tunnel-road'. He told me about a fire near his grandmother's house, where people were looking from behind curtains, laughing and squabbling to get the best viewing position. He told me a nightmare in which a boy was lost and is found again. My first impression was that here was an excellent candidate for psychotherapy, but further reflection made me question whether the scintillating tit-bits he gave me really squared with another impression I had, namely his embroidering of the account of the dream, his controlling accuracy and verbosity, and his facility with lies! I then began to understand something of how his mother felt about him, when she found she could not 'think straight' when he was there, on account of his excitability and frequent lies. In this case, the child conveyed a quality of intrusiveness like an invader within an opposing camp. Understanding his first experience of the hospital was integral to an understanding of some aspects of the family problems.

The place of the child within the community

For over 25 years it has been the rule that children have come with their parents to the hospital. At first, this was with the aim of keeping mothers and children together. Soon children who required psychotherapy and were regarded as the primary patient were referred. Generally, the parents would not be able to support similar treatment in an out-patient setting. In some cases, especially where the child suffered from phobias, particularly about school, the parent / child interaction became of importance. Fathers then became important, and the emphasis has now shifted to a full study of family interactions in all cases.

We can ask, how does the child fare in this transition to in-patient life? When the child becomes an in-patient, he or she will have significant adjustments to make. He or she will have a hospital room, perhaps shared with parents, or brothers or sisters, or children of the same age from other families. He or she will change school, attending for a short time, or perhaps for the duration of the stay, the hospital Day Unit staffed by a teacher and nurses, and attended by some day patients from neighbouring areas. The child may attend a local school, especially if there is the special need to keep outside friendships or maintain continuous academic progress throughout school. Contacts with home life will be broken; even though the child will go home most weekends, sometimes he or she will stay in the hospital with the family if there is a particular crisis. This will mean losing contact with schoolfriends and dependable, significant people, such as relatives, teachers and family friends. The child will be thrust into a large, changing and amorphous patient group, which will comprise a frequently imbalanced children's group. There may or may not be children of similar age and sex amongst the five or six families there at any time, although the composition of the group will be affected by the numbers and age of the out-patient group in the Day Unit. The child and his parents may strike up friendships with single adult patients, in the two adult sections, or adolescents, with whom they may share some meetings and activities. Whatever benefit the children themselves get from this, it is clear that they can be a stimulus to growth in other members of the community, re-introducing the sanity of everyday needs to in-patient community life and focussing attention on the 'actual family'. The presence of children can bridle the regression which can occur in in-patient settings, introducing a valuable and relevant reality perimeter for parents with severely neurotic, borderline and psychotic features.

Overall, making these adjustments will cause a strain for the child, so that great attention is needed by parents to help the children settle with the minimum of stress. This is not always easy for parents who feel under stress themselves. The child also frequently experiences further stress which emanates from parental unwillingness to recreate within the hospital a safe environment for the child. When children fall down or get lost in the building, our concern is alerted.

Two central accounts have been given of the child's place within the community by Lydia Tischler (née Folkart, 1964,1967), a co-founder of the Children's Unit in 1962, with Salo Tischler. It had always been a central tenet in Dr Main's thinking about therapeutic communities that patients should retain as many responsibilities and ties with their outside life as is compatible with their illness. This basic premise was extended to families too, so that whilst they are in-patients, parents continue to look after their children. A prime focus of work is on disturbances of 'mothering' and 'parenting' and their effect on the development of the child. Despite dangers that the parents' 'acting out' may precipitate too quickly or inappropriately their requests that staff give individual attention to the child, including treatment by the child psychotherapist, it is still important that these decisions be left to the parent, though of course how parents arbitrate such decisions will be a focus of treatment.

The contrast between the in-patient and out-patient psychiatric settings, the out-patient hospital or child guidance clinic, is important. In the in-patient setting a number of families with shared or separate disturbance are brought together, and the work of the community breaks down defences and opens up wounds. The child sees his parents as more exposed and will be aware of the effects of their treatment on them. The level of shared anxiety can be intense, is felt by the children, and is communicated in their individual therapy and demonstrated in the community. The parents' reaction to their children's therapy opens up unusually intense feelings of guilt, so that the child psychotherapist is frequently viewed with an unusual idealization or denigration. This, of course, has important implications for how the child psychotherapist may set up individual psychotherapy times for children. It is important to realize that treatment success or failure then cannot be gauged as due to the effects of psychotherapy rather than the protective environment of the hospital and the work of the therapeutic community, or vice versa, but as due to a composite effort and the intricate relationship between different branches of treatment.

Also, in contrast to the out-patient setting, where the transference relationship between therapist and child is the way of understanding the child's emotional life, in the in-patient setting equal attention needs to be given to clarifying the relationship of the child to his or her parents and others in the community. The child psychotherapist is a member of that community, with roles and responsibilities which extend outside the consulting room. This is a complex task, especially as the child psychotherapist has to evaluate not simply the child's view of the psychotherapist as transference object, but a host of qualitatively different information from separate sources, including from the parents' therapists and the family nurse.

Observations of the child's daily experience, (whether in the family, the children's group, the whole in-patient group or the group of children in the Day Unit, with other families, in teaching groups and outings, with the nurse, or with other nurses and in the patient community), can be evaluated at a weekly children's meeting. Views distilled from all parts of the hospital can be shared by staff and thought about here. Some children have individual psychotherapy sessions (three times weekly for 40 minutes); others do not. However, the way in which all children adapt to or react to life within the community is of special concern to the child psychotherapist. It is the psychotherapist's task not only to offer assessment, but to make observations about the progress and psychological state of the children, which will increase the therapeutic possibilities of the hospital treatment. This function of the child psychotherapist of assimilating the in-patient experience of the child is so important, as life in a therapeutic community with several types of therapeutic input can be bewildering for the child, requiring a patient who, to quote Montaigne, 'is a good swimmer, so that he would not be swallowed up and drowned by the depth and weight of his learning'.

Perhaps it is because the child psychotherapist is identified with the work of the Families Unit in providing not only a therapeutic but a supportive environment for the child, that he or she comes to be seen in a parental role. Given the feelings not only of the children, but of the parents, the stage is set for the idealization and denigration I described earlier. Such views about the therapist will of course become expanded in daily contacts in the hospital. There may be a view of the therapist supplied by this community life which is carried by the child, but which may be distinguishable from the child's own view. However, the former view may dominate over the child's view. An example of this, culled from many sources, is the occasional fantasy that parents have that the child psychotherapist is not fit to see the child, that the psychotherapist is too lax, or too strict, or harms the child. Such group fantasies make for difficulties, not only for the child who has individual psychotherapy but for the child psychotherapist. To minimize the difficulties which may result from such fantasies and work with them in a therapeutic way, it is necessary that the child psychotherapist be, and be seen to be, flexible, accessible and unmysterious, in the necessary contacts with families and staff alike.

To appreciate the currency of beliefs about various aspects of the treatment, to minimize splits in the therapeutic approach, and put splits which occur to therapeutic effect, there is a need to understand the daily life of the child in the community and to examine working relationships with other staff. Such an approach alters the psychotherapist's understanding of the concepts of transference and countertransference in the in-patient psychoanalytic setting.

Briefly, for there is not space to go into this issue in depth, the child psychotherapist will need to be aware, not only of the child's transference and his or her own countertransference in the psychotherapy session, but of the child's 'transference' to the hospital and individual staff members, in particular, to the family nurse. In supervisions too, the psychotherapist must pay attention, not only to countertransference to the child, but feelings towards other workers, with whom the child may also have a significant relationship.

The experience of the child within the hospital

People outside the hospital always react with surprise at the idea that children should be in a psychiatric hospital, and that families should undertake such an intense therapeutic experience together. Frequently, it is asked, 'What do whole families think about going into hospital together?' and 'What does this mean for the children?' The children themselves give diverse answers which reflect changes in their inner experience of events, in addition to changes or disruptions to time-honoured patterns of personal and family life. Children are clearly concerned with the minutiae of their daily life, and ask questions such as 'Why are we staying here overnight?' 'Where do we sleep?' 'What will we eat and who cooks it?' 'Who will we have to share with?' 'Who will we have as friends?' The children may form views and make adjustments before their parents, giving valuable indicators of their feelings and those of other members of the family. Such indicators are vital in our assessment as to whether the child and family's use of the in-patient setting is likely to be therapeutically successful. I shall give some examples from my initial assessment of children when they come to hospital to illustrate this.

The hospital as a place of containment

Two children, a boy of pre-school age and a girl in first infants' class, showed in separate ways their awareness of family events during and after the transition to hospital life. In my first meeting with the girl, she drew a picture of a fish tank with a bullet-like frog in it, along with a vacant-looking fish. Outside, a pig looked on in the garden with fruit around. Patrolling the house was a rather shrunken-looking tortoise. The tank seemed to represent her sense of confinement, with characters as follows: the frog herself, the fish her brother, the pig her mother and the tortoise her father. The passivity of the mother was represented as sloth, while the paranoid armour of the father was represented in the tired old tortoise. The family was not functioning or moving forward, and the children were captives. I had warmed to this girl in this first meeting, but I had found her play very stereotyped when she was not very excited, so that overall I felt I was being drawn in to become a captive with her. However, a week later, she was expressing herself more in her play.

She used a Lego set to construct the family home and then the hospital, showing as the significant change a shift in perspective from a house where all the windows look in to one where they look out. This signified an opening up from the nervous defensiveness of family life and the shared fears of that family, about types of food, intruders and much else. She then developed a game with animals which were all locked in a pen, saying 'They are so overcrowded inside . . . they can't move . . . they can't even open the door'. I felt her describing something not only about her internal world, how feelings and thoughts are locked inside, but her external family which was restrictive and confining. She now ventured an admission; she said that she liked to eat steak, rather than the vegetarian diet that her parents required them to eat. I felt she experienced the restrictions on her diet at home as restrictions on her omnipotence, shown in her flaunting attitude to male staff, her severe physical punishment of her younger brother and her lack of responsiveness to a caring approach. The restrictions were now being challenged in the community as a result of open divisions in the family; thus her fear was that removing the restrictions may be tantamount to giving way to unrestrained expression on her part.

The change in perception for the boy was more marked, for as he began to develop play, his behaviour in assessment and subsequent psychotherapy sessions moved from chaos or stony withdrawal towards construction and expression. In our first meeting he disturbed me because he was so cut off and unresponsive. His anxiety was at first latent and he spent his time nervously moving from object to object, from toy to toy, fingering it and putting it down. Only with the playdough did he linger longer, trying fervently to wrap it up again. He emptied everything out of his cupboard as if completing a thorough search. He had a nervous way of wiping bubbles away from his mouth, as if the end of a feed were most uncomfortable. By the second week his awareness of painful psychic reality was evident. In our staff meeting it had been reported that now he spent time crying on his own. He told me he had no friends and seemed to shy away from me, like a boy before his headmaster, not giving anything away. Only when he crawled under the table did he relax and smile. I felt he responded from now on to containment without being over-close. He drew a child and a rocket, the two sides of him, mildly withdrawn and maniacally explosive.

In our third meeting, he developed further drawings and sequences of play. He began to experience strong feelings of anger when separating from his mother, and expressed anger to his parents at the weekend. In the fourth meeting he began to play mealtimes with me as if he had felt there was a real dialogue with me, in contrast with the counterfeit relationships within the family, without mutuality, where, for example, the child was not allowed by his father to eat the same meat as his mother. His drawings were now of a shaky house showing, I felt, that he could find some containment in the hospital and in the psychotherapy which was now planned for him. Both children had experienced the family as a place of confinement. The girl had shown me first the fish tank drawing, whilst it was soon revealed that the boy had one night suffered the traumatic experience of getting himself locked in a trunk with water at the bottom for a considerable time. The girl's drawing, no doubt, alluded to this incident, which seemed to epitomize the child's experience of family relationships. At first, the family were obsessed with views about hidden forces, but would disregard the everyday evidence of cause and effect. In such circumstances, the everyday structures of community life were of first importance in establishing a more open communication. The family's view of themselves influenced their view of the staff, so that, at first, the parents expected therapists and nurses to convey messages amongst themselves on issues regarding the children which they, the parents, could convey, thus assuming the staff to have a secret system of communication. Work with this family continued for several months; the boy received individual treatment, as the parents had too, before progress faltered; the family closed ranks again as deeper secrets were being revealed.

The hospital as a dangerous place

Many of the views expressed by the children at the beginning of treatment reflect fears of the hospital, of their own badness and fears of loss of control. Two boys in one family had been circumcised shortly before in an admission to another hospital, for which they had had no preparation. Their initial reaction on admission was one of panic and shock. The elder boy, six years old, had felt betrayed by his parents and the doctors. He would only come to assessment meetings if he had fully negotiated with me on his own terms. He seemed to feel no confidence in his parents' powers of negotiation and his initial reaction to me, of suspicion and fear, was rooted in his belief that I would not be able to offer sufficient containment for his acute feelings. A week later he felt a greater degree of safety. He built a spaceship in which he no longer needed airbottles, (i.e. like the dreaded oxygen cylinders of his earlier hospitalization). He also felt that I could probably understand what it was like for him in hospital because, as he said,

'When you were a little boy you were probably in hospital sometime'.

For his younger brother of four years old, the recent hospitalization for circumcision was just one of a series of hospitalizations for adenoids, tonsillitis and grommits, which had heightened severe separation problems for him. He was wetting his bed and he seemed to me to be a confused and disorientated child. Inside the room, he flicked electric switches in an aggravating way. His play about ambulances becoming 'firebirds' and crashing into the playroom walls, damaging the plaster, clearly expressed his anxiety about being in hospital. Side by side with his attacks on the fabric of the playroom, he showed a wish to use the therapy room as a safe place for his anger and his confused feelings. At a deeper level, his belief that the playroom could be dangerous, and his fear of entering within, seemed connected with his fantasies of killing off the baby within. He seemed highly aware of his parents arguing and fighting and he was curious as to his parents' sexual behaviour. Yet his fear and that of many children was that he was in hospital because of his 'badness'.

The hospital as a place of comfort and security, to keep away conflict

Other children often see the hospital as having an interesting and varied life, where difficulties can become diffused. Early relief leads to patterns of idealization. Reception into hospital can then be experienced as a form of seduction, which is enjoyed and then regretted, so that deeper anxieties about intrusion are soon heralded. For one school-phobic girl, these fears about intrusion became focussed on the therapy, so that she became unable to communicate in the therapy room. By contrast, she banned all entry to her hospital room, to forestall any intrusion. Only when staff, after much disagreement, could share the view that this girl was using a splitting mechanism, dividing rooms into totally safe and totally unsafe, was progress made. The girl was then given a room with others her own age, at first with much protest. Work in therapy sessions and in the community could then come closer together. In fact, in view of her limited concrete way of showing her feelings, it was only by concentrating on the minutiae of her daily living that progress could be made, so that the work of her individual psychotherapy was to focus on her adjustment to life within the community.

A six-year-old girl who attended the Day Unit and came for psychotherapy three times a week found the privileges of the in-patient children intolerable to bear. She was from a children's home and had not yet been found a new home. The fact that other children had their home with their school was insufferable for her. She frequently played out her conflict about being the intruder in stories about Goldilocks and The Three Bears. She expressed strong wishes to stay in the hospital, eat with patients and sleep there. The hospital became idealized as 'the safe home' and intensified the conflict that the children's home, her natural parents' home and any possible foster home would not be good enough. In a way, this child experienced a conflict which centred round the breakdown in the child's idealized notion of a family, which other children from in-patient families also have; however, for this child it was most concrete, as she did not have a family.

The hospital as a place which allows the child his individuality in his family

The way the child is wrapped up in the conflicts of his ill parents can sometimes also be observed in his or her views about the hospital. One boy from a large family drew airships and seemed concerned with how one design of airship led to the design and production of another prototype. It struck me that his interest sounded like an account of early genealogies in the book of Genesis. He was worried about himself and his brothers and sisters being the cause of the problem. The airships he drew seemed like the stream of babies that came along. He told his nurse that the family were coming into hospital because 'the children are mad'. At eleven, he was still eneuretic. He was a helpful child, whose concern for his family significantly contributed to them managing at all. But he lacked the individual interest he felt he needed. All of this was reflected in his first views of the hospital. He liked the food and found the hospital very interesting, as he had discovered that there were many ways to get from the ground floor to the central rooms. I felt that here the hospital was being seen like a large body, which feeds, and has special bottom and middle passages, perhaps linked to fantasies about procreation and excretion. It was especially significant then that referral for in-patient treatment was made after a final attempt at help by marriage guidance, and on admission, no mention was made by the parents about sexual difficulties in their relationship, even though there were many. It was as if then, the child not only cared for the other children of his parents, but in struggling with his own childhood sexual fantasies he carried the preoccupations about sexuality which his parents had disowned. Coming into hospital appears to have enabled him to work unconsciously on his fantasies about birth, procreation and what it means to be a child in a large family. The main work of therapy and community treatment concentrated on his parents' illness and their functioning as a family. He was encouraged to express his needs as a child, including his anger, and to have his own interests and more attention from his parents, so that he could develop individually and not be so dominated by his parents' illness.

A case example

I shall now describe some features of a nine month period of psychotherapy (three times weekly) of a boy, Mark, aged five, in the in-patient setting. This was the second half of an eighteen month in-patient stay. I shall lay stress on features of the treatment when the transference relationship to the psychotherapist illuminates the child's life in the community, and vice versa.

Briefly the history was as follows. There had been difficulties from the start when breastfeeding broke down, as Mark's mother had an inverted nipple. She had described this as a feeling 'there was nothing for the baby to hang on to'. The mother was young.

Her marriage to Mark's father had not lasted long, and she became highly dependent on her own family.

The mother had taken a number of overdoses and had had frequent admissions to psychiatric hospital. Mark was separated from her, being looked after by her parents or going into residential care and being fostered. For eighteen months prior to their admission here, Mark spent the whole day at his mother's parents and only slept at his mother's home. Mark and his mother were admitted to see whether they could live as a family. In the home visit just prior to admission, the nurses recall how the house was bare of furniture. In relating to each other, mother and child had numerous angry bouts. Even at the time he came for psychotherapy, there was a question of whether Mark's violence could be contained, doubts about whether mother and child would be able to live together and about whether Mark attend an outside infant school. The issue of whether mother and child could connect with each other was still central, from the time of the earliest disconnections in infancy. It was now clear that mother and child would only face their biggest challenge after they had left the hospital, for until then the difficulties of being together would be mitigated by life in the community. This was especially so since Mark, though frequently unmanageable, was very well liked, and his mother was very active in taking responsibility in community affairs. This degree of adaptability to the social environment reflected previous dependence on the mother's family.

There were, however, bizarre elements in the mother, such as rapid and stark changes of image and repeated periods of mental abstraction, even during the course of otherwise normal conversations. The mother wanted Mark to have psychotherapy, but she had mixed feelings. She and Mark strongly felt the loss of the male nurse, who along with her psychotherapist, had run play sessions, focussing on their interactions. The nurse had now moved to another unit. The mother seemed afraid that the psychotherapist would take Mark over, as her family had done. She was particularly alarmed that in psychotherapy, Mark might experience the depth of his feelings. Another family with whom

Mark and his mother had become friendly were just leaving, and they were worried about their own lack of preparation for life outside the hospital, as well as this family's.

My first impression of Mark was of an attractive and boisterous child, who seemed to slur over and deny his feeling that I was taking him away from his mum, and could not believe he could make an attachment to me. He could see me as having a function, as a 'wheely-mind man', who would talk to him about his 'wheelies', i.e. his losing his temper. However, then he would become furious when I did not hear something he said: 'Are you deaf?' he would shout. The feeling in early sessions was that Mark enjoyed the rapport but wanted this without regard to me, in a taking-over sort of way. Also, he chose safe toys and there were few glimpses of him developing forms of symbolic expression. Although very intelligent he was unimaginative, so it was not surprising he communicated through ruthless action. It became clear that Mark's troublesome, noisy behaviour in the hospital had the function of stimulating the mother's attention. He engaged wholeheartedly in his sessions, which led to the rapid establishment of a quite intense dependence on the therapist. But soon his main complaint was that the psychotherapist stopped him from thinking.

Mark was a mixed-race child. He sometimes mockingly spoke in an African accent and coined a new name for me, 'British Beef'. As time went on, he appreciated his black relations more, particularly after painstaking work by his black nurse. But at this stage, the missing white father was idealized. When I had to be away for a short period in an unscheduled way, Mark was observed to eat no meat at all in the hospital. His wish for a father and his fear that his aggression towards me had damaged and driven me away, brought out deep-rooted guilt about his oral aggression.

After the first break, Mark told me a dream in which: 'I saw a man with a moustache. I walked up to the man wondering who it was. The man looked at me and said "Oh, it's you!" The boy then turned into a nasty batman.' The man with the moustache reminded him of his favourite uncle. The anger seemed to be because the man paid too little attention to him. He was angry about the break and the psychotherapist's indifferent attention to him.

As time went on, Mark became most unsettled about the arrival of other children on the Unit. He felt that his territory, both inside the therapy room and inside the hospital, was being taken over. He now began to want to go into his mother's bed at night. He also became furiously angry about the fathers in these families having any involvement with him. His mother would not accept it either, so both adopted a collusive withdrawal. At the same time, Mark would frequently create a disturbed situation before his sessions, so that various means were needed to get him there. Once there, he could begin to play, to respond and to get some relief from the irritations and angers he could not express outside. But the crises he precipitated meant bringing mother, nurse and psychotherapist into a series of arrangements which were successful not just in getting Mark to his session time, but in working through some of the conflicts within the community. Mark had begun to see different combinations of couples, each excluding a third person. Sometimes he saw the psychotherapist or nurse and mother as conspiring against him, sometimes it was Mark who was allied with mother making the psychotherapist into a intruding father. The fact that Mark had a strong relationship with both nurse and psychotherapist meant that such combinations were deeply meaningful. Mark attempted again and again to split the parental couple, denying that it could be visible and effective.

Mark asked about his real father and for a couple of weekends he came back into the picture. It was telling that in describing his father to me, Mark said he looked like one of the patients in the hospital. It was clear that life in hospital, despite its difficulties, was the only home Mark and his mum had been together in for any length of time. A focus of work in the therapeutic community was on the difficulties which came up in the times they were together, particularly regarding the mother's unresponsiveness and Mark's refusal to accept his mother's authority. Mark experienced any restrictions as a fear that his relationship with his mother would end, so the searing level of his protest had the function of controlling his mother. He now did some drawings of an aeroplane which might crash. Inside this plane was another smaller plane. He also told me that he stayed up until twelve midnight watching a film 'with my mum all on her own'.

There began a phase of harsh sadistic attacks on the therapist and on other children's toy boxes. Even when he had appreciated the session, being able to reconstruct some toy he feared he had destroyed or overcoming his nameless irritation, he sometimes said 'the session was crap' as he left the room. Throughout this time there were a number of incidents in the hospital of toilets being smeared with faeces and one toilet door being smashed down. Frequently, Mark was tuned into the sadistic fantasies of those around him and had re-enacted in his session in sadistic attacks on the psychotherapist what was going on in the community.

In a sense, he was not just the 'barometer' of community feelings but 'detonator' too, for Mark could own up to his destructive wishes, so that they were available for therapeutic work, when other patients could not. As so often, it is the child who expresses what others cannot or will not, who invites an immediate response to himself, who becomes of special service to the ill patient within a psychiatric hospital, as a vehicle of neurotic acting-out or schizoid communications.

Mark's lack of creativity came more into focus as it became apparent that if he could not recreate the same good object he would not try or attempt anything. He also felt that without magic he could not do anything himself, it was 'only shit'. This lack of creativity and his very active mode of functioning made Mark into a useful vehicle for projections in a schizoid way.

For a time, he attacked the therapist mercilessly, sensing the plans for the family leaving and wanting to test the quality of containment. His attacks were a provocation, testing whether he was to be forced out of the hospital he considered 'home'. He now began to talk about other hospitals, where his mother had gone after her overdoses. He remembered how he was sick too and how 'a chip came up with the sick', and how it was 'runny and lumpy'. The memory he had was of his fear that he had driven mother to her overdoses. For Mark, being in hospital seemed to mean there was always a fear of his mother's death around.

When some younger children were admitted to hospital Mark began to regress, talking in a baby voice, playing with soft toys and becoming more clingy. This regressive change occurred when the nurse from his earliest time in hospital, with whom he had had play sessions, moved to the Day Unit so Mark had renewed contact with him during school time. Mark's regression then was comprehensible in relation to finding contact with this previously valued person. Soon after this, Mark and his mother were able to make plans together to enjoy each other's company, and still be able to separate and let go, aware they could come back together again. Mark also was now able to come to his session times more easily. He drew a series of buggies which had brakes. They were partly 'baby buggy' and partly 'moon buggy'. The brake lights signified the capacity for some self-control. As the buggies got bigger they were to have bigger brake lights.

Both mother and child had work to do towards the ending. This was shown not just in their plans about leaving but also in their attitude towards work in the hospital. Both feared they could not retain what had been learned. Mark was particularly helpful preparing for the hospital garden party, to which staff and some former patients may come, carrying five loads of materials from the *inside* of the house *outside* to the garden. Quite out of the blue he paused and said to a nurse standing by, 'You know, I like Mr Flynn . . . but he hasn't helped me'. He seemed infected by his mother's pessimism, but he was anxious about the new outside school he visited in preparation for his leaving. He had been unable to go into the school for fear of the other children. In his play it became clear he expected them to be as aggressive as he could be. His mother too, was clearly worried about how well she could make the plans for herself and Mark. This was illustrated in the following incident. After the school visit, Mark's mother provoked a dispute with the community nurse and walked off. As Mark's mother was responsible for ordering hospital provisions for the cooking which patients do, this was delayed. In fact she later adjusted to the task so that the provisions were ordered.

Near the very end of his stay, Mark produced some of his richest drawings. One in particular was a story about pirates on the high seas. He was showing that he could anticipate dangers and difficulties outside, so that when I asked him what he felt about seeing a child psychotherapist in an out-patient setting, he said he would like to. On leaving the hospital, the family did in fact make contact with the child guidance clinic we had put them in touch with and they proved able to negotiate a new form of therapeutic contract.

Conclusion

The child who comes into hospital with his family will have many adjustments to make. Even if he or she does not have a particular need for in-patient psychotherapy, there will be many opportunities to reflect on experiences within the family. There will also be an opportunity for special nurturing help within the hospital Day Unit, which for many children is a compensation after many years of being embroiled in family problems. The child's particular experience of hospital life can be a valuable indicator of his or her inner emotional life, which enables hospital staff, psychotherapist and nurses, to make appropriate provision for their needs and treatment.

[13]

Observations on Family Functioning in an In-patient setting

Lydia Tischler and *Trevor Hartnup*

This paper arises out of our work as child psychotherapists at the Cassel Hospital. We are therefore, particularly interested in the development of and possible disturbances in children growing up in families where family functioning is seriously distorted or has broken down.

The families who come to us have either appeared unable to make use of out-patient psychotherapy, or do not experience themselves as having the kind of problem which would lead them in that direction; that is, they do not as a rule fall into the category of patients whose problems present as essentially personal and intrapsychic and who see psychotherapy as relevant to their complaints. They also have great difficulties in seeing the children's problems as separate from their own, and can therefore take particular advantage of the Cassel's admission of the whole family, and the Cassel's general attitude of keeping the child's own interests to the fore.

There are a number of individual and family characteristics which should be mentioned. Such families rely heavily on externalization and on splitting, and attempt to rid themselves of their conflicts by trying unconsciously to change others or to force them into certain roles. At such times the boundary between internal and external, between the self and the other, becomes fluid or indistinct. In our experience, if individual psychotherapy is undertaken with members of such families without a period of preparatory work, it usually fails.

The pathology is often not experienced as such by the nominated patient, or is experienced as lying within another family member. There is often no clear symptom formation, the problem often lying in interpersonal conflict or social functioning – such as the children's refusal to attend school, the parents' poor care of the children etc. In the consulting room, a number of adolescent girls we have seen have presented as empty or 'not knowing', and are sometimes just as uninterested in the therapist as in any other figure outside the family circle.

It follows that, where the family members have partially suspended the boundaries between them in order to deal with anxiety, their capacity to engage in a treatment alliance with a therapist is correspondingly diminished because it would be experienced as a threat to the family's defensive system, which each family member unconsciously feels the need to maintain. Therapeutic interventions are therefore experienced as an interference with the defences of all the family members, and there is sometimes a denial that the difficulties lie within the family. Usually excessive ambivalence has some part to play in this constellation, and is dealt with by splitting and projection of the hostility on to people outside the family. In this context, separation is often conceived within the family as a hostile act, sometimes resulting in excessive closeness between family members and crippling interferences in individual psychosexual development. The internal world of fantasy as it unfolds in psychotherapy often remains a closed book, partly perhaps because it is not felt to belong to one individual but is experienced as common property within the family. Thus, different members often feel that they can literally know what the other is thinking and feeling, and verbal communication is seen as superfluous.

Patients rarely come to the in-patient setting because of a shortage of out-patient facilities. Almost always, there has been a simultaneous breakdown of individual internalized structures and family structures to the extent that the continued existence of the family as a viable unit is at risk. The degree of anxiety or potential for physical danger generated has proved uncontainable in the out-patient setting and by social work agencies. Although patients come to the Cassel only by their own choice, they often feel that they had *no* choice and that there was no alternative. This represents in part a wish to invest the helping agencies with characteristics of their own internalized parents, and is accompanied by feelings of hostile dependency and feelings of being controlled by the professional workers. In the families under discussion, there tends to be a concrete delegation of parental authority and responsibilities. It is not in the first instance therefore a psychotherapy setting which they seek, but a whole hospital setting, a physical and social setting in which a feeling of safety can be re-established. In one way or another the families are all seeking an environmental solution, i.e. the use of material or physical surroundings, or the social setting, to bolster or substitute for their shaky or deficient holding or containing functions. It perhaps takes its starkest form where parents have been unable to perform the psychological function of home-making, as well as the material provision of living accommodation. A number of families, during their stay at the Cassel, have tried, sometimes successfully, to relinquish their own accommodation and begun to make their plans for their future in and around the hospital. Unless we engage vigorously with this aspect of their regressive dependency wishes, their apparent work within the consulting room usually proves illusory and turns out to have been a way of 'paying the rent'.

Introduction to case examples

As child therapists, we are particularly alert to the child's point of view. This balances the tendency of staff experienced in adult work to see children's behaviour as an expression of infantile aspects of their parents.

It is our intention to focus on a major grouping of families, where achievement of psychological and emotional differentiation between family members appears to be a major stumbling block. In our experience, this appears most clearly in families where the children are in the newborn and up to age 2 range. Normal child development here presents the family with the conflicts of the separation individuation phase. It also appears in families with adolescents, where adolescents are faced with becoming separate sexual individuals in their own right.

It has often been observed in the literature on the subject that parenthood re-awakens in the adults the conflicts which they experienced at the equivalent phase in their own childhood, and that it provides them with a second chance to find new solutions to them. It follows that the child's or adolescent's growing psychological differentiation requires of parents the capacity to tolerate and resolve these conflicts from their end. If they are unable to do so, the conflicts which are re-awakened in the parents are liable to interfere with their perceptions of their child. In extreme cases, the parents may treat the child as an aspect of themselves; children cope with inappropriate parental behaviour and projections as best they can. If the children attempt to accommodate the parents' distorted perceptions of them in their development, they are to some extent engaged upon taking care of the parents' problem for them. Clearly, this may have serious consequences for the child's individuation. The capacity to detach and to differentiate, seems especially to require the constructive use of hostility. It also requires the capacity to maintain a positive relationship in spite of heightened ambivalence and envy, to be able to tolerate difference and to have differences.

When children become the instruments by which parents deal with their own conflicts over separation and separateness, we can sometimes see, in the in-patient setting, the process of the child's age-adequate adaptation to his pathological environment. This sometimes gives rise to formulations about family functioning which may accurately reflect the parents' failure to recognize the child's separateness, but which do not do justice to the child's own experience, i.e. the formulation itself obliterates individuality.

Jacob and Melanie

After their usual weekend at home, Jacob aged 2½ and his mother, Melanie, returned to the hospital. Jacob had a series of bad nights when he awoke crying. Some staff suggested that it was because Melanie's therapist had just gone on leave and that Jacob was experiencing his mother's feelings for her therapist, as Melanie herself denied any feeling about it. This turned out to be both true and untrue. It emerged that Melanie had left Jacob's transitional object at home by mistake and that he was missing it. Her omission made sense in terms of her therapist's absence, especially when we learned that the transitional object was called 'Bye'. Her attempts to deal with her own feelings by denial brought inevitably in their wake her scotomization of similar feelings in Jacob. In this context, the formulation that Jacob was expressing his mother's feelings runs the risk of agreeing that Jacob was an extension of her, rather than that he had his own reactions to her moods and behaviour.

The Chalk family

Mr and Mrs Chalk had been in the hospital for seven months when they asked for help with James. James and Jeremy, his twin, were 18 months old. Mr and Mrs Chalk were being seen twice a week by their individual therapists. They had come to the hospital because of Mrs Chalk's puerperal depression, marital problems, and what the referrer called 'their personal adaptation to adult life'. The twins had been premature. James, the younger and smaller of the two, had to stay in hospital for several days after his mother and brother had been discharged. According to the mother, James had never taken to the breast. When he was four months old, she could not stand this any longer and abandoned an attempt at breastfeeding which must have been frustrating and painful for both of them. A split developed in the relationship between the parents and the children. For mother, James was the bad one and Jeremy the good one, whereas father preferred James.

The parents themselves spoke of what they described as their own traumatic backgrounds. The history they related betokened their feeling of unsafety about their environment, both as regards people and place. Mrs Chalk had been brought up by a 'strict and poisonous housekeeper' as the only surviving child of her mother's eight pregnancies. The others had all resulted in miscarriages, including one set of twins. Her father was now dead and she had had sporadic and uncomfortable contact with her mother and the former housekeeper.

Mr Chalk, also an only child, came from a 'globetrotting family'. When he was 16, his mother committed suicide; he was left stateless and with no nationality. He felt that his father had always turned him away as not being in need.

During the first six months it was observed that the parents were more like rivalrous twins themselves than a couple who had chosen to be together and who wanted to sort out their problems, consumed as they were by mutual anger, envy and competitive feelings. Mr Chalk used the flexibility of his hours as a research worker to remain in the hospital and take over the care of the children from his wife. Both parents seemed rigid and obsessional in the performance and organization of their domestic chores, feeling angry and frustrated when the newly-cleaned kitchen was then used by other patients. Both parents acknowledged their underlying depression.

In the first assessment meeting four weeks after admission, the nurse noted that Mrs Chalk talked about the twins as if they were much older than their chronological age. One example of this was when she accused James of waking his brother in the night and laughing at her when she could not get him back to sleep. Linking this with the parents' obsessionality, the consultant commented that the parents were frightened of infantile material, which felt to them like emptiness or madness. In other words they felt they had to impose their own order on things; this made it hard for them to relate to the relatively unorganized state of their babies.

Over the next few months, the nurses reported that the other patients who occasionally looked after James were bothered by his behaviour. They described how, when he was frustrated, he would throw himself backwards on to his head. We had the opportunity of observing him when he attended the playgroup once a month. We were not alone in observing that James was very preoccupied with jigsaws and with turning wheels, in such a way that he seemed completely detached and difficult to contact. Generally he seemed an unhappy and difficult child to whom development was an arduous task which he would only accomplish reluctantly. His parents always compared him unfavourably with his brother, who seemed more confident and was beginning to walk and talk.

These observations were discussed in the staff group. The therapists of Mr and Mrs Chalk viewed the situation from the perspective of the parents' internalized world and saw James's behaviour in terms of the parents' projections. This quite valid point of view nevertheless had the disadvantage that it reduced the children to the status of an externalization of the parents. No doubt this arose from the fact that the therapists did not receive from the parents any view of the children as separate people with a life of their own, children who were internalizing a world which would belong to them alone. It was felt that a lengthy period of individual psychotherapy would be the most effective response to the *parents'* difficulties. However, Mrs Chalk did not want this. Moreover, this particular in-patient setting does not favour treatment which lasts more than about 18 months. Also, of course, if one sought to help James by means of a lengthy treatment of the parents, it would be quite out of phase with the urgency of *his* developmental needs.

There remained the problem of how to engage with the parents about our concern for James. We decided to let the nurses and the other patients convey our own and their worries and observations to the parents, without offering advice or treatment unless the parents asked for it. We hoped that this approach would give some support to Mr and Mrs Chalk in their role as parents, instead of assuming ourselves responsibilities which might be seen as parental, rather than clinical. Fortunately, Mrs Chalk wrote to the child psychotherapist some three weeks later asking for an appointment. The nurse and the therapist met once with the mother and James, and once with mother and Jeremy. The meeting with James was extremely interesting. Mrs Chalk sat down with James on her knee. Both seemed tense, and James fidgeted around in an uneasy way. After several minutes he got himself into a position which did not seem all that comfortable, one leg across his mother's lap and the other hanging down the side of the chair. He fell asleep, his head resting in the crook of mother's arm, as if he were at the breast. His mother played almost no role in this. She asked the nurse and the therapist if she should wake him so that they could see him. They debated this aloud, eventually concluding that they wanted to see James as he was and that he was showing them what he wished. The mother could not understand their interest in this situation. She replied to the therapist's question by saying that James never fell asleep in her arms. If he was sleepy, she would put him in his cot. The nurse and the therapist noticed silently that it was very difficult for Mrs Chalk to remain silent and pay attention to her son. She continued to talk to them about the past as if compelled to do so just as at other times she seemed compelled to keep herself busy in the daily life of the Unit.

It seemed possible that Mrs Chalk kept herself busy not only because she had two children of the same age, or simply to deal with her pain and anxiety, but also, unconsciously, to preserve the idea that James was rejecting her – that is to say, to preserve her projection. According to this point of view, she organized her life to keep herself separated from James, a course of action which prevented the development of a more positive relationship. Since the parents were not yet responding to interpretations of their way of thinking about the children and managing them, it was decided to intervene at the level of Mrs Chalk's care of James. The terms of the offer to the parents were that James and Mrs Chalk could have a meeting *with each other* twice a week for half an hour in the consulting room, in the presence of the nurse and the child psychotherapist. By this means the staff sought to provide the more positive aspect of James's relationship with his mother with the opportunity to manifest itself and to develop. It also meant that the nurse would be able to support Mrs Chalk in bringing her everyday life with James into the child psychotherapist's room, and in carrying the experience and understanding gained there back into the wider setting of the hospital.

Mrs Chalk had the idea that James had not wanted to be born. It seemed that she needed him to fill a hole in her, to be a narcissistic extension of herself. By the physical severing of the umbilical cord and the failure to achieve a mutually satisfying feeding relationship thereafter, James and his mother seemed to be establishing instead a mutually hurtful relationship, substantially distorted by Mrs Chalk's projections of her own hostility. The aim of the meetings was to focus on the process of the interaction between them, in order to highlight some of the obstructions to more effective communications, as it were. In particular, this meant drawing Mrs Chalk's attention to the way in which she constantly put people, ideas and things between her and him like a barrier, rather than as a medium for communication. The work concentrated on fostering a play space between them, to use Winnicott's terminology, in which there might develop some room for response as well as reaction.

In this example, we see how Mrs Chalk's ideas about James's destructiveness completely altered the nature of the interaction. James crawled up to her and touched her foot. Mrs Chalk froze. She explained that she thought that he was going to hit her. When, on the other hand, James happened to find a nail on the floor, she became animated, urgently reaching out her hand and asking him to give it to her. He too became animated and smilingly teased her, inviting her, or so it seemed, to come and catch him. We can see that the maternal behaviour in these two examples tended to strengthen the negative relationship. The mother could see the child's behaviour only as destructive, and we can glimpse the mechanism by which the child began to conform to his mother's projections.

Similarly, Mrs Chalk continually placed the child psychotherapist in the way by maintaining that she brought James to see him rather than to see her. Whilst recognizing Mrs Chalk's envy and the connection with her husband's rivalrous mothering, the therapist resisted the temptation to interpret this to Mrs Chalk, firstly because Mrs Chalk already had a therapist and secondly, because he recognized that Mrs Chalk's attempts to engage directly and sometimes greedily with him would foster a mother/child dyad in the transference, which would detract from the real one between Mrs Chalk and her son.

Mrs Chalk came to the second session talking excitedly of James's achievements, his walking, talking and drinking from a cup. She and her husband had said, 'See what happens after one session with Mr Hartnup! Knowing that Mrs Chalk had previously been unable to recognize James's four or five tottering steps as walking, the child psychotherapist wondered if it might be Mrs Chalk's view of the child which had changed. He continued to point out how Mrs Chalk placed the child psychotherapist between herself and her son.

It was also important to demonstrate to Mrs Chalk James's capacity to receive from her. The nurse and therapist encouraged Mrs Chalk to find games she could play with James. On one occasion she brought a clock. She put it to James's ear, saying 'tick tock', which he repeated. She gave him the clock and then wanted him to enter the game of giving it back to her. His refusal awoke feelings of complete failure in her. However, she was able to accept the comment that she had been able to give James 'tick tock', which directed attention away from the material clock, towards the fact that he had taken in and enjoyed the 'tick tock' words she had given him.

The most important symbolic obstruction was removed by Mrs Chalk herself, when in a later session she told the nurse and therapist that she was not wearing a bra that day and was pleased that James had noticed the different feel of her whilst he was playing on her lap. In view of the failure of breastfeeding, this was clearly a crucial point for Mrs Chalk and represented her willingness to get in touch with a soft and vulnerable part of her own experience and risk opening herself up to James once again.

The history of their failed relationship began to unfold. The parents had noticed from early on that the pattern which decorated the side of James's cot had attracted James's attention. They made sure that this pattern was available to him. Mrs Chalk sensed that in turning towards this pattern, James was turning away from her, but she encouraged this alternative, because it supported the split in her ambivalence and also helped her to accomplish the heavy task that a mother of twins has. It seemed that James had stared at this pattern, a probable forerunner of the jigsaw and the wheel, whilst he had been at her breast. We could therefore offer the mother a different version of the history from her own, a version in which the cot pattern represented James's original tie to his mother and not simply a rejection of her. Of course, we know it is not sufficient to say to mother, 'It isn't like that at all', in order to reconcile her to her child. We know that her experience depended upon her own internalized structures and not only on external reality. Nevertheless, from the mother's point of view the approach which we have described must to some extent have modified the means by which she was dealing with an internalized conflict – namely projection accompanied by behaviour which tended to reproduce in the external world her own internal reality – that is, a child who rejected the mother.

There is an interesting aspect of the possible implications for other members of the family when a two-person relationship changes in this way. Two members of staff independently observed that the position of the twins in relation to their mother began to be reversed at some point during this period. Mrs Chalk apparently beginning to prefer James to Jeremy, and Jeremy was becoming discontented and irritable. We did not hear this observation until after the series of meetings with the mother and James had ended, although Mrs Chalk may have mentioned some worries about Jeremy at the time. This shift in the projection did not continue. It does seem likely, however, that it represented a last attempt to preserve the projection before modifying it. It was clear to Mrs Chalk's therapist that as a mother, she became increasingly able to tolerate the two sides of her ambivalence. It seemed to us that the elaboration of her relationship with James and of its history must have provided her with an opportunity to work it through, not only within herself, but also at an interpersonal level with James.

As for James, he became steadily less tense and more confident. During the session, his approaches to his mother became increasingly lively and conformed less and less to his mother's projections. He no longer threw himself backwards on to his head with the same frequency, and his motor and social development progressed again.

How do we understand this improvement on the child's part? We think that the physical presence of the mother and her growing psychological presence were enough to reawaken the developmental processes in James. Although in the first instance his behaviour in turning away from people, and in being overwhelmed by his own feelings, had seemed to have potentially drastic consequences for his future development, his capacities for recovery were unimpaired. Just as families may sometimes use the hospital literally as home in an unhelpful way, parents may use cots, playpens, highchairs and so on as physical containers, turning them into substitutes or even replacements for maternal care rather than aids to it. After James's birth, his mother was unable to provide him with a satisfactory space within herself, which hampered their capacity to use the physical environment creatively to establish a 'play space' as Winnicott calls it, between them. When James threw himself backwards on to his head or stared at jigsaws, he may have been internalizing the physical environment as a 'container' and stimulus barrier. He could relinquish them when mother opened herself up to him and became a more satisfying object.

From the whole family point of view, it was remarkable how space was made for this effective intervention. James had preserved his capacity for babyhood, and mother hers for early motherhood. Jeremy had to some extent adopted the position of the older brother, and although Mr Chalk felt extremely excluded, he was able to tolerate another couple helping his wife.

The nurse's presence and the emphasis on James and mother as a couple may have been important in this respect. The family co-operated to give Mrs Chalk and James a second chance.

A family with a school-refusing daughter

As our second example, we will present a family which illustrated some of the features common to families referred to this hospital. In particular, a shared symptomatology, presenting in somatic and behavioural forms, and problems in maintaining appropriate boundaries between family members. We have selected some phases from a year's work, of which only a small part went on in the consulting room.

The presenting problem was that Theresa, aged 13½, developed recurring abdominal pains, which eventually resulted in her refusal to go to school. Her GP referred her to the local child guidance clinic, where an attempt at family therapy over a period of six months resulted in the exacerbation of Theresa's symptoms. She became increasingly depressed and excessively concerned about her mother's welfare. On one occasion, after a family upset, Theresa badly scratched her arm. The anxieties became greater than the family and the outside agencies could contain and it was then that they were referred to the Cassel Hospital.

The composition of this family itself was consistent with the lack of clarity of boundaries which characterized relationships between the family members. The immediate household consisted of Mrs Holmes who was divorced from her husband, her two daughters, Theresa (13½) and Diana (10), and her cohabitee of the last 6 years, Mr Stevens (himself a divorced man and father of three daughters, who did not form part of the household). Mr Holmes continued to be a frequent visitor to the family, and both men spent a great deal of time together. Maternal grandparents were also very involved in this household and Mrs Holmes and her mother were especially close.

It subsequently emerged that Theresa was not the only member of the family to have somatic complaints. Both Mrs

Holmes and Mr Stevens suffered from nervous frequency of micturation and Mr Stevens had a travelling phobia.

Mr Stevens did not come to the out-patient consultation, and refused admission for himself. The offer was, however, accepted by Mrs Holmes and her two daughters. A family's response to admission often has important significance as regards their pathology. It can of itself represent an enactment or an avoidance, and it is a matter of clinical judgement whether the absence of a family member will interfere with the work to an unacceptable degree. In this case, we noted that Mrs Holmes was removing herself and her daughters from three important people: Mr Holmes, Mr Stevens and Mrs Holmes's mother. Its meaning was unclear at this stage.

Theresa emerged as a soft-hearted girl who worried about other people's upsets and was distressed by violence. Her sexual development was forward, and was accentuated by her style of dress and her hairstyle. On the home visit, the nurse describes Theresa as 'dressed in a low-cut tee shirt. She had a red rose tucked in her long hair and she was carefully made up'. 'She looked physically much older than her 13 years, with a lacy bra on and her cleavage showing'. In the hospital, both the mother's and Theresa's appearance was striking in contrasting ways. They wore identical bras under their transparent blouses. Theresa's elaborate hairdo and made-up face was in stark contrast to her mother's short bobbed hair and miminum of make-up. The mother's appearance was invariably immaculate, and her bearing almost stately. It was soon clear how deceptive such appearances can be. In ego development and object relationships, Theresa seemed more like a latency child. As for Mrs Holmes, she set more value on her niceness as a mother than on her authority.

The other daughter, Diana, kept to herself as far as staff were concerned, adopting a rather hostile stance to staff interventions. Diana did not want to know about anything which might disturb her or the family.

On admission, Mrs Holmes attended, in addition to the nursing meetings, a group with a psychotherapist. In the group, a patient's capacity to engage in individual psychotherapy might emerge. Theresa and Diana attended the hospital day unit which serves a similar function among others. During this first period, staff felt they made little impact on the family. The problem had apparently disappeared. Theresa liked being in the hospital and the tutorial unit, provided that she was in the company of her mother or her sister. The inseparability of this threesome and their unfailing 'niceness' effectively kept staff in ignorance of the relationship between them. In particular, the nurse felt quite frustrated and unable to make any meaningful contact with the family.

In retrospect, however, this can be seen as a crucial period. Firstly, it enabled Mrs Holmes to move from a position of relief at the admission to hospital, to a growing awareness of the dynamics of her family relationships through internalization of the therapeutic culture of the hospital in its different group settings. A decisive aspect of this for the Holmes family must have been the constant exposure to the expression, containment and resolution of hostile and angry feelings between the other patients, as well as the acknowledgment of feelings of failure. Very gradually, Mrs Holmes began to recognize her own problems and make links between them and Theresa's difficulties. Towards the end of this period she began, albeit with difficulty, to attempt not to be on hand for Theresa at all times.

Furthermore, our observations of the family over this period continued to accumulate. Staff continued to work together at constructing a coherent formulation. It was soon clear that the appearance of niceness and closeness were the behavioural expression of an attempt to defend against psychic pain, in particular against feelings of intense shame. The attempt was not altogether effective in the case of Theresa and Mrs Holmes, and hence perhaps the presence of somatization.

Now, two further observations could be added. One was the theme of mistaken identity (i.e. the deceptive appearances), and the other was Mrs Holmes's lack of appropriate authority. Theresa had on occasion been mistaken for her father's girlfriend. Soon after admission, she commented anxiously that one could not tell the staff from the patients. Indeed, on one occasion Mrs Holmes had been mistaken for a member of staff by a visitor; however, Mrs Holmes's apparent competence concealed a lack of any sense of her own authority.

We began to hold meetings of the family and all the staff working with them: the child therapists, the nurse, and the teacher from the day unit. Our aim was to engage with the family's denial of a generation gap between mother and daughters. Here, through taking up practical issues such as who felt responsible for notifying the teacher if one of the girls was away sick, the staff could attempt to draw out the meaning of mother's omissions. Two things now emerged. We learned of Mrs Holmes's inability to assert her authority with Mr Holmes and to regulate his visits to the family home. He would arrive unannounced, or he did not come when expected. Upsetting other people by a display of annoyance was felt to be wrong. Similarly to voice one's hurt or upset feelings seemed like making a complaint, i.e. like telling someone else to 'stop it'. It became clear that hospital staff were experienced in the transference as figures of authority, before whom all the family felt they had to behave themselves. We could now understand that in this family, mediation and conciliation substituted for parental authority as a way of dealing with infantile feelings of oedipal rivalry and jealousy.

Clearly, Mrs Holmes held a central position in this constellation. This is how she herself describes the family dynamics: she wrote how she did not realize that Mr Stevens did not accept, spelled 'except', the children nor they him. 'And I was in the middle' she went on 'trying to keep everyone happy, which I realize now was wrong'. With Mrs Holmes's growing understanding of the family's dynamics, we had reached a new stage in the treatment of the family, and individual sessions for Mrs Holmes were now introduced into the treatment plan.

In her sessions, it emerged how Mrs Holmes had been unable to assume adult status in relation to her mother, who continued to represent an internalized unattainable ideal.

The child psychotherapist had acted as convenor of the family meetings. Mrs Holmes understood the word convenor to mean 'someone who comes between', and thus her feelings of inadequacy emerged in the transference, based on her experience of a mother who continually undermined her authority with her own children. Similarly, she felt that Mr Stevens was brainier than she. In the transference this appeared as a fear that she would not be able to 'do it properly', by which she meant psychotherapy. The material moved on to the problems of her own adolescence, especially her feelings of being shamed at school when she could not answer questions, and how she tried to restore her injured self-esteem by resorting to daydreams of becoming a dancer. However, when she wanted to take dancing lessons, her narcissism suffered a further blow. Her parents disapproved because they thought it might lead her into 'bad company'. It then transpired that an aunt had disgraced the family by going off with a married man whom she had met at a dance. Mrs Holmes also remembered falling and hurting her back when she tried to do a handstand for the first time, but she concealed this from her teachers and her family because she was afraid that she might have to visit the family doctor. She then revealed that currently she was worried about a visit to the family planning clinic and had concealed from the staff in the hospital for the past three weeks she had had continuous menstruation. Eventually this brought into the transference her fear of loss of control, of not being in charge, that is her fear of sexual excitement.

From the foregoing, we deduced that Mrs Holmes had never been able to complete the adolescent task of overthrowing parental authority in order to make it a part of herself. Coming between people in order to keep the peace was also her way of controlling in others her own projected envy, rivalry, sense of inadequacy and loneliness – aspects of her oedipal conflicts which she had not been able to resolve. In her adult life, her defiance of the internalized parental prohibitions was enacted in doing what her aunt did, and setting up house with a married man.

The psychotherapeutic work with mother in turn enabled Theresa to move forward in her own development, presumably relieving her from the unconscious burden of carrying mother's unresolved, adolescent conflict. Theresa now requested individual sessions for herself, and for a short period was seen by the child psychotherapist.

In her sessions, some elements of the family mechanism of 'deceptive appearances' of which Theresa made use, became apparent. In Theresa's case, her sophisticated appearance was covering up ego interests and object relationships of a latency girl with a severe super-ego.

Theresa's presenting problems indicated conflicts of some severity over aggressive drives related to achieving separateness. Gradually, in the safety of the tutorial unit, she began to express her feelings more openly and vigorously, especially in relation to her family situation. In the transference, this emerged in the following way. Theresa took in hand an eleven-year-old patient of the child psychothrapist's, and gradually helped her to change her appearance, for example, by varnishing her nails and changing her hairstyle. At the same time, in her sessions, she often gave accounts of another girl of her own age in the hospital, who flaunted her nascent sexuality; this shocked and frightened Theresa very much. She was also very troubled by the then prevailing hospital culture, in which patients often belittled the importance of their own sessions, and denied any positive feelings for their own therapists, as a way of dealing with their fear of envious attacks by other patients. By then, the teacher in the tutorial unit began to work actively with Theresa about returning to outside school, and this was gradually achieved. For a time, Theresa had difficulties in leaving the hospital, and her anxiety at this point took the form of obsessional questioning and delaying tactics. When we became aware how mother colluded in this, it was decided that helping Theresa to get to school could be a useful nursing task, and this proved to be so. Unlike her mother, when Theresa was being anxious, the nurse would tell her that this was not the time to discuss these matters, that they belonged in her session, but that now she had better think about getting off to school. The anxieties, which had originally precipitated her school refusal, were then brought into her sessions.

The belittling of 'parental figures' came to be seen to relate to the original upsets in school, where it emerged that Theresa had become very upset because the girls there called her names. These related to her mother's co-habitation. The usual conflict inherent in a threesome relationship, including the oedipal triangle, assumed great complexity in this family. Theresa attempted to avoid this conflict, albeit unconsciously, by 'dressing up in her mother's clothes', but she seems to have assumed the identity of an adolescent of her mother's generation.

This makes some sense if the problem is seen as spanning three generations. Whilst maternal grandmother was seen to hold parental authority, mother and daughter could be 'as if' of one generation. It was only when mother began to assume adult authority, that Theresa felt free to make moves in her own development. In the absence of a developmental history and an account from Theresa of her own early experiences, we are left with some gaps in our formulations, especially regarding the interplay of specific internal and external factors which led to the formation of her very severe super-ego. However, an important factor must have been fear of loss of the object. In order to please the adults she wanted to remain 'a good latency girl', but this made her feel out of step in her more sexually aware peer group.

One of the interesting factors about this family is that Theresa was the referred patient, but from the initial period in the hospital it was Mrs Holmes who emerged as the one who could own a problem and work on it. The initial work of nursing made psychotherapy possible and Mrs Holmes became increasingly able to set limits on Mr Holmes and her own mother and her daughters. She was able to assume greater responsibility for letting Mr Stevens know that she wanted them to be married, which they did at the time of the family's discharge from hospital. All these changes were a great relief to Theresa, as a card written to the child psychotherapist a year later attests. Here are some quotes: 'I thought I would write and update you on how I am getting on. My fifth year at school was the best and I have really enjoyed it. It's the only year at school that I have had without any worries and I really felt part of the school instead of an outsider.' She then describes how she took part in a mock interview for a job and, to her great suprise, she won first prize. After leaving school she started work as an office junior at a solicitor's. The card is signed Theresa S., the initial of her stepfather.

Clearly, we need to account for the improvement in Theresa. We think it was due to a combination of external as well as internal factors. Most importantly, we think it was the mother's increased capacity to become an effective parent. This reinforced and helped Theresa in her internal struggles and relieved her persecutory anxiety and guilt feelings, arising from her oedipal conflicts. In the hospital, Theresa had the experience of feeling understood for the first time and this must have enhanced her self-esteem and contributed to her capacity for a more reality-oriented view of herself and her family.

Summary

In this paper we have described work with families in an in-patient setting. We have tried to show what makes the setting therapeutic. In our view, it is the integration of nursing, educational and consulting room settings which facilitates the psychotherapeutic process with the family and its individual members. We have illustrated this process by detailed accounts, tracing the disturbances in the separation individuation phase in early childhood and its resurgence in adolescence.

[14]

Good Baby, Bad Baby
Exploring a Mother's Perception

Sheila Ashley

THE FOLLOWING PAPER describes part of my nursing work with a family who were admitted to the Family Unit at the Cassel Hospital. My work was in conjuction with Sister Biancardi, who nursed the family for the first six months, and the psychotherapy staff, in particular Trevor Hartnup, child psychotherapist, who gives an account of some of the work in his paper with Lydia Tischler (see p. 228).

This paper primarily focusses on my observations and work with the mother, and on the relationship between mother and one child.

The Chalk family: events leading up to admission

Mary Chalk had become depressed after the premature birth of her twins, Jeremy and James. At the time she was treated with drug therapy but she, and her husband in particular, expressed a desire for psychotherapy. Mary and her husband, Alan, openly acknowledged their difficulty in communicating with each other. Both, with good reason, felt their childhood experiences had been traumatic and damaging, and were contributing to their difficulty in relating now. They were quick to blame each other, and angry exchanges could end in violence.

Mary experienced difficulty with feeding and managing James, the smaller and second-born twin. Mary and James were separated at birth when he was put in an incubator. Due to his prematurity, his sucking action was poor and this made breastfeeding unsatisfactory. Mary felt actively rejected by James. He slept less and cried more than Jeremy, whom she saw as placid and good-natured. The twins were one year old when the whole family were admitted.

At the time I took over the nursing of the Chalk family, the family had been in hospital for 6 months. I felt I had already established contact through my work as community nurse at nights and weekends, and this was helpful to me during the transition.

My observations of Mrs Chalk

If I was asked to sum Mary up during those early days, the things that come to mind are: too nice, too good, no mess. Mary projected a 'sweet little girl' image which did not openly acknowledge conflict, frustration or irritation. She was always neat and cleanly dressed, which must have been difficult to maintain with twins, who were by then 18 months old.

During my first weeks of nursing the family I had frequent contact over day-to-day events such as the cleaning of the unit, the feeding of the twins, and over Mary's job as Firm Chairman of the Family Unit. We also embarked on a project together, to be responsible for the plant stall at the hospital's annual garden party. This involved the taking, rooting, planting and general care of plant cuttings.

Mary's childlike way of dressing and her inability to choose her own clothes, seemed to illustrate how little sense she had of herself as a woman. She complained that she did not even know what clothes she liked but would often say to me 'You look nice in that'. This problem seemed related to her not allowing any time for herself. If she gave herself anything, she felt tremendously guilty. She was always busy. She kept her diary neat and full. At the end of the day, exhausted and dissatisfied with her efforts, she became depressed and tearful. The Unit kitchen, her work area, would be sparkling several times each day. Tears of disappointment ensued after other people 'ab-*used*' the kitchen.

Mary's conscientiousness was nearly obsessional. The need for perfection led to depression at her constant failure to reach this goal. Any comment to her was perceived as criticism. She then withdrew like a hurt, angry child.

Mary's desire to be perfect and to keep things nice excluded the recognition of her own anger and led to her rejection of her husband, Alan, when he became angry. Her anger was very evident to others in her high flush of colour and general agitation. She and Sister Biancardi had begun to recognize together the 'sugar-coated bitter pills' she would deliver. For instance, she would say, 'It's nice to have quiche for lunch. Is it yesterday's?'; or 'It's nice to see so much of you, but you still don't feel like my nurse'. I adopted the 'bitter pills' phrase and it became humorous and a remaining link with Sister Biancardi.

Mary lacked self-confidence and needed constant reassurance, a need which at times was hard for me to recognize. As she attempted to reach her own high standards, I often felt 'not good enough'. Mary attended the Monday evening pottery group on a few occasions but found it difficult to relax and use the clay and, quick to criticize her efforts, wanted to throw her pots away. I had to encourage her to finish the two pots and we only succeeded in this just before her discharge.

Observations of James and Jeremy

The twins were gaining their developmental milestones adequately, although both were still physically small for their age. While concern for the emotional attachment between Mary and James had existed from admission, it was not possible to engage actively with this without first making a relationship with the family and respecting Mary's and Alan's individual problems and feelings of deprivation. I feel this task was well underway when I began to nurse them, and was consequently able to approach the problem between mother and son.

James was physically very small for his age, noticeably smaller than Jeremy. He was responsive and quick to smile at people, but far more interested in things and how they worked. He was irritable at times; he clearly knew what he wanted to do and what he did not. He was a little aloof and not so easily lovable as Jeremy. Mary found him difficult in many areas.

She felt his slow feeding, his not sleeping and his throwing himself backwards were James's deliberate attempts to annoy her. She called him the 'bad baby' who did not want to be born and who rejected her. She continually anticipated problems with James; for example, at nappy changing time whe would say, 'James is bound to scream'. If he did not, she would say to him, 'why aren't you screaming?' She seemingly could not appreciate the negative attachment, and could not see anything positive unless it was blatantly obvious. For instance several people on the unit had seen James take a few steps, but it was only after he had walked halfway across the room that his mother noticed this. Alan identified with James as the 'bad twin'; it was Alan that was often left to cope with James's irritability and slow feeding. James was difficult to comfort when upset and turned more readily to his patterned sheets or picture cards on the wall than to his mother. He had made no attempt to talk.

Jeremy was quite different to James. He was an interested, responsive child, quick to smile and eager to play. His vocabulary was expanding, he could recognize certain objects in books and liked to draw on the blackboard. He was walking, was strong and well co-ordinated. He responded well to people and would turn to his mother or father when hurt or upset. Mary called Jeremy 'the good baby' saying he was little trouble, affectionate and that he wanted to be born. Jeremy behaved like an older brother, often generously giving James what James wanted.

For the main part they played happily, doing separate things or 'in parallel'. Mary coped very well and efficiently in the physical caring of the twins and they were always clean, neat and tidy. She found mess distasteful. She treated both children as older than their years; she expected them to sit and listen to a story. This seemed inappropriate given their obvious prematurity, which seemed to represent to Mary her imperfection as a mother. Mary was totally unable to play with the babies, which was paralleled in her serious relationship with her husband. Mary appeared to need rules in order to keep things in control and therefore 'good', 'nice' and 'not messy'. This limited the spontaneity which is so vital for children's play. I was constantly made aware of how like the twins Mary and Alan were themselves in their inseparability and their wish to remain childlike, each paralleling one child: Alan as James, the 'bad baby', Mary as Jeremy, the 'good baby'.

The nursing process

Very little of my nursing intervention with Mary was in the form of formal one-to-one sessions. I mainly used the opportunities which arose from day-to-day living and the relationship between the two of us. Some formal sessions were used to facilitate Mary's and Alan's communicating with each other, particularly in the face of their anger and frustration.

1. *Presenting Problem:* Mary's inability to buy her own clothes.

Underlying Factors: i) Non-acceptance of her own sexuality.
ii) Denial of her adult self.
iii) Not knowing herself, and not allowing herself time for this.
iv) Her difficulty in being an individual, separate from her husband.
v) Repression of her own feelings.

Objective: For Mary to buy her own clothes, to begin to recognize and value her individuality.

Action: I did not mention Mary's appearance until she complained to me of not knowing what she felt comfortable wearing. She then talked at length about her insecurity about her appearance and the need for Alan to approve. She felt his dress sense was good and she therefore felt secure in his choice. Through talking, she decided that she would like to buy something for herself and recognized the childlike manner in which she had given this responsibility over to Alan. However, she felt unable to reclaim this, as she felt herself to have no dress sense. I offered to go to the shops with Mary to look at what was fashionable and to maybe try a few things on to see how she felt in them. Some weeks later when this offer had not been taken up, I realized the complexity of the situation and decided to slow down. I brought in some magazines and we sat down casually together. We often spent more time criticizing the horoscopes than looking at the fashion pages, and most comments on clothes were of a negative nature, for which Mary felt she had to apologize. I assured her that it was useful to know what one did not like. I began to give feedback on how she was looking.

However, I felt I was slipping into Alan's role of dictating her dress and so I stopped this interaction. If Mary commented on my clothes, for example, 'Is that new?', I would use the opportunity to ask her opinion and would then share my own feelings about them. At first, Mary would always be positive, saying she liked them, but could offer little else. There were many such interactions before Mary could say 'I don't like you in that, the colours are too bold'.

Outcome: Mary never took up my offer to go to the shops with her. However she did buy three pretty Indian cotton skirts of different colours. Though she did not try them on in the shop, they did suit her, she looked softer and more feminine and she liked them very much.

2. *Presenting Problem:* Exhaustion, resentment and depression.

Underlying Factors: i)Inability to allow herself any time, and the guilt she experienced if she did.
ii) Guilt linked with not feeling good enough because of failure in her aim for perfection.
iii) Her tendency to say 'yes' when she meant 'no'.
iv) Her inability to openly acknowledge her anger and frustration.

Objectives: i) For Mary to recognize the need for, and allocate, time for herself.
ii) Mary's tolerance and acceptance of her own and of other people's imperfections.
iii) To be able to express anger and frustration directly.

Action: Mary became Firm Chairman of the Ross Unit – a job which she carried out with great efficiency. She was reliable and supportive of patients and staff. This job, however, highlighted her obsessional organization and her negative use of her organizing ability. Her investment was in organizing her timetable so that she did not have any time for herself. When asked to do something, for example, to babysit or to help in the kitchen inventory, she would always say 'yes' and then appear noticeably angry and resentful when she was rushing around trying also to get the twins fed and bathed. It proved difficult to work with Mary's need for her own space while she was engaged with the Firm Chairmanship, as she shouldered the responsibility gravely. I worked out with her the Firm's needs, her family's needs and tried to help her to delegate when the pressure was too much. Towards the end of the term of office she was more able to delegate the Firm's needs in favour of her family's, but unable to recognize the importance of her own needs.

My working with Mary for the garden party stall served many functions. It allowed her to do something she enjoyed without Alan or the twins. It gave her the experiences of frustration and resolution inherent in working together with someone else. It provided a flexible goal and achievement. When we first began, Mary would frequently check that the twins were sleeping, even though they always slept at that time of day, and she complained that she felt that she was neglecting them. Mary was very efficient with plants, and fortunately so was I. However, I was frequently rushed and had to leave certain things for a few days before finding time to attend to them. At first, Mary silently accepted my shortcomings and perhaps because of my own guilt I did not question her restraint. The tension between us grew. Eventually, after another patient became angry with me for spending so much time with 'those bloody plants', Mary was also able to get angry with me for not spending enough time with them or with her. The angry torment was considerable but the tension was relieved and the planting continued.

Mary was also involved in preparing a special muesli breakfast for the community, weekly on Wednesdays. Mary worked with the nurse tutor over this and, again, the relationship was stormy, with periods of silent resentment over their different ways of doing things which eventually erupted in anger from Mary, who then wanted to give up the job. The tutor acknowledged Mary's feelings of wanting to give up the job, but she felt that they should go on trying to work together.

Outcome: Mary was able to defend her care taking of the plants against Alan's wish for her to be elsewhere. She also began gardening at home during the weekends. She found this relaxing and allocated time for it.

Mary was more able to be directly angry with me.

Between us, and with a little help from other people, we produced 300 cuttings for the garden party, which was a success. Despite my shortcomings and imperfections, the plants still grew.

Mary was able to thank the tutor for helping her to stick with the breakfast job, which survived despite the different ways of working and the angry outburst.

3. *Presenting Problem:* A difficult relationship with James.
Underlying Factors: i) Mary's inability to play.
ii) A desire for the twins to be the same, not individual.
iii) James's use of patterns, not people, when upset.

Objectives: To recognize a positive attachment with James as well as a negative one.

Actions: Mary had formally asked for help with James from the child psychotherapist, Mr Hartnup. The request was to 'stop James complaining about life'. We decided to respond to the request by an assessment of Mary with each child in the presence of myself and Mr Hartnup. We consequently arranged sessions for Mary and James on a twice weekly basis for half an hour. I felt these sessions to be invaluable for the mother/child relationship by providing time for them together without the demands of Jeremy's presence. James used his first session to curl up against his mother's breast and go to sleep. Mary felt this to be a completely new situation, as she would normally have put him back in his cot and carried on with something else. The sessions also provided me with a time to observe and reflect with Mary, and together to formulate some tasks.

Mary's lack of spontaneity was evident in her difficulty in converting James's game of pushing a plastic handle into her mouth into a game she felt comfortable with. We began to have to think of games to play. I planned times outside of the sessions to spend with her and one child, though not always with James. On one occasion en route to the duck pond, we encountered several puddles and I suggested that we played one, two, three jump with Jeremy over each puddle. Mary could not understand what I meant and found it hard to comprehend using the environment for play. In one session she handed James a clock and said 'tick tock', holding out her hand for him to return it. When he did not, but carried on saying 'tick tock' she felt fed up that the game had failed, until it was pointed out to her that she had given James 'tick tock', with which he was playing.

Here I will list some of the tasks formulated:

i) Inventing new games, first using herself and then the environment in conjunction with toys or in place of them.

ii) To make time to be with each child on their own for at least half an hour, twice weekly.

iii) To identify a new achievement from each child and acknowledge her own contribution to this.

iv) To identify ways in which James and Jeremy were different and what she liked and disliked about this.

v) To spend some time 'babying' James, i.e. to feed him on her knee occasionally.

The family were away from the hospital for a period of six weeks during the summer, and I suggested that Mary continue with these tasks.

Outcome: Mary became more able to recognize James's achievements and give him praise; I feel this major step was facilitated by recognizing her part in his development.

Mary felt more able to comfort James, who resorted to patterns less often; she stopped verbalizing to James her negative expectations of him.

James's bouts of throwing himself backwards were diminished though not completely stopped.

Mary continued to reprimand James for being difficult if Jeremy was being good.

Mary appeared more relaxed in her care of both twins.

The experience of leaving the hospital

In view of both Mary and Alan's experience of an emotionally deprived childhood, the staff group were apprehensive that a leaving date from the hospital would be experienced as total rejection and render both parties incapable of integrating any insight or change in their lives at home. We were also concerned that the twins should continue to thrive in their home environment. We therefore suggested to the family that they go home for six weeks over the summer period, and we arranged a final leaving date for six weeks afterwards. After the initial anger, they accepted the decision. Mary felt quite excited about going and said she would find it very difficult to return after the break. They arranged a week's holiday at the coast with friends and to spend the other five weeks at home. Prior to departure, they were both anxious and required a lot of nursing time. I told them that they could telephone the hospital any time during the six weeks. There was only one telephone call from Mary, who spoke to their second nurse as I was off duty. She spoke of their family situation which sounded as difficult as in the pre-admission period. The nurse felt Mary had needed to telephone to try and identify and focus on the problems and to help her to communicate with Alan. On my hearing a report of the telephone call I felt pessimistic. I decided to restrain myself from the impulse to telephone them.

On their return to the hospital, my most striking observation was on how much more mature they both appeared to be. Although Mary found returning to the hospital difficult, she was excited to see everyone again and said how much she had missed the other mothers, two of them in particular. The twins were also excited but rather shy at first. Alan was friendly and very approachable. Both were certainly more able to face problems and to think about them constructively. Their relationship seemed more open and communications less strained. They both appeared happier people. Both twins had made adequate progress and Mary's interaction with both boys was noticeably more relaxed, though mess continued to be a source of friction for her. The holiday with friends had been enjoyable and successful which contrasted with a disastrous holiday earlier in the year. My previous pessimistic mood lifted, though did not totally disappear.

As anticipated, both viewed their leaving the hospital seriously and worked hard in their last six weeks. All Firm and community jobs were handed over to other people in good time and with a detailed description of the job. They certainly behaved as 'old hands' encouraging and supporting other patients, though at times it was possible to feel their resentment, such as during the admission of a new patient. My worry during this time was that things seemed to be going too well which was a bit reminiscent of the quality of Mary on admission.

As a goodbye to the community, Mary and Alan cooked a vegetarian supper, and Mary, with a nurse, prepared a special breakfast which most of the community attended (a most unusual occurrence). On their last afternoon, Ross Unit gave the family a tea, during which Alan and Mary gave presents to what seemed to be everyone. The event seemed like Christmas and became a little embarrassing, but it appeared to indicate their need not to be forgotten. In saying goodbye to the family, I felt a sense of loss. I had grown to like them through the work we had done together, and they had at times been supportive of me, particularly with community issues.

It is always a privilege to be allowed to see into the painful areas of personal vulnerability and I learned many things, both professionally and personally, from the experience of working with this family. Perhaps it was the two-way process which made such work both challenging and exciting.

[15]

An Account of the Early Stages of Treatment with a Family in In-patient Treatment

Petrie Thompson

This is an account of the early stages of in-patient work with one family at the Cassel Hospital, the main purpose of which is to illustrate some of the ways in which the family's disordered functioning manifested itself in the day-to-day community life of the hospital and the way in which the material arising from this was used in their engagement in treatment. This was in a family which were not containable in out-patient treatment, and needed the Cassel's intensive programme.

As a basis, it is necessary first to describe the family's background and the situation which had been reached by the time of admission. The members of the family are as follows: Mr X, aged 39, at referral working as a sales representative; Mrs X, aged 33, the principally referred patient; and their four children, John, aged ten; Jane, aged seven; Adam, aged five; and Thomas, aged two. The referral came from a consultant psychiatrist whose patient, Mrs X, had been in difficulties for about 18 months, dating from shortly after the birth of the youngest child. She had been depressed after the birth and had difficulty bonding to the baby, who was sickly, with eczema. At first, things had seemed to improve but Mrs X did not regain her usual self. She had apparently coped well through the first ten years of the marriage and the birth of the first three children, only suffering a transient lowering of mood following the birth of the eldest child.

Before Thomas was a year old, Mrs X began a progressive

deterioration in her ability to function as a mother due to an increasingly low mood, difficulty in going out and tendency to panic in crowded shops. She also began to abuse alcohol in bouts of heavy drinking. She had been treated psychiatrically, first as an out-patient and then as an in-patient, being prescribed antidepressants (tricyclic and MAOI) and then having ECT during her first admission lasting seven weeks. She was only slightly improved on discharge and continued to rely heavily on support from her GP, psychiatrist, community psychiatric nurse, social worker and health visitor. Individual sessions were also arranged with a clinical psychologist at that time. The observation was made that she split the professionals involved with her into those she liked and those she did not. The clinical psychologist noted that she seemed motivated for help when the focus was on herself, but that she opted out when the attempt was made over several meetings to include her husband. This ended in the psychologist feeling that there was no alternative but to end the sessions because they seemed to be getting nowhere and that somehow Mrs X did not want to be helped. Similarly the health visitors' services were withdrawn around this time by the GP because it was felt Mrs X only abused them, taking the opportunity to stay later and later in bed and not going to bed until the early hours. She became increasingly isolated from her husband and began drinking again as much as before. Mr X reportedly felt increasingly helpless and burdened by having to take on much more of the day-to-day care of the children then he ever had done previously. At this time, he opened a credit card account for his wife and she began to use this freely, quickly running up considerable debts which have remained ever since as a burden on the family.

Mrs X now began to write extensive letters to the professionals involved expressing suicidal wishes and raising their anxiety as a group until a second admission was offered. This lasted for twelve weeks, concern being expressed about Mrs X's 'negative attitude' and denigration of all help offered. A further attempt was made at joint meetings with Mr X but with similarly unsuccessful results. Separation was seriously considered by them at this stage, but they resolved to try to continue their relationship. Professional concern for the adequacy of the children's care increased, and even more careful plans for supporting the family were made following this second discharge, including Mrs X's attending a mothers' group regularly with Thomas, and frequent meetings with community psychiatric nurse and social worker. This did not prevent Mrs X again deteriorating; she now complained of not being supported by her husband. Conjoint meetings with the couple were arranged which at first seemed helpful to Mrs X and the children. However, these came to an end because of Mr X's reluctance to continue them and his claim that they conflicted with his work commitments. The psychologist conducting the joint sessions noted that any attempt to explore sexual problems in the couple's relationship was resisted, especially by Mr X, who seemed so threatened that it was suspected that this was the underlying reason for his withdrawal. The family's debts and other practical problems continued to intensify. Mrs X now refused to take medication prescribed by her GP and consultant psychiatrist. She did, however, take an overdose of tablets which she had stored up. She said that she felt that killing herself would be in the best interests of her children and that she had been trying to distance herself from them to prepare them for this.

It was felt by the professionals that the children were subject to very great emotional strain but that this was largely unrecognized by both parents. It was at this juncture that referral to the Cassel Hospital was decided on, the referring psychiatrist underlining in his referral letter that Mrs X continued to cause considerable worry and that her treatment was getting nowhere.

After initial consultation and home nursing assessment, some doubt was felt about the family being able to sustain motivation for in-patient family treatment in view of Mrs X's tendency to denigrate all previous efforts made to help them. However, it was clear that the daily structure of the family's life at home had broken down and a date for admission was agreed for a four-week period of in-patient assessment.

The workers involved with the family were two therapists meeting jointly with the parents, a child psychotherapist assessing the children, and the nurse who would be principally working with them (the 'first nurse'). These staff met together with the whole family on the day of admission. It was immediately noticeable that Mrs X was very quiet and passive. Mr X spoke for the whole family. Both parents were emphatic in their view that the problem resided completely in Mrs X and that Mr X had no difficulties in his own right. He did, however, give us some cause for consternation by blandly announcing that since the consultation he had given up his job and had no immediate prospects of further employment. It had been agreed very clearly with him that he would be expected to continue in his work from the hospital during the family's stay. His abandonment of his role of breadwinner in the family was seen as the first manifestation of his wish to establish dependency on the hospital in his own right.

Arrangements were made for sessions with therapists during the assessment period, the decision being made to see the parents conjointly twice weekly. The first important observations, however, came immediately, in the family's relationship to their nurse and in their behaviour within the hospital community. On the first night of admission Mrs X drank a half bottle of rum (which she must have secreted into the hospital) but did this in a way that could not possibly have avoided detection; indeed, she handed in the unfinished bottle to the duty nurse. During the family's first weekend in hospital, she handed in another unopened bottle of rum and some razor blades, having threatened to cut herself. This seemed an immediate attempt by her to establish how such issues would be dealt with and it was plainly stated to both parents that such behaviour might indicate that they did not wish to be treated at the hospital. Mr X did not see his wife's behaviour as having anything to do with him; he saw it as part of an illness that remained a total mystery to him. Mrs X, however, responded well to this confrontation, not drinking again during the remainder of the assessment period. She had been taking diazepam and chloral hydrate regularly on admission; these were successfully reduced and finally stopped during the first weeks of admission. She quickly established a very clinging kind of relationship to her first nurse, putting great pressure on the nurse to take over control and responsibility for her daily activities with her family in the hospital. The nurse constantly felt it very difficult to remind Mrs X that she retained parental responsibility while in the hospital.

For his part, Mr X seemed equally keen to have the nurse effectively assume responsibility within the family. He assumed that his needy wife would now be taken care of without any involvement from him. It was quite dramatic to observe how the couple managed to be hardly ever physically together in the hospital. At mealtimes, Mr X would be with the children while Mrs X would be elsewhere (she also created concern at her lack of proper eating). At bedtime, he would stick rigidly to his customary time for retiring while she would remain out of bed for half the night, going as far as she could in eliciting contact and concern from anyone but her husband. In any activities such as outings with the children, which they had been encouraged to plan together, it would characteristically turn out at the last moment that for some reason they could not go together as a family. Mrs X seemed to prefer the company of young adult patients in another section of the hospital rather than that of her husband during the day. Mr X resented the reminders given to him that he was expected to retain responsibility in his family as a husband and father, making it clear that he felt it should be the staff's responsibility to deal with his wife's need for support and comfort. Both nurse and therapists were often left feeling that they carried anxiety about the family which would usefully be taken on by the couple together.

Meanwhile, the children as a group seemed remarkably composed and self-sufficient, giving much less cause for immediate concern than either of their parents. The eldest, John, aged ten, seemed particularly to function as a competent caretaker or surrogate parent for his younger siblings, to the extent that it was not at first easy for the children's needs as individuals to be seen. It was felt that hidden beneath a brittle pseudo-maturity in the children there lay a shared anxiety about being able to keep access to supplies of attention, nurturance or even simply to food.

Further information came to light in the parents' sessions which began to provide some background for understanding the behaviour and attitudes that each brought to their present predicament. Mr X was the only child of an unmarried mother and had never known his father. He had been sent to a boarding school at the age of seven and had become a rather wild adolescent. As a young man, his disreputable and carefree ways had been an important part of his attraction for Mrs X. Mrs X was the eldest of nine children and had taken on a great deal of the caretaking of her younger siblings as a child. She had rebelled against being put in this role by her mother when her fourth sibling was born and had strongly murderous fantasies about the fifth and sixth of her own siblings. The rather unusual circumstance existed that her children were of similar ages to her own younger siblings and she had remained quite closely involved with her parents who lived nearby to the X's home.

It also became clearer in the couple's sessions that Thomas's conception was the result of a joint mishandling of contraception and had not been planned. After the third child, there had been an agreement that Mr X would have a vasectomy but he had equivocated over this, much to the annoyance of Mrs X, who responded by taking her contraceptive pill irregularly and consequently becoming pregnant. She had been offered a termination but refused it, perhaps because it would have been too much like acting out her murderous fantasies towards her younger siblings which had been of such concern to her.

There were indirect hints from Mrs X at some sexual difficulty between them and it seemed likely the couple had currently had no sexual activity. They seemed to feel their sexuality was unmentionable and continued, at this stage, to make it unavailable to exploration in treatment.

All the children were assessed individually by the child psychotherapist. The three older ones also attended the hospital's Day Unit which provides daytime activities, including schooling, in a nursed setting. Each of the children was felt to show quite marked disturbance in their own right, underlying the initial impression they had given as a group of apparent self-sufficiency. It seemed likely that individual treatment for the children would later be required if the family remained in the hospital.

At the point of the family's definitive assessment and acceptance for treatment after one month of admission, an attempt was made to make a focus for working with the family using the formulation that every member of the family was in his or her own way convinced of the inadequacy of the resources available within the family – the children in effect feeling that they must parent themselves because of lack of parental resources; Mrs X feeling that her husband had nothing to give her and she nothing to give to her children; and Mr X feeling helpless to provide, the most concrete expression of this being his giving up of his job and loss of income while the family's large debt remained. An important aspect of this formulation was that Mr X himself must have had an unacknowledged sense of need and that his investment in maintaining his wife as the sick member of the partnership constituted an important part of his defence against the pain of his unsatisfied wish for dependency.

In practice, this meant taking up his reluctance to look for new work in order to begin to deal with the debt and repeated attempts to help the couple face their difficulties in doing anything together or being together. Repeatedly, it seemed that all efforts to modify the situation were fruitless and that the state of affairs with the family in the hospital was just as intractable as the situation that had existed before admission.

As a means of engaging with the couple's difficulty in functioning co-operatively, it was suggested to Mr X that he undertake construction of a Wendy house which would be used by his own and other children in the unit. This allowed a concrete expression of his tendency to exclude his wife from any productive activity that he undertook in that he resented her involvement in the project. He had remained impervious to interpretations of this tendency but its enactment in this way gave an opportunity for the nurse to confront him with its occurrence, and help the couple to have an experience of modifying their customary pattern.

Supervisions of nurse and therapists together were a very important part of what enabled this effort to be sustained, especially in diminishing the ever-present tendency for splits to occur between workers in relation to the family's problems. For instance, on several occasions Mrs X indicated to her nurse that she would like to impart special secrets that would be their private knowledge and unknown to the therapists or her husband. Only by insisting that knowledge must be freely shared between workers could such divisions be avoided. During this long period, the pattern continued as it had established itself during the assessment period, without there seeming to be any beginning of movement. The sense of frustration of the workers could be intense, with frequent doubts about the capacity of the couple to make use of the treatment. One important theme to emerge from nurse/therapist supervisions was that the nurse felt burdened by the family and particularly by Mrs X, and that she felt unsupported by the therapists. This was seen to reflect Mrs X's sense of being abandoned and unsupported by her husband, the recognition of the same dynamic between the workers helped to keep the focus explicitly on the conflict between the couple. While this led in part to some improvement in the couple's co-operative functioning, it also led to their underlying mutual hostility becoming more flagrantly manifest.

An important shift seemed to come when the first nurse announced that she would be leaving the hospital. This resulted in both parents being unavoidably confronted with the real loss of a person on whom they had come to depend more than they liked to acknowledge. In this circumstance Mr X's imperviousness to interpretations of his wish for dependency diminished. Just at the time of the nurse's leaving he expressed his sense of need in a session by breaking down in painful sobs; for a brief time, at least, was capable of relinquishing his facade of coping. At first, this seemed too much for Mrs X to bear. She had to leave the session at which it occurred, but she managed to return to voice her fear that now her husband had 'caught her depression' everything would go to pieces: herself as an individual, the marriage and her husband. When this did not occur and the experience was survived, she seemed to some extent to find a new capability in hrself and a greater readiness to remedy the shortcomings of her care for her children. She had been elected to the post of Family Unit chairperson and now improved steadily in her confidence in this capacity.

This juncture could be seen as the culmination of the initial phase in the treatment of the family in which, gradually and against great resistance, both parents were beginning to gain awareness of previously unconscious anxieties which had found expression at first through acting out in the dysfunctional pattern of their relationship. With his partial acknowledgement of fear of being abandoned and left in a despairing and helpless state, there had occurred a necessary dismantling of defences creating the possibility of change in the pattern of mutual projection in the marriage, with the promise of improvement of their joint capacity to function as parents and as a couple.

[16]

Notes on and Vicissitudes of a Confused and Confusing Family

Luigi Caparrotta and *Judith Burman*

In this paper, we describe some aspects of the treatment of an in-patient family, who induced in the workers a sense of confusion and almost of boredom, which was put to therapeutic use by the workers in the therapy of the family. The parents of this family were able to become more separate from each other and then attend to the children's needs. The treatment included both attending to the couple's paranoid fantasies and also providing reality-based support for parent-child differentiation.

The family was composed of Mr P, a 32-year-old computer designer; Mrs P, a 42-year-old housewife; B, a boy of four and a half, and G, a ten-month-old boy. Mrs P referred herself for a consultation. This was an unusual step for a family presentation. She had previously had group therapy as an out-patient at the same hospital; subsequently she was seen for a few sessions with her original therapist.

The complaints that led to her self-referral were 'constant persecutory and paranoid ideas that her husband was unfaithful to her, that he did not love her, that he had "unconscious motivations" which indicated his basic negativity towards her and that he might be homosexual'. The husband, on the other hand, protested vigorously against the reality of these accusations, and seemed to make no indication that he would have liked the marriage to break up. Mrs P was, however, unable to comprehend why he did not want to leave, as she felt she had caused him so much trouble, and she seemed intent on producing evidence which would have proved her point of view.

Both Mr and Mrs P were worried about the effect of their regular constant bickering on the children. Mr and Mrs P had lived together before getting married, when Mrs P was pregnant with B.

Mrs P was one of two siblings. Her parents separated when she was an adolescent. Her mother was a dominating and sometimes frightening woman, who had died of cancer of the kidney a few years before. She remembered her father as quiet and in need of protection; she last saw him in the 1960s. Her brother had problems of a neurotic nature. She claimed that she was sexually abused by him when she was 13, which she recalled with horror. Mr P was the only child of living parents. His mother was described as strong-willed, overpowering and over-possessive. His father, of Jewish descent, was described as subdued and dominated by his own father. Mr P had difficulty in mixing with his peers and shied away from any activity or sport involving competition. He regarded his wife as an extrovert character who brought him out of his shell. However, he also experienced her as very controlling and demanding.

The children did not show any major signs of disturbance in their own right. B was developing signs of mistrust, stemming from his mother's suspiciousness. It was thought that his mother was preventing him from reality testing and gaining mastery of these feelings. G's delayed weaning was limiting his capacity to take interest and develop curiosity in the environment beyond his mother.

In the assessment home visit, the nurse readily detected the difficulty of involving Mr P, while Mrs P readily conveyed the urgency to have help. It was then felt that, with Mrs P's problems of mistrust, the experience in the hospital community of sharing household duties and the care of the children with other mothers might make her pathology more available to the therapy, and hence facilitate some treatment process.

Assessment after the first month

From the outset, both therapists and nurse shared reservations about Mrs P's idealization of treatment and her inability to let it be of use to her and her family.

The result of the assessment was to focus as follows:
(1) To help Mrs P get in touch with and integrate the part of herself which she projected onto her husband.
(2) To help Mr P to become aware of his anger and contempt towards women.
(3) To achieve in each of them a separate identity as parents, and challenge the fantasy that being separate individuals would lead to disintegration.

Experience on admission

Mrs P was quite ill on admission. It was felt that she wanted treatment because she seemed to have had glimmerings that she was affecting the children, and that they were at risk of experiencing something dangerous, i.e. an arrest of their development. Nonetheless, her delusions took the form of projecting dangerousness into her husband, in her fears of his threatened violence to the children and his infidelity to her. The children were both at critical phases for her: the baby needed to be weaned some time soon and the older boy was due to start primary school.

Early stage of treatment

A pattern soon emerged in which Mrs P kept her sense of dangerousness encapsulated in the marital violence. The emotional battering at weekends and strained relations with her husband in the week confirmed the paranoid anxieties aroused for her in situations of intimacy. She kept herself essentially apart from people, eating alone and never using public transport.

Mrs P was difficult to treat directly in conjoint psychotherapy, and indeed in psychotherapy. This was because her idealization, as well as her envy of it, stood in the way of her using it. It soon became painful both for her and for us to acknowledge that psychotherapy could not take the place of the ordinary mothering and fathering. This was an issue which was maintained all the way through; indeed the nurse was not allowed to be part of this process, but made to feel left out, almost to the point of being redundant. Mrs P, in fact, was always putting off and deferring and not making anybody aware of the degree of her fears, so that the nurse could not manage to become acquainted with these fears. This was possibly to defend herself against enormous issues of dependency which she could not bear to disclose.

Focussing on difficulties in physical intimacy gave some sense of direction. This relieved what had become, after five to six months in the hospital, psychotherapy encounters which were generally sterile and came close to boredom. This focus led to renewed prominence being given to Mr P, viewed as an ineffectual man with passively expressed conflicts towards mother. One felt that his confronting her would have engaged with her aggression and would have had the best hope of counteracting her tendency to regress into madness.

Later stage of treatment

It was only six months later that a treatment review came to recognize how much their own unresolved oedipal problems, particularly Mrs P's, had stopped them from functioning as a family. This led to modifications and more specific co-ordination of the therapy with the nursing, by offering a monthly meeting between the nurse, the therapist, the parents and the children, to highlight the parents' role.

This made it possible to broaden the focus to encompass the fathering, the mother's weaning of the young son and the reconstitution of a family setting where resentment about professionals and authority figures could be safely worked with.

More direct aggression also became generated for the first time in Mr P towards the therapists. Mr P experienced defiance and competitiveness when he felt his fathering was being looked at. This was however, thought to be less threatening approach to him than taking up their joint sexual difficulties.

Admission can then be seen to have averted a chaotic state of affairs which Mrs P unconsciously fostered, where the authority of the parents was overthrown and the guiding principle was the children's arbitrary wishes. For example, there was the older boy's inclination to choose father's seat in family meetings and to openly exclude him.

The therapy sessions continued, but they were laboured, with an apparent sterility and lifelessness in terms or linking of achieving understanding of either Mr or Mrs P's personality make-up, or their interaction with each other. What had to be consistently tolerated, beyond the idealization of psychotherapy, was Mrs P's hatred of being observed, and the narcissistic humiliation it caused her. It became clear, as one had expected, how the precariousness of the couple's mutual self-esteem had inhibited any movement towards separation and individuation. The couple re-enacted this in the separation issues around the ending of treatment. Throughout the entire period of admission, the couple were beset by doubts that the hospital would continue to persevere with them. Hence our proposal of a three months' leaving date, which served to confound this fantasy that they would end by provoking us to get rid of them suddenly, or that we would not let them know.

Gradually, through the nursing work, Mrs P came to have more adult expectations of herself, whilst her 'precious' position in the hospital community and her family was challenged. The child therapist provided her with some realistic feedback on B and G's development, on the phases of development reasonably negotiated. It was pointed out to Mrs P that B's aggressive tendencies might be helpfully dealt with by providing appropriate play material through which he might more safely discharge aggressive feelings. B was now settled in school and G more or less weaned, indicating the mother's greater tolerance of the children's movement towards independence.

Although it was not apparent at the time, the follow-up six months after discharge indicated that some change process was generated.

The husband showed greater independence from Mrs P, letting her know that he considered leaving her, or in any case that he felt like it. He took a short holiday on his own. This demonstrated to her his capacity for being separate which she wanted to deny, and which temporarily dumbfounded her. Her omnipotence over her family and over the hospital was substantially challenged. By now the sense of danger in the children's developing independence, and her suspicion of evil intent in other people had dissipated.

Understandably, the idea of discharge rather than her experience in the patient community now preoccupied Mrs P far more. Leaving the hospital was tremendously feared. This was eventually an experience she handled in a split way, conceding less feeling towards the male therapist, while reserving tearful dependence for the nurses and the female therapist.

Conclusion

One could say that this admission in a co-ordinated way served to help modify Mrs P's very frightening inner world, one in which her image of herself as a woman was damaged and distorted by her partial identification with a failing mother. She defended against these fears by omnipotently reconstructing an identity as an ideal mother. Therefore, she kept observing both herself as a mother and the development of her children, rather than experiencing them and accepting her failures.

The staff worked with her resulting deadness of affect and fostered some spontaneity by exposing the conflicts of aggressive withholding. When confronted with these issues, she became more aware of how this could be tolerated, and then perceived her husband and children's capacity for independence as benign, and belonging to them, rather than the destructive consequence of her omnipotent control.

Nevertheless, we could see that what we still had to struggle with to the end was her chronicity and identity as a patient while she was in treatment. From this, she drew 'psychological weapons' in order to unconsciously undermine the therapists' attempt to be therapeutically effective. What we had needed to make an impact on was her narcissistic omniscient facade, with its slippery quality, which shifted from a 'blunt, blasé' attitude to an almost 'naive' one.

The encounter with the hospital would seem to have been experienced essentially as productive, since it could be looked back on as an experience of consistency with which the couple were able to identify. The effect of a follow-up appointment as a means of evaluating the experience of admission with the therapists enabled them to see their independence as more co-operatively achieved, rather than stolen or reached by over-turning and spurning the hospital work.

One last aspect of this was the couple's wish to share with us how they valued the chance to come back and reflect with us on what leaving had been like.

[17]

Facilitating a Child's Removal into Foster Care

Irene Wineman-Marcus

THE PURPOSE OF this paper is to illustrate how the in-patient Family Unit provided the setting for the assessment, treatment and eventual separation of an extremely precarious mother/child dyad.

A brief summary of the relevant history is given. Our main focus is on the treatment plans that were designed to facilitate the viability of this mother/child relationship and the failure of these plans due to an inability to keep the child, Simon, safe from his mother Penny's abusive behaviour. Finally, we will discuss the work done to prepare Simon for placement in a foster home.

All this will be described from the unique perspective of the in-patient facility which provides ongoing contact with other patients, nursing and medical staff, and child psychotherapists, all of whom contribute towards the understanding and monitoring, but most importantly, the mutually reinforcing treatment of the case.

As this paper is based on the work done by the child psychotherapist on the unit, my emphasis will be largely child-centred, and although some aspects of Penny's pathology and individual treatment will be touched on, this will be only in as far as they pertained to the mother/child relationship.

Finally, some follow-up material will be given which illustrates how even though the original aims of the treatments could not be achieved, the team work on the Unit allowed for some measure of success and optimism, at least regarding the child's future.

HISTORY OF THE PROBLEM

Penny had been depressed since the birth of Simon. She felt hostile toward the baby and would occasionally throw him in the cot. She also felt like strangling him. In describing Simon's early years, Penny's affect was either flat or irritated. She commented that he slept through the night from two weeks onwards, but added, 'because he was so exhausted from crying all day'. In the same vein, Penny reported that Simon was only breastfed for two weeks because 'he was never satisfied'.

Penny was seen by a psychiatrist for the first time when Simon was 8 months old. She continued to be depressed. The main problem was seen as being within the mother/child relationship. The psychiatrist reported that Simon was a difficult baby who rejected Penny's efforts to care for him and who behaved better when his grandmother, aunt or father took over his care. The difficulties between Penny and her son were aggravated by the problems in Penny's marriage as well as within each parent; in turn, adding tension to the already existing marital problems.

Penny was admitted to the hospital two months later, during which time her husband left her and the marital home. Simon was watched over by Penny's twin sister. Penny attempted several overdoses at this time as well as attempting to cut her wrists and her throat. Following discharge from the hospital, Penny returned to her mother's house. The marital home was up for sale and Simon was on the 'at risk' register. The local authorities attempted to take Simon into care because of concern not only for Penny's aggressive feeling towards Simon, but also because Penny's sister was expecting a baby and it was not considered in Simon's or the new baby's best interest for Simon to remain in the sister's home. However, Penny contested the care order and was granted custody for a trial period.

It was at this point that the local authorities contacted the

Cassel Hospital because of their concern about Simon's safety if Penny were the sole caretaker.

Aims of treatment and treatment plans

Penny and Simon were admitted into the Family Unit with the aim of offering treatment to Penny to help her with her difficulties and with the aim of reducing the risk to her child.

More specifically, several issues were of concern and would have to be addressed if maximum use was to be made of the Family Unit by mother and child. There was concern among the nursing staff about Penny's dependency and the passive way she agreed to enter the hospital. They were concerned that Penny should not just use the hospital as a place to take over the caretaking of Simon, as a replacement for her sister and mother. From the child's perspective, there was concern for his wellbeing not only in terms of his physical safety, but also because he had been removed from his familiar caretakers. At this point, it was unclear whether it was Penny or Simon's grandmother who fulfilled the role of Simon's psychological mother. Furthermore, in all considerations of this mother/child dyad, the issue of whether Simon would eventually have to be placed in care had to be taken into account. Penny was offered individual treatment for herself with a medical therapist in the hope that if she could make enough changes, particularly in the realm of understanding and not projecting the 'bad' part of herself onto Simon, there might be some possibility of the two of them remaining together. It was also hoped, if this were not possible, that individual treatment might enable Penny to give up Simon of her own accord and make enforced removal of Simon into care unnecessary.

The child psychotherapist's role in the treatment plan was not to offer Simon individual treatment, but to facilitate the mother/child interactions. When the mother and child had initially been seen together, it was reported that 'there is little sign that Penny can perceive Simon's needs or behaviour as anything except as an interference of her own needs'. The mother and child were thus to be seen together in order to:

1. Help mother see Simon as the two year old he was.
2. Work as a mediator between the two in order to enable the mother to decipher the child's language and the feelings behind the communications.
3. Facilitate Penny's perception of Simon as an individual, who was not just the externalized bad and messy parts of herself.

Working with the two of them would also enable the child psychotherapist to keep a close personal monitor of Simon's development and his difficulties, giving the opportunity for direct interventions with Simon whenever necessary.

Furthermore, the child psychotherapist would work closely with the nursing staff, who had more contact with Penny during everyday activities such as the playgroup, mealtimes and bedtimes. Thus the staff could mutually enhance their understanding and hence the adequacy of their interventions with the mother and child.

THE HOSPITAL AS A PLACE OF SAFETY

All the previously elucidated plans depended on the hospital's ability to keep Simon safe and contain Penny's aggressive impulses toward him. At first, although not officially a 'place of safety', there was some confidence among the staff that the structure of the hospital (the group meetings, the intense relationship with the nurses assigned to each patient and the use of other patients to caretake and monitor), would enable Penny to use others to help her to keep Simon safe from her own impulses. However, after a very few months in the hospital, although those working directly with Penny were not feeling extremely anxious for Simon's safety, the patients, nursing and medical staff not as directly involved were becoming increasingly concerned. It became clear through discussions in meetings with the Family Unit that Penny's intense dependency needs induced in those working more directly with her a wish to mother and protect her, and hence some denial of her danger to Simon. The individual work done in the two-month period had highlighted the fact that the only person whom Penny felt comfortable in expressing her rage and anger at was Simon. This situation necessitated clarifying; who was responsible for Simon's safety? It became apparent that the social worker who had put Simon on the 'at risk' register, and who had been and would be the mother and child's social worker when they returned home, was the one who should be responsible for Simon's safety.

The social worker thus became an important part of the work done in the hospital. She was involved in all decision-making meetings about Penny and Simon and took part in considering, for example, the sleeping arrangements of the mother and child. These were designed to keep the mother away from Simon at night time, and to allow another patient to take care of Simon's needs. She was also the one who, in consultation with the Unit staff, had to make the decision as to whether Simon's safety was in jeopardy and if, or when, he would have to be put into foster care. This mutually supportive arrangement also meant that as far as was possible within the limitations imposed by the law and the courts, the social worker was concerned to implement our recommendations and to ultimately keep us appraised of the results of our work outside of the hospital.

Description of Simon

Simon was an attractive 2½ year old with blond curly hair, big brown eyes and a perpetually serious expression. At the beginning of his hospital stay he was seen as being orderly, organized, and precise, with little warmth. In the playroom, he began by being watchful and quiet, but soon progressed to extremely aggressive behaviour. He would push the other toddlers or pull their hair. Mothers would then retaliate with the same action. When angry with his mother for frustrating his wishes (for example, he would want to jump off a chair), he would scream loudly with no tears. He did not hit his mother; instead he would bang his own head. In the playroom, Simon would often be seen playing by himself. These games seemed to involve an identification with his idealized grandfather and father. Simon would drive his grandfather's coach or his father's tractor, using pretend keys; he would smoke crayons instead of a pipe.

During the time at the hospital, Simon woke frequently at night with nightmares of fire engines and ambulances. It appeared that the nights were particularly frightening for him; he would say things like 'Mummy bye bye, Mummy dead'. Nights were also the time when his mother couldn't contain her aggressive impulses. She found it hard to comfort him when he woke at night, once putting a duvet cover over his head to try and keep him quiet.

Another form of behaviour that was of extreme importance, because of its adverse effect on his mother, was Simon's frequent requests for a drink or the potty. These were, of course, intimately related to one another.

Penny had reported at the initial interviews that she had always been concerned about Simon's toilet training. She had begun to try to put him on the pot from age five months onwards. A great deal of nursing work was done around helping Penny toilet train Simon in a consistent and appropriate fashion. Simon had become relatively clean and dry during the initial part of their stay in the hospital; however, any accidents would throw Penny into a rage. Toileting eventually broke down as Penny became more stressed. Furthermore, she had the same difficulty taking him out because of her embarrassment at his using the pot in public. All of these issues caused great tension between mother and son.

Treatment

Because of our fears for Simon's safety, treatment which was aimed at facilitating the mother/child interaction lasted only a few months. The work which took place once a week involved helping Penny limit Simon in an appropriate manner, elaborating for both the mother and the child the fears he seemed to suffer from at night, and attempting to encourage Penny to play with Simon rather than watching for any misdemeanour he might do.

One of the main areas of work during the brief treatment was on Simon's aggression. This was particularly worrying, because he had begun to head bang and because of the nightmares from which he suffered. Verbalizing Simon's anger when he became frustrated and began to scream and hurt himself was surprisingly effective. The mere act of understanding this child's feelings and making them conscious had dramatic effects on his behaviour. Thus in one session when his mother had said 'no' to something that he wanted to do, Simon stopped screaming, leaned towards his mother and then away from her. I could point out that although he wanted a cuddle from Mummy to make sure she was not angry with him, he was so angry with her he had to move away. In this vein a great deal of work was done on Simon's fears of the noise of ambulances and fire engines. Simon would verbalize in conjunction with the noises 'Mummy bye bye, Mummy dead'. It became possible to link for Simon his fears that Mummy would go away and die, especially at night time, and his own anger with her and wish that she would go away and not say 'no, Simon' any more, and not pinch or hit him. We were also able to elaborate the distinction between his pleasure at seeing his mother after the playgroup, the good Mummy and his fear of the witch Mummy that came at night time and scared him.

Through the course of these few months it became clear that Simon was in many ways an intact child; he was at the anal phase of development which was an appropriate age for him to be in. There was some evidence that he had the potential to move into the phallic stage. This ability seemed based largely on his identification with his grandfather. However, it also became clear in sessions that Simon withdrew into fantasy play as a means of escaping from his mother. This fantasy of grandfather seemed to keep Simon self-contained and separate from his mother. Simon would also speak in sessions of his cousin who was only a baby. It became apparent that he was jealous of this cousin because he had been told that his cousin was grandad's baby and he, Simon, was grandad's big boy. Simon quite clearly wished to be grandad's baby, indicating that grandfather represented not only a potential oedipal figure for rivalry and later identification, but more importantly that grandfather represented the idealized nurturing figure towards whom he did not feel the intense ambivalence that he did towards his mother.

However, Simon did attempt to be close to his mother and gain her attention. As mentioned before, he would repeat frequently throughout the playgroup 'Mummy coming'. Besides his obvious relief at her arrival, there was also his pleasure in being with her which, unfortunately, was not reciprocated by his mother. Simon's incessant demands on his mother for his bottle or the pot were attempts to connect with her, to gain her attention and have some measure of control over her; they did not seem to be a wish to battle with mother. However, despite the work done in conjoint sessions, the mother continued to be extremely provoked by Simon's demands.

Furthermore, in Penny's individual treatment she was being required to confront some of the realistic difficulties that she would have to face if she wasn't a patient at the hospital. That is, she had to find a place for herself and Simon to live and to spend some time there together over the weekends. This, of course, required liaison with the social worker in the area to ensure Simon's safety.

Issues around the weekends became central to the mother and child sessions. However, over time, the entire staff and patients became increasingly anxious about Simon's safety on these weekends. As Penny became more in touch with her feelings of emptiness when without adult support, the more lonely, hostile, depressed aspects of herself began to break through, usually in the form of aggressive outbursts toward Simon. In the face of this, Simon began to appear less resilient and more withdrawn.

It was at this point that the staff involved with the case recommended that Simon no longer visit with his mother on weekends and suggested the possibility that Simon be taken temporarily into care. However, it was still hoped that we could delay putting this into effect until Penny could come to this decision herself. This was particularly because of the fear of what harm Penny would do to herself if she didn't have Simon with her.

However, within the next month when Penny and Simon's social worker visited to assess their situation again from her perspective of Simon's safety, she felt that we could no longer wait for Penny to decide to give up Simon, but to move towards foster placement for Simon.

Recommendations for placement

Following the meeting with the social worker, the following recommendations were laid out as being maximally beneficial to Simon if they could be practically arranged:

1. That there be some time to work on Simon's removal to foster parents. That he be given an opportunity to visit with the foster parents once or twice possibly with his mother and the social worker, and stay overnight and/or a weekend to get used to the people.

2. It was further recommended that once Simon was placed with the foster parents, Penny would be allowed to visit relatively frequently at first in order that Simon would know that she was still alive. The reason for this recommendation was Simon's belief in the power of his aggressive wishes and his association of goodbyes and death. It was feared that Simon's nightmares, which were related to his aggressive wishes, would increase unless he had some reassurance that she was still alive. It was considered that this contact would not be too detrimental to Simon establishing a relationship with his foster parents, particularly once Simon felt secure in his new environment.

These recommendations were given with the understanding that they were dependent on Penny's mental state and on her ability to tolerate Simon's presence in the hospital after the court decision, as well as considerations for Simon's safety.

In the event, a few days prior to the court hearing we were informed that if the decision of the court was to put Simon into care, he would be placed immediately with the foster parents and would not be allowed to return to the hospital.

WORK TOWARDS SEPARATION

The knowledge that Simon would not be returning to the hospital if the court decided he was to be taken into care had profound effects on the whole Family Unit. Many families on the Unit had children who had been in temporary care. For many families, putting the child into care was a threat and wish on the part of the parents and yet, of course, also a fear in terms of what it would mean to that nuclear family. Furthermore, many of the families had been intimately involved with Penny and Simon. Some mothers had had the role of caring for Simon at night time to avoid his mother going in; others had supported Penny in all her attempts to look after Simon. Many of the patients were angry with the social worker, who was a little-known figure to the patients and hence easy to direct their anger and hostility towards. However, they were also angry with Penny's psychiatrists for putting her under pressure to function on her own at weekends and, to some extent, with the nursing staff. The child psychotherapist seemed to escape this anger and upset, probably because she clearly represented the best interests of the child; no one felt secure about Simon's safety with Penny. They just felt upset and furious for Penny. Furthermore, Penny had always maintained a good relationship with the child psychotherapist, as the one who would understand and respond to the child part of herself. Penny's inability to respond to Simon's needs without feeling that they intruded and negated her own needs had always been one of the limitations of treatment.

The lack of blaming of the child psychotherapist left her in a unique position to deal with the issue that was troubling both the staff and patients. How do you tell a two year old what is going to happen to him so he can assimilate it?

In the event, when mother and Simon came for their session the therapist chose to tell Simon a story. It was the story of a little boy whose mother loved him very much, but she couldn't look after him because she was so scared she would hurt him although she didn't want to. The story told of the foster family that he was going to, the names and ages of their children and that he was going to live there not because he was naughty or bad, but because his mother wanted him to be safe.

It was hoped that this story would connect with some of Simon's concerns, for example, that his mother did love him and that he wasn't being rejected because he was bad or angry; that his mother was also a good, caring mother who wanted him safe and not just the witch-like attacking mother whom he had seen so much of in recent weeks. It was hoped that de-emphasizing the purely negative mother and allowing for the ambivalence would give Simon a better basis to separate from his mother and eventually learn to deal with her unavailability.

In fact, the story had a far greater impact than was anticipated, for two reasons:

1. Because the story was non-judgemental, Penny was able to hear it and repeat it to the other mothers who were very involved in how Simon was to be prepared for the separation.
2. The structure of the Unit and the involvement of the patients and staff meant that, having been given a way to tell Simon about the separation, they too wanted to use it to help prepare him.

Thus Simon heard this story many times in the next few days; as a bedtime story, in the playgroup and so on. Interestingly, the story seemed to prepare not only Simon, but also the rest of the patients, who felt they now had a way of looking at the situation which did not require anyone to be judged as bad, just unhappy and troubled. This was of great importance to them because of their own family situation.

Aftermath

The court decision was for Simon to be removed to foster care. Penny was to remain in treatment at the hospital for a time, seeing the medical therapist for her individual treatment and the child psychotherapist to talk about her fortnightly visits to Simon. The visits were always extremely difficult for Penny; she would also wait around the foster parents' house when she did not have a visit arranged, hoping to get a glimpse of Simon. There was a deep concern at the hospital for Penny's suicidal potential now that she did not have Simon.

However, fortunately, the picture was not so bleak for Simon. A month after being taken into foster care the foster mother on her own accord sent the social worker a report of Simon's progress. Because of the very close work that had taken place between the social worker and the hospital, the social worker sent the hospital a copy of thc report. It was a simple, yet moving account of Simon's adjustment: Initially, there was a continuation of his nightmares and although Simon no longer head banged he still had a tendency to hurt himself in accidents. The account also described Simon as saying 'Mummy bye bye, Mummy better now'. Although only a hypothesis, one could understand this as the gradual fading out of the scary witch-like mother that was aroused by her aggressive behaviour towards him; thus, Mummy was nicer and better. Simon was not as disturbed by his mother's visits as by those of the social worker. This would fit in with the social worker being seen as the one who removed him from his mother, which is what the social worker had to do in the courtroom. In many ways, although it was uncomfortable for the social worker, this view enabled Simon to preserve his mother as the good person. It was evident from the foster mother's account that she was able to tolerate and accept Simon's regressive and infantile behaviour. She could also accept his upset. 'Last night, Simon woke and cried really hard. I took him into our room and just held him. He cried for a good ten minutes. It was as if it just had to come out.'

By the twenty-second day of Simon's stay two incidents that his foster mother quoted gave some insights into Simon's adjustment, particularly taking into account his age. The foster mother wrote that when she went to the toilet, Simon would say 'knock,

knock, Simon here'. She also commented that Simon said 'Hidihi!' a lot. There are, of course, various possible interpretations of this behaviour. One interpretation is that Simon needed to make sure his foster mother to whom he must have felt a growing attachment, had not gone or disappeared. Furthermore, the 'Hidihi!' seemed to represent this same struggle with the disappearing, yet appearing person. The emphasis in this example was on the pleasure of reuniting and of saying 'Hi' to the person.

Just before the foster mother closed her account she reported that Simon told her that he did not like her. This seemed to be a very positive sign in the relationship in that Simon could express both his liking and disliking for the same person. He no longer had to split these feelings as he had to with his mother, nor did he have to turn his anger on himself as he had when he banged his own head. The foster mother had clearly become a safe person who he could have ambivalent feelings towards without violent repercussions. This was confirmed by the final entry, where the foster mother wrote 'I think Simon has accepted us. After breakfast he used the toilet'. (Toilet training had eventually broken down in the hospital with Penny's difficulty with responding to Simon's demands for the pot). 'It will be pants today.' Thus, from Simon's point of view there was now a secure environment and a person whom he wanted to please enough to entrust his body products to. It was Simon's newly reacquired toilet training that told us how he was adjusting, more eloquently than any report or communication could have done.

Conclusion

This case has been largely described and elaborated from the point of view of the child and his eventual adjustment to his foster placement. This had meant that the details of Penny's individual treatment and complexities of some of the difficulties in nursing her have not been detailed.

However, despite the narrower focus, our intention has been to illustrate how it was only within the Family Unit, with ongoing nursing work, other patient involvement and eventual involvement of the local authority social worker, that the work of the medical therapist and child psychotherapist could have been attempted.

At the time of entry into the Cassel Hospital, this mother/child dyad had no other facility that would have offered them the opportunity to assess the viability of the relationship. If they had stayed in 'home territory' Penny would have continued to use her extended family as caretakers for Simon. She would have probably gone in and out of mental hospitals and Simon would have been moved back and forth between his grandparents and his aunt. The lack of clarity as to who was Simon's psychological parent at the time of entry into the hospital is indicative of the changes in his caretakers. Furthermore, although no mention has been made of it in the body of the paper, none of the professionals who met with the aunt and the grandparents felt that they would be suitable parents for Simon, because the family pathology was extreme. It was also considered that even from Penny's point of view, it would have been more destructive to her to place Simon in the care of her twin sister than in the care of a stranger.

The work done on the Family Unit took place under the constant shadow of anxiety for Simon's safety. Much of the nursing work focussed around plans with Penny to help her keep Simon safe. Much of the time, she was unable to use her nurses or other patients to stop her from abusing Simon. Initially, those working closely with Penny denied the extent of the danger to Simon. It took the involvement of the entire Unit and the Unit meetings to bring it into the open and highlight this danger.

With the greater awareness of the danger to the fact that the hospital could not act as a 'place of safety', it became clear that the individual work with Penny seemed to put her more in touch with the disturbed aspects of her personality and increased the danger to Simon. Furthmore, despite the work done with the mother/child dyad, it could not counteract the effect of the individual pathology. It was at this point that the decision was made that Simon would have to be placed in care.

However, what conjoint sessions did in some measure achieve was a consolidation of the dyad. They helped put the mother more into the position of the primary psychological object for this child. It could be argued that although Simon had to separate from mother when he went into foster care he now, at least, had a primary specific object to separate from. Thus, although Simon had intensely ambivalent feelings towards his mother, these would hopefully be worked through at a later stage; at least they were directed at one person rather than a diffuse amalgam of aunts and grandmother. Grandfather/father, who seemed to be possible primary psychological parents to Simon, were both in reality very unavailable; his father visited rarely and never alone, and his grandfather was away from home a great deal for work. Thus, although they were idealized figures for Simon, they could not adequately fulfil the role of primary caretakers or psychological parents for him.

The mother/child sessions also served the more unusual functions of alleviating some of Simon's anxiety through the understanding of the meaning of his nightmares, verbalizing his affects, and interpreting the defences against, in particular, his aggressive wishes. However, perhaps the most important piece of work was that done after the danger to Simon could no longer be tolerated by the hospital or the local authority social worker and he was placed in foster care. Moreover, the one or two sessions that were available prior to the court hearing would have been totally ineffective as a means of preparing Simon. To have told the story described previously without any other follow-up would have had little reverberations on a child so young. Thus, it was the feeling of the story within the context of the Family Unit that made it so effective. It could then serve as the stone thrown into a pond that had a ripple effect, which ultimately was what impacted on Simon and Penny. This allowed for some measure of resolution on the Unit, which although not of a longlasting sort, particularly for

Penny, enabled Simon to leave the Unit with some feeling of calm. With the help of the obviously very caring foster mother who took Simon in, and through the work done on the Unit, Simon had the opportunity to cope better with what might otherwise have been a devastatingly traumatic episode.

Acknowledgement: Irene Wineman-Marcus would like to thank Paul Marcus, Ph.D., for his invaluable assistance in writing this paper.

[18]

The In-patient's View of the Cassel Experience

Vivien Biggs

> 'It struck me as awful . . . yes awful, awful; this long corridor and these rooms and kids everywhere.'
>
> 'That was a great chance I was given . . . and the most valuable thing of the whole time was the life with all those other people, and the time to make friends honestly. Give me a Firm meeting now, and I would really use it.'
>
> (Two ex-patients of the Family Unit)

THIS PROJECT WAS undertaken because I wanted to study how patients perceived their experience of life in the Family Unit, and compare their perceptions with ex-patients' memories of it after leaving the hospital. Although it was a small project, I understood that no study of this kind had been made before at the hospital.

The study was based on interviews with 13 inpatients, ranging in age from 11-41 (the rest were too young); seven members of staff (three medical psychotherapists and four nurses); and 17 ex-patients from 25 families. The other members of these families either did not respond or refused to be interviewed. One of the latter wrote: 'I'm immensely grateful to the Cassel for the support it gave me and my family at a very difficult time. But it *was* a difficult time, and a painful one, and not one that I would want to recall in any detail. I hope that you will understand.'

I used a combination of research methods to meet certain objectives: to record my own observations; to collect data on how patients experienced life on the Unit; to compare these views with those of ex-patients, and to consider how staff thought patients experienced their life in hospital. A modified participant observer approach, and non-standardized interviews with open-ended questions satisfied these requirements, and were sufficiently flexible to accommodate any emerging hypotheses.

The in-patient group was a heterogeneous one with diagnoses ranging from multiple problem families and marital pathology to individuals with schizoid, obsessional and hysterical symptoms. There were two cases of puerperal breakdown and one of possible non-accidental injury to a child.

The ex-patient group whom I interviewed similarly had had a variety of problems and symptoms. There were, in addition, inadequate and socially deprived patients, and one patient who was described unclinically but colourfully as a 'Kensington bitch'.

The ex-patients who did not wish to be interviewed had most of the same problems but on inspection of their hospital records, an additional common factor emerged. They were nearly all patients with 'secrets' which they had not revealed during their stay; most of them had left with many of their problems unresolved. I speculate therefore that they had no wish to be any more open with me than they had been in hospital.

The interviews covered aspects of patient and staff experiences on the Unit and in the wider community. These included their expectations of life on the Unit before admission; their first impressions; sharing living accommodation and facilities with other families; caring for and supporting other adults and their children; receiving care and support from other patients; violence and aggression on the Unit and its handling; having to take official responsibility in the hospital; and the long-term effects of being in hospital as a family.

When invited to make further comments, almost without exception all the patients and ex-patients wanted to make some statement about the relationship between the community life and psychotherapy, and which was the major influence on their recovery.

Margaret Mead (1950, p.206) has said, 'One of the problems which confronts the field anthropologist, and which by its very nature can never be solved, is that the only perfect language in which to describe the behaviour of the Apache or the Eskimo is the Apache or the Eskimo language'. Accordingly, I learnt while at the Cassel to use Cassel language – a sub-cultural 'ideolect', including a simplified form of psychoanalytic imagery, some psychoanalytic vocabulary, together with unusual terms for areas, activities and relationships peculiar to the hospital. This was not only of use to me in the hospital, but also in relating to the ex-patients.

The interviews were all tape recorded with the permission of the interviewees. Very few people said they were anxious about them, and many seemed reassured that no-one in the hospital would hear the recording. Some of the interviews were as short as 20 minutes; some as long as 45 minutes.

Ethical dilemmas

A problem confronting research in the field of human emotions must be: how can we avoid harming the people under study? Any such research carries with it the danger of damaging the individual's self-esteem and invading his or her privacy. I was anxious to avoid loss of dignity to the people whose perspectives I was studying; however, being a participant observer and declaring openly my intention to study and record the experience of patients seemed to avoid fears of deception.

Confidentiality was another ethical issue. After discussion with staff and patients, I agreed that nothing would be revealed to staff without a patient's prior permission. In the event, this was a problem in only two cases; one patient revealed fears about another patient, and agreed with me to raise this at a meeting. Another discussed her intention to discharge herself and agreed that I could discuss this with her therapist, which I did.

Another dilemma presented itself in the case of the ex-patients. I emphasized that this was a purely private study and not an official follow-up by the hospital. However, as I was still in touch with the hospital, I was prepared (with their permission) to give purely social news or messages to staff who had known then. All of them agreed, although none sent messages. They showed much more interest in news of other ex-patients whom they had known, with whom I was in touch.

Epistemological issues

The greatest problem in this area is to decide what we can know about reality. Is subjectivity a negation of objectivity, or is all knowledge edited and ordered by the observer?

In choosing a standardized interview technique with open-ended questions, I allowed the respondents to express themselves in their own language, at their own speed, and at whatever level was appropriate to them.

In recording the views of my interviewees in their own idiom, I hoped to acknowledge the whole person, responsible, capable of choosing what he or she says, and with valid perceptions. I did not think it would increase my understanding of the patients' experience of the Unit to look at it through a haze of interpretations.

Findings of the study

Patient interaction and relationships

Nearly all patients said that they arrived in the Family Unit with minimal information about what to expect. Many of them said that they could not comprehend what they were told because of their disturbed state before admission. 'I was too groggy-headed'; 'I was so involved in my own state', 'I was so screwed up', were typical comments. One woman said, 'I was very overwhelmed with the idea of coming in anyway, and extremely depressed about coming into . . . what I though was a psychiatric hospital. So a lot of what I was told didn't sink in properly'. The consultant psychotherapist in charge confirmed, 'It's important they know nothing . . . because if they visit the Unit, it gives them an opportunity of organizing their defences against coming in'. Certainly, this official policy seems to have the desired effect. However one patient commented, 'I wanted to come in and see, and I was told categorically "No, you can't"; if I'd seen it, it might have been worse, and yet I felt terribly cheated'.

Several patients had specific reasons for wanting to be admitted, most commonly a desire to remain together as a family. One man said he was told, 'If you three want to stay together this is the only place'. Another man said, 'The main thing I knew was that it was a place which would take families – I didn't want us to be separated'.

Most patients' first impressions on admission were of shock at the 'dirt' and 'disorder' of the Unit, but pleasure at being met officially by another patient, usually the Firm chairman. They said, 'I was horrified at first by the general mess and dirt, but the first thing that happened was that somebody wanted to pick her up . . .'; (the patient is referring to her baby) 'I was pretty horrified . . . so dark and dingy'; 'As we walked through that door and saw that great long corridor, it felt like a prison . . . all the people, people and children, all around'.

However, many said that they felt relief: 'Soon as you get in and meet the Firm chairman, someone to talk to straight away'; 'I found it very offputting. I felt very insecure. But it was up to the other patients to gather round and look after one'.

So patient support is immediately felt, and it was clear from what they said that patients had a sense of relief and safety in the company of others who were expected to be involved in caring for them. An ex-seaman commented, 'It's like a youth hostel or a trip to sea'. Other patients said, 'I liked the people around me';

'Very often I was coasting round looking for where there were other people . . . and it was usually in the kitchen'; 'If you wanted someone to talk to, they were always there'.

An ex-patient, now living a fairly isolated life, reflected nostalgically: 'There is one thing there . . . people are honest and friendly, and there's a very nice feeling . . . lots of people around, but you can just sit back and cry if you want to. Yet, I'd like to go back now I'm well again'.

In a sense this little community comes to resemble a form of extended family. The close links of kin are absent of course, but the descriptions given by patients of their mutual support and care of each other's children is curiously reminiscent of those by people in other cultures who live in close association with their extended family. I observed that adults would care for the Unit's children with a remarkable degree of common concern and affection. Their attitudes to these children, not their own, with whom they lived and whose problems they knew well, was caring and uninhibited. It reminded me forcibly of African and West Indian families where multiple mothering is a common feature. One mother expressed it in exactly these terms: 'When I first went in, I couldn't ask other people to help . . . I felt they were my kids, and I should be looking after them . . . It takes a bit of time to get into the extended family idea, but in the end it helped me to separate from them.'

A father commented: 'I would expect my children to be disciplined by anyone on the Unit, if they were seen to do wrong.' The children themselves clearly accepted care and discipline from anybody on the Unit, and the parents, almost without exception, felt that the children benefitted from it. A single mother said, 'She benefitted enormously . . . from the care and all the people . . . always being picked up and cuddled . . . an enormous amount of life. She'd been very isolated before, and I'd been depressed.' Another mother reflected, 'She would go to anybody when she came off Ross' (Ross is the popular name of the Family and Adolescent Unit, named after Dr T. A. Ross, medical director of the Cassel in the 1920s and 30s). 'I suppose the Unit benefits the children . . .

wouldn't it be better to be with grandparents, or is it really much the same thing?'

Indirectly, the mothers, many of whom had found it very difficult before, learned a good deal about how to care for their children, as in an extended family; and as in that setting too, children were not harmed physically, because there was always someone there to prevent things going too far. The reverse was also true; a very protective mother said: 'Seeing the way other people treat their children . . . I am gradually letting him do things a bit more, and I think that over the time that we're here, he will become much more independent.' A father pointed out, 'To know how other children behave is useful. It helps to know what you might expect from your own.' Two ex-patients made the same point: 'Certainly it was helpful to me . . . in fact, I did become a childminder after that'; 'It's very useful now when I go babysitting. It doesn't worry me as it would have done if I hadn't had that experience of being responsible for other people's kids'.

The constant companionship and interaction of the Unit seems to be very important to many patients, whose isolation and loneliness was both a cause and symptom of the distress which brought them into hospital. One mother summed it up: 'It's nice to feel needed. Well, if other people value or need you, it's a boost to your ego and your self-esteem; but what I value most is the ready-made friends and the company. It's there, built-in, whereas at home you're cut off.'

The mutual support which patients give each other is clearly a matter of vital importance to the ideology of the therapeutic community. At a primitive level, as we have seen, the very proximity of other families, their availability and presence at all times affords a form of comfort and security. But patients also use each other more positively for counselling which they both seek and give: 'I would go to a patient . . . always . . . I felt closer to patients . . . I felt at ease with them, because I had helped them, I'd established an easy relationship with most people there'; 'Personally . . . knowing that patients were in the same boat, you felt you got more support from them . . . even if you didn't trust their advice . . . but it helped you sort out your own problems, using others as a background'; 'I felt I wasn't a patient really . . . but I went to see people when I felt down . . . Of course, I went to see a patient, not a member of staff'; 'In actual fact an enormous amount of help comes from other patients. Little things that people said to you . . . just in the course of the day . . . sort of friendship . . . *that's* what you remember helped'.

Giving support and advice clearly is satisfying and pleasurable to most patients. It is often a significant discovery for many people to find an ability in themselves to help and support others in distress. The patients commented: 'I didn't know if it helps really sharing everybody else's problems to such an extent. Quite often I'm so burdened with other people's problems, I've lost sight of my own . . . which may be a good thing, of course . . . I don't know'; 'I think it gives me confidence, and I find it quite rewarding to feel that I'm being useful and I can do things like that'; 'There is an aspect of myself . . . I do that sort of thing because of the gratification . . . in a way you get a kick out of it'; 'I found it quite satisfying, caring for others in distress . . . Yes, very helpful . . . marvellous really . . . before I went I would have run away from any difficult situation'.

One interesting patterm emerged from this part of the study. In-patients were very concerned about their relationship with the staff, whether hostile, dependent, good or bad, and talked at greater length about it. Ex-patients, however, spoke more of the mutual support experienced with other patients. The longer they had been away from the Cassel, the more they spoke of the help they received from other patients, and the care they were able to give. A mother who was discharged five years before the study said: 'That was the most valuable thing in the whole . . . I didn't realize at the time . . . I mean, I thought I was crumbling. It made me realize how much strength I had left compared to the state that some of the other people were in.'

On the subject of rotas, patients differed widely in their views. Some said it was alarming to be with a patient who was confused or unpredictable: 'It can be very frightening . . . the fear of physical violence, you understand . . . you know, real fear'; 'I was scared stiff . . . I don't find it particularly helpful. It's depressing'. But others said: 'I would join in if the person wasn't too upset'; 'If there was a crisis, everybody rallied round'; 'I did it sometimes because it was a duty, but mostly I regarded it as helping friends who were in trouble . . . you know, really sad trouble'.

On the other hand, a few patients, perhaps because of their own difficulties, found it a chore, and one of the most difficult parts of life on the Unit: 'I'm very reluctant to try to help people . . . everything I say is empty and meaningless'; 'People who had been . . . you know . . . troublesome and difficult . . . you really felt, why should you give even more of yourself to this person, who was giving nothing to anybody else, never mind you . . . you did feel a certain resentment'.

Staff/patient relationships and staff roles

In this area, I found that my own first impressions were shared by the patients. I have no doubt that many reasons can be found for the patients' hostile feelings towards staff, and for the irritability and lack of compassion which they perceive in the staff; there is the inevitable dependency, inequalities of status, the sense of failure and hopelessness common to most psychiatric illness, and the need of staff members to reinforce their superior position. I have mentioned elsewhere that I came to recognize that some of the hostility was in fact the expression of reality confrontation common to therapeutic communities, and I have also commented how difficult it is to express the conflicts and tensions inherent in this work in a spirit of humanity and also of honesty. The patients are likely to provoke powerful and primitive feelings in the staff, and defences are likely to be built up against them, denying the full extent of the patients' problems. This is inevitably anti-therapeutic. However, these comments are mine, and arrived at only after some time and a lot of consideration. During my interviews of staff, there seemed to be no hint of hostility or lack of concern towards the patients.

Hostility towards staff was, however, a striking feature of life on the Family Unit from the view of the patients' sub-culture, and almost every patient and ex-patient I interviewed commented upon it: 'I was very self-conscious and very much in awe of the doctors particularly . . . I mean, it was a bit of an invasion, a most extraordinary sensation . . . that tramp, tramp, tramp of the bearded black-suited doctors. I mean you could *never* get used to it'; 'Somehow the staff should share in the life of the patient'; 'I found it very odd that we discussed our problems, but the staff never talked about theirs. None of the staff ever talked about their home lives. If we had known that they had problems, it would have made everything much more normal'.

Not only was the distancing of the staff resented by the patients, but the apparent lack of time which the staff gave to them personally: 'I felt they were very rushed for time, very harrassed . . . that annoyed me extremely. When I first went I used to look for them . . . and then I began not to bother. They hadn't time for you'; 'The staff are not on Ross anything like as much as they should be . . . on Tuesdays, you knew you wouldn't see a nurse all day – and the *anger* you would feel! They were in their meetings all day long, and here were all the patients . . . perhaps all of them in a bad way, and no nurses to call on . . . You really needed them, and you knew other people needed them, but they didn't seem to care'.

The lack of sympathy and understanding, like these other complaints, may reflect the neurosis of the patients, but they were nevertheless a subject of great concern to the patients: 'My main criticism of the Cassel would be that although the place seems streets ahead of . . . anywhere . . . other psychiatric hospitals, there was a lack of sympathy . . . an awareness of people's suffering . . . of the positive side of people . . . their creative side. We are talking about staff. They tended to concentrate on the negative aspects. My own experience of people who are neurotic . . . they often have a lot of creative aspects about them, and find it hard to discover these things about themselves. The staff should help'; 'They [the patients] all talked about important things . . . the best bits of themselves . . . in the kitchen when the staff were out of the way. *They* wouldn't have understood'.

One ex-patient with considerable insight said: 'There was a feeling I'm not very proud of that I would have preferred to be a member of staff. There is a slight . . . not glamour, more status . . . about being a member of staff . . . Something about *forcing* them to care'.

One of the principles of social therapy is that it is a way of overcoming the lack of confidence, the low self-estimate and the over-dependency which all too frequently characterize the patient in the psychiatric hospital. However, some of the patients I interviewed commented somewhat ruefully that, while their confidence was greatly enhanced very often by their interaction with other patients, their relationship with staff was actually anti-therapeutic. One young mother typified the rest: 'The only time I resent other people having anything to do with the children is when I feel thay are completely taking over, or if I feel they are succeeding where a few minutes ago I was failing miserably. Then I mind . . . mostly the patients are all right. Often with the staff I am made to feel inadequate.'

The relationship between staff and patients is highlighted at times when violence breaks out between patients: 'Things were getting very explosive, and it was a quarter of an hour before a member of staff arrived on the scene . . . It did worry me when I thought that someone could have been hurt, and there wouldn't have been a member of staff present'; 'When people get into conflict . . . the staff opt out too much . . . to some extent they want people to sort things out for themselves, but the patients can only go so far, because they have no authority'; 'Although there is violence between patients, the real friction is between staff and patients . . . the violence sort of highlights it'.

One community within another

The Family Unit was, at that time, to some extent a self-contained community. It was physically separated from the rest of the hospital by a 'no-man's land' in the form of a small corridor and a staircase. There was a small gate to keep children in, and a heavy fire door. The families shared kitchen, toilet and laundry facilities, and the sleeping accommodation was all contained in the middle of the Unit. This is the only Unit in the hospital admitting whole families, and all these factors bond the Family Unit patients together.

At the same time they are also patients in a larger community of the whole hospital. Main meals are cooked and eaten by the whole hospital together. Leisure activities are generally arranged by and for the hospital as a whole.

The Family Unit patients seemed to be divided in their feelings about how much they felt part of the Unit community, and how much part of the community of the whole hospital. As I interpreted it, patients who felt themselves to be married or parents were able to identify better with other married people or parents; they saw the community of single people as a threat, or at least 'different'. Those who either rejected their married status or parental role identified better with the single adults. Occasionally, those who were trying to shake off the fetters of their marriage or children, felt closer to the adolescents who were being helped to separate from their families.

One mother, very aware of her children's needs and her role as a mother said: 'I tend to stay on Ross . . . I don't go up to Centres [the adult unit] . . . It's not for me or my children'. Others, in the same vein, said: 'I got the feeling that Ross ought to be with Ross . . . They didn't like children on Centres . . . I felt pushed out . . . The adolescents had left their parents in the hospital'; 'I only felt part of Ross . . . I just got on with it. It didn't worry me. I think it was due to age differences'.

Sometimes patients longed to be part of the young, free community but felt unable to: 'That was something that was wrong . . . I remember someone saying you felt as if you need a passport to go from Ross to the Centre . . . that was a very fair comment'. A man who was separating from his wife, however, said: 'After the first six weeks the numbers on Ross dwindled [not correct] and I got to know people on Centres. I didn't spend much time on Ross at all. I felt more part of Centres . . . I did feel I was abandoning them, I think'.

A woman who was anxious to give up her children to someone else's care said: 'I felt much more part of the whole hospital community. In the evening I found it practically impossible to stay on Ross . . . people's preoccupations were far too domestic'. Another mother, who resented caring for her children because of her own immature personality, commented: 'I feel much more part of the singles and adolescent unit than I do a part of Ross. I can feel just as at home there, in fact sometimes a lot more comfortable, than I do down here'. A young mother, separated from her husband before admission, began to face life as a single person again during her stay, and described her development: 'I didn't feel part of the whole hospital community for a long time. For the first three months, I only felt part of Ross, and to walk through the Common Room was a terrible ordeal . . . and then I got to know a whole group of people on Centres, and then after that spent more time with them . . . and then the Common Room became the place where I spent most of the time . . . I felt isolated having a child . . . people in Centres were . . . sort of . . . young men. I got very fed up with Ross before I left'.

Patient responsibility

Decision-making by consensus, patient responsibility for aspects of administration, catering and domestic duties are accepted parts of social therapy, and I found it interesting to talk with patients about how they experienced this part of their time in a therapeutic community.

Most of the patients accepted their domestic tasks without question, saying, 'I was willing to play my part'; 'It satisfied the feeling that you ought to be doing something'; 'I just do it because I have to'; 'I volunteered for that job, so I don't mind doing it'; 'I just like cleaning the place up a bit, it's such a mess'.

The more responsible tasks clearly evoke more emotional responses. Some patients felt that they had been pushed into them against their wills, others that they had taken them on reluctantly but still came to value them. Others tried to understand their usefulness in recovery. One woman said of Firm chairmanship, with considerable anger: 'I felt very bitter about it, because at the time there was no-one who would do it . . . I really had no choice'. But others said: 'Looking back . . . public spirit, I suppose . . . I was blackmailed into it really. I was sure I wasn't ready for it . . . very frightening thing . . . But in the end I enjoyed the power and to know what was going on'; 'I felt I had to be Firm Chairman to keep them off my back . . . the patients, that is'.

Two men, both struggling for insight and an understanding of the purpose of the community made the folowing comments: 'I feel I'm doing my part in the community . . . If things don't get done I have to leave it . . . it's hard for me to accept . . . It's part of the therapy, struggling with other people. The place has to be run . . . for instance, supper has to be cooked. A minimum of hygiene has to be maintained. Then it's either the responsibility of the hospital to make sure that everybody is properly fed . . . or they can leave it to us . . . The treatment requires the co-operation of the patient'.

One patient pathetically told me: 'When I got there, I said I feel so ill I can't do anything. When I get better I shall leave. It didn't work like that. I never was well enough. Perhaps I should have tried. Perhaps they were right. It might have helped'.

There were various social and creative activities also arranged in the hospital (games, art, pottery, gardening, music) but nearly all the patients commented that they were therapeutic in the social interaction or the confidence gained in organizing them, rather than in themselves. I think this has some implications for occupational therapy, art therapy, and games organized *for* patients in psychiatric institutions.

Community life and psychotherapy

When designing my standardized interview with the patients, I did not anticipate discussing with them their views about the relative value of psychotherapy and the community life. However, almost without exception, every patient and ex-patient raised the subject in some form – either when discussing some aspect of life in the hospital – or, more commonly, when I asked them if there was anything they would like to add at the end of the interview.

The patients whom I interviewed differed in their perspective on this from the ex-patients. The in-patients were very conscious of the fact that the events of community life are the material for therapy, and also extremely aware of the confrontation in therapy which makes living on the Family Unit meaningful. They said: 'I don't think you can separate living here from the sessions . . . They can help to clarify what is happening elsewhere'; 'Whereas before I just did what I wanted to do and bugger everybody else . . . now I stop to consider what effect it will have on other people . . . because here if I go off and leave the children, someone will ask me why . . . Everyone here asks you *why* the whole time'; 'The row feels very destructive at the time . . . but can be very constructive if you sit and evaluate it afterwards . . . But the value is not in the things the tension is about . . . it's in working out its meaning'.

The ex-patients were less inclined to value the sessions so highly, or the interpretations of the psychotherapists. They nearly all said that it had been the community life which had been most valuable, and their fellow-patients who had been the best therapists. Most of them said that the change in themselves, so necessary for them to leave the hospital and return to life in the outside world, came from the interaction with other patients and the life of the community, rather than from their experience of psychotherapy. They saw the community as doctor, therapist, nurse and friend.

This view strengthened with the length of time they had been discharged. This phenomenon can be interpreted as the gradual loosening of the bonds of dependency or as a denial of the need for professional help, but whatever the reason, it was extremely striking in the results of my study. One woman discharged five years before my study said: 'When I got to the Cassel I got more relaxed, because I was at ease. I liked a lot of the patients . . . not all the staff. You were sharing it all with the other patients you know, not the staff, and the patients cured you. They *knew* how you felt'. A woman, three years after her discharge, recalls: 'I talked to anybody who happened to be there . . . I got more help from the patients and just living there . . . J was wonderful. She was always in the kitchen having cups of tea; I would go in and . . . grrrrr . . . out it would all come. They were marvellous, and turned me back into myself . . . but like ships that pass in the night, I have new friends now'.

Others said: 'It was something we hadn't experienced before as a family . . . to live with other families . . . like a commune. Living as a community was more helpful to me than therapy . . . There was a spirit about the place. It lifted you, people being so open about themselves. Yes, damn it all, there *was* a spirit about the place'; 'It's very difficult to say, but it was the time I spent with the other patients and in the community which helped, not the therapy . . . I suppose the therapy could be helpful to somebody, but it wasn't there for me . . . My social life is now all with Cassel ex-patients. They are people I have been close to. There is a sort of common understanding'.

A woman who said her whole attitude to life had been changed attributed it to the close community living, an experience she had never had before. Here is how she summed it up: 'I think I came to realize that people who you initially find very unlikeable can be of immense value . . . much more than therapy. It's the living together – you care for me and I'll care for you – it's how the community works, and you can come through this hating to a close relationship . . . If you can do that, you can do anything'.

Staff understanding

After interviewing all 13 in-patients and 17 ex-patients, I interviewed seven members of staff – three psychotherapists, three nurses and the matron, all of whom either were working or had worked on the Families Unit. I asked them how they thought patients experienced life on the Unit; I used the same subject headings that I had used with the patients.

The staff were clearly aware that patients knew very little about the Cassel before admission. One doctor said, quite accurately: 'My impression is that they usually have an expectation . . . that they will be cared for in a much more practical way – they being more passive and the staff being more active than it actually is'. The staff were also aware of the disappointment and distress that most patients described as their first impressions. However, the relief and containment which some patients felt was mentioned by two nurses. One doctor commented: 'The patients find it cosy and reassuring to have the proximity of other people, much more than they consciously admit'.

All the staff were aware that patients find conflict and violence very alarming. A doctor commented: 'Particularly early on, if they are pretty anxious about their impulses – aggressive and sexual – they are really quite alarmed at seeing something which is like a parents' argument looks to a child'. This echoes exactly a patient's thoughts: 'It reminded me of my parents rowing . . . with me in the middle unable to do anything about it'.

Discussion of how much patients feel part of the hospital or part of the Unit produced some interesting interpretations from some members of staff: 'Occasionally a member of a couple is somehow having an urge to act out . . . wanting to be an individual and not accept the obligations of the relationship of marriage, and goes off to the Centre which they see as embodying the identity of single and possibly free patients'; 'A lot of women prefer the single adults, maybe to get away from their families and husbands . . . to feel free'. Their views reflect exactly my own findings from the interviews I conducted.

The issue of mutual support and care in the patient community was an area where the staff seemed to be less aware of the patients' feelings, and of the value to patients of this aspect of the life of the community. Several of the nurses' comments were: 'If a member of staff is around with a patient in distress, other patients retreat

. . . perhaps because they feel humble and incompetent'; 'Sometimes they'd rather not know. There is a reluctance in the Firm to take it on'; 'It depends on the person in difficulties . . . How they relate to them, and how long it goes on . . . then they get to a point that *they* want to be looked after'.

Two doctors commented: 'It will vary with how the patient's own therapy is going – if it's going well, they can enjoy rescuing somebody else, or maybe see some point in tolerating and helping someone else. But generally it's a bit of a chore'.

Asked whether patients look for support from other patients, most of the staff felt that they probably didn't: 'Some people say other patients can be helpful, but not much'; 'Probably they go to staff if it's an acute thing'; 'Patients look for a member of staff first, I'm sure'; 'I imagine that patients feel the quality of help from staff is something special, and would grasp for that in a rivalrous fashion . . . and defend against the threat by being more pally with each other'.

Two members of staff said that the objectives of the community were the interdependence of patients: 'To learn to do less with magical sustenance from staff . . . and have more interdependence . . . that's what we're aiming for'.

In spite of acknowledging this as a principle, not one member of staff said that they thought that patients might value the help and support of other patients more than that of staff. I wondered whether perhaps they were unable to accept an equal role with the patients in caring for each other?

The 'extended family' pattern in the Family Unit was acknowledged and accepted by most staff, although none expressed it in those terms. They were, however, aware of the reciprocal nature of sharing the care of children and the interaction between patients in making these arrangements.

On the question of whether the community life or the psychotherapy was more valuable to patients in recovery, most members of staff emphasized that there was a framework of psychotherapy for which the happenings in the community were 'grist to the mill', as one doctor said. Three nurses said: 'The community life has to be useful, or we'd have them as out-patients'; 'You can see how a family operates . . . how mums deal with their kids. It all helps us to understand them'; 'The whole thing is that each family brings in their way of living, and the way it jars very much shows up the family difficulties. The way mums handle their children can be observed'.

The doctors commented on the containment effect of admission: 'You can have people here who don't have sessions . . . I think the effect of being in a hospital is often very reassuring . . . The culture of tolerating the whole range of human impulses, emotions and fantasies has an extremely powerful containing effect. It can allow other things to happen'.

Altogether, I felt that the staff were closely in touch with the patients' experience of life on the Family Unit, but considerably underestimated the strong bonds of the patient sub-culture: the friendships, the mutual support, and the therapeutic effects of sharing so much. I also noticed that they seemed to be totally unaware of the anger and resentment which the patients sometimes feel towards them, for whatever reasons.

Conclusion

Some findings of my study I found particularly interesting:

1. Patients felt a sense of relief and safety in being welcomed by other patients who were expected to care for them.
2. The Unit came to resemble a form of extended family, with multiple mothering.
3. It is a significant discovery for many patients to find that they can help and support others.
4. Current in-patients were very concerned about their relationship with staff, but ex-patients spoke more of their interaction with other patients. The longer they had been away, the more they spoke of the mutual support they experienced.
5. Patients often commented on their hostile feelings towards the staff, and the lack of sympathy they felt in the staff.

6. Patients' confidence was more often increased by contact with other patients than with staff.
7. Patients who were rejecting their marital status or parental role felt more part of the whole hospital than of the Family Unit.
8. Ex-patients valued psychotherapy less than in-patients. They saw the community itself as therapist, and this view strengthened with the length of time they had been away from the hospital.
9. Staff were fairly accurately aware of patients' experience, although they underestimated the value placed by patients on their mutual support.

As long ago as 1938 Rowland wrote, 'The fact of the matter is that the mental patient must associate every day with other mental patients. From the sociological standpoint, this is of greater importance than all other aspects of life in a mental hospital' (Rowland, 1938, p.323).

Part Three
The Therapeutic Community
Some Theoretical Considerations

[19]

A Sexually-Charged Clinical Problem

Social, Structural and Classical Psychoanalytic Approaches

Oliver James and Alan Wilson

THERAPEUTIC COMMUNITIES aim to use their organization as a means for helping disturbed individuals. In deliberately planning a therapeutic environment, the allocation of who does what with whom, when and where (social structure) is a key aspect if the institution is to be reasonably sure that it is going to have the effect it desires, consistently. There are social factors other than structure within an institution, such as culture or what Bateson (1936) called its 'ethos', but here we shall be concentrating on how the structural affects, and is affected by, the personal.

Many things happen between two or more people in any institution every day. Some of these 'happenings' become the object of a great deal of feeling and speculation by many of the members for days or weeks on end. The promotion prospects of particular people within the organization when a post falls vacant, gossip about sexual relationships between two members of the institution, these and many other matters may become the focus of widespread informal talk. When such happenings become cathected widely in this way, we call them 'events'.

The identification and analysis of such 'events' is one of the tasks which we have proposed for the individuals and groups of the therapeutic community. In this paper we present an example of an 'event' (Section I) which occurred in a psychoanalytically orientated therapeutic community, and we analyse the role which the community's social structure performed in its genesis and subsequent interpretation, from two contrasting perspectives.

The first perspective (Section II), that of classical psychoanalytic functionalism, views social structure as a function of the biological and social needs of individual members who use it in order to defend themselves against unwanted anxieties. Menzies (1959) provides a definitive example of this approach.

The second perspective (Section III), that of Durkheimian sociology, views social structure as coercive, and independent of the individual member. Stanton and Schwartz's study (1954) remains the most systematic application of this view to the mental hospital.

In examining the 'event' we are about to present from these two perspectives, the interplay of pathological individual needs with ineffective structural rules, roles and relationships emerges. The practical implication is that the staff of a community must deliberate consciously about the effect of its structure and subject it to regular overhauls if they are to be reasonably sure that it is therapeutic.

I. An example of a community 'event'

1. The happening:

Time: Late afternoon on a Friday.

A girl of five years old belonging to a family on the Family Unit speaks to her mother. She tells her mother that an adolescent boy, also a patient on the Unit, had put his hand down the back of her pants and asked her to put her hand on his penis.

2. The response to the happening and its representation in the community as an 'event':

The mother called the duty nurse to the parents' bedroom and represented the happening as an assault. Placing the girl on a bed, the mother removed her daughter's pants to show the (male) nurse an allegedly reddened vulva. These further happenings occurred:

(i) the original happening was now referred to, first as 'an assault', then as 'a sexual assault'.
(ii) its elements now included first, touching of the girl's genitals by the boy, and then, the notion of penetration by him; in the subsequent week, some criticism in the staffroom focussed on the nurse for having examined the girl; it was held that this was a job for the duty doctor and not for the nurse.

The duty nurse telephoned his superior, the duty nursing officer, who supported him and attempted to calm the situation. Demands were already being made to discharge the adolescent boy and to arrange police prosecution, as requested by the parents of the little girl and in many ways endorsed by others, both parents and staff. With support and encouragement, the family of the little girl went home for the weekend. The duty doctor was informed, but in a way which did not arouse his anxiety. The duty nurse went off duty, staff and patients returned after the weekend, but did not have an early meeting with the duty nurse involved. Attention continued to be focussed on the 'event', the prospective criminal proceedings featured prominently. The hospital GP was requested to examine the little girl and is reported by the mother to have said that the condition of the girl's vulva was consistent with an attempt to penetrate.

The adolescent boy's account of the afternoon now began to be heard and followed through in detail. She had been playing with him with other children in the room he shared. A guitar, which was not his, featured in their play. He had occasion to be cross with the little girl in an attempt to control her. She left to go to her mother.

This 'event' included wide discussion throughout the community. In the weekly whole staff meeting, it was viewed with considerable but decreasing anxiety. The discussion showed a marked tendency to dwell on the detailed content of the 'event'.

The family did not return to live in the hospital but had some appointments with staff. Other happenings became focus of attention, creating new events.

3. Background information relevant to the 'event':
The 15½-year-old adolescent boy was admitted to the hospital some nine months before the 'event' with school refusal and travel phobia as his principal symptoms. He was described by his therapist as physically small for his age, lacking confidence and without sexual experience. He remained in the hospital for a further eleven months after the 'event'. By the time of his discharge, he had developed a sexual relationship with a girl his own age. During his stay he denied consistently that he had had any sexual contact with the little girl during the 'event' and it is the opinion of his therapist that this is probably true.

The 34-year-old mother of the little girl involved had been admitted with the whole family one month before the 'event', her general practitioner having reported her to be depressed and frightened that she would seriously damage her daughter, whom she hit frequently. Her therapist described her as hypo-manic with depressive features, and as not suffering from a neurotic illness. Almost two years after the family discharged itself from the hospital, her therapist received a letter from her which made no reference to the 'event' and in which she described herself as a 'new person, symptom-free', a recent change which she attributed to discontinued use of the contraceptive pill.

The little girl involved in the 'event' was described by her therapist as eager to please, frightened of her mother but with a desire for physical contact. She could play 'very flirtatiously' at times. She is described as not having been unsettled by the 'event' and in her mother's letter of two years later, is reported to have had a reading age two years in advance of the average.

4. Initial conceptualization of the 'event':
The original happening was rapidly labelled as an assault (touching of the genitals, not then the girl's buttocks) and then relabelled a sexual assault (genital penetration). This inflation took place without anyone stopping to consider whether or not the original 'happening' actually happened as described by the little girl. Considering that the hospital is a psychoanalytic one, this is

surprising, since one of the most important breakthroughs which Freud made in developing the theory of psychoanalysis was the realization that many of his patients had invented accounts of being sexually interfered with by their parents when young.

This inflation can be further conceptualized as a widespread breakdown in the capacity of those involved to think: to retain a sufficient level of detachment to be able to reflect on the feelings which the event evoked in the participants, and on its meaning. This loss of the capacity to conceptualize was the consequence of high levels of anxiety and uncertainty which were evoked in those people involved. In the place of thought was put rote application of a crude morality (the boy had done something 'wrong') and of the law (society's rule book prohibits this kind of behaviour).

II. The psychoanalytic functionalist perspective

1. The psychodynamic use of the structure by its members:
A woman uses scissors to cut up a jigsaw in order to make the pieces fit.

This is a good analogy for the psychoanalytic view of the use to which disturbed members put the external reality which the social structure represents. Rather than adapt to the rules involved in completing the jigsaw, the woman achieves a short term release from the anxiety which the structure of the jigsaw represents by cutting the pieces to fit, but at the price of an incomplete picture at the end. Likewise, the disturbed patient in the short term is constantly seeking ways to cut up and cheat the structure of the community to make it fit his or her wishes, but at the price of being an incomplete and maladapted person in the longer term.

The opposite of a Durkheimian approach, psychoanalytic functionalism views social structure as used and effected by the members of the social system. Whereas for Durkheim structure is external to and constrains the member, in psychoanalytic functionalism the structure is seen as an expression of the individuals; its form and content are understood as functions of their needs.

This functionalist approach is most eloquently and vigorously exemplified in Menzies's (1959) paper entitled 'The *Functioning* of Social Systems as a Defence against Anxiety' (our emphasis). Following Jaques's (1955) original thesis, Menzies analysed the ways in which the nurses employed in a general hospital used its social system to defend themselves against depressive and persecutory anxieties which were evoked in them by the nature of their work. The particular forms and contents of the social structure were presented as the consequence of a compromise between the need for support for intrapsychic defence mechanisms in the form and contents of the social system on the one hand, and the need to perform the primary task of providing nursing care on the other.

Whilst in Menzies's case, the defence adopted was formality and rigidity, Tonnesman (1979) demonstrated that the opposite of these may be adopted in other social structures (informality, extreme flexibility, 'generalized positive regard', and so forth), but equally, may be used to the same end.

Another example of psychoanalytic functionalism as an approach is to be found in Winnicott's (1972 p.112-21) paper 'The Location of Culture', which presents cultural phenomena as an expression of the need and capacity for creativity in the individual. Although using different assumptions from those of the Kleinian school of psychoanalysis, and consequently, drawing attention to the creative as opposed to defensive needs of the individual, Winnicott's account is essentially of the same form as that of Menzies: he sees the effect of the early infantile experience of members and their needs as the explanation for (in this case, the culture of) the social system.

The standpoint from which we view the relations between members and social structure has a very significant effect on how we view the role of social structure in therapeutic treatment in communities. If structure is seen as determining, then its effect on therapy must be great; if it is seen as determined (by psychodynamic forces in the members), then it does not affect the progress of therapy in an active way (as a cause of effects), at least not in the same sense. A determining structure is used directly to bring about desired changes (for example, reducing the degree to which patients' lives are run for them by the hospital in order to avoid institutionalizing them in the ways described by Goffman, 1961). The effect of a determined structure is indirect, that is, one can interpret the defensive *use* to which a structure is put, (Hinshelwood and Manning, 1979).

2. A psychoanalytic functionalist view of 'the event':

Many factors contributed to the inflation of the girl's original alleged statement, as reported by her mother, but a psychoanalytic view would regard the nature of the statement's subject matter as foremost amongst these: erotic involvement with a little girl.

As noted above, several significant changes occurred in the content of what was supposed to have happened as the 'event' developed. Firstly, the adolescent boy's alleged wish for the little girl *to do something sexual to him* rapidly was reformulated by the adults of the community into *the boy doing something to the girl's genitals.* Secondly, there was a three-step progression from a request by the boy to be touched, to his having touched the girl (an 'assault'), to him having penetrated her (a 'sexual assault'). Thirdly, no-one stopped to ask whether the girl's story was true. These embellishments were added by the adults, and it seems possible that they expressed the fantasy wishes or the fears of these adults: their own paedophiliac urges were aroused by the story and they added to it what they would unconsciously like to have done or happened. They avoided realizing this by acting precipitately and unthinkingly.

Further support for this view can be deduced from the fact that there developed a widespread and precipitate desire to punish the boy for his wicked acts. This was an exaggerated desire, since from the moment that the girl allegedly spoke to her mother, the boy was treated as 'guilty until proved innocent', even though nobody had stopped to ask whether there was any charge for him to answer. This ready assumption of guilt, coupled with the overblown desire to punish, would be consistent with the interpretation that the adults were indeed the possessors of the unconscious wishes evident in their work of embellishment; these primitive reactions were defences against consciousness of their own wishes and the guilt at their possession.

Thus, their unconscious wish to do to the girl that which they attributed to the boy was also accompanied by guilt at having such wishes and a fear of being punished for them. The wishes, the guilt and the need for punishment were projected onto the boy, and the adults were freed to obtain the unconscious pleasure, by proxy, of the acts which they attributed to the boy, simultaneously, they could consciously bask in the mindless and rote application of those structural mechanisms which society at large provides to help protect citizens from such impulses: morality and legality.

The foregoing makes the assumption that the happening was inherently anxiety-provoking: from this assumption we have been able to offer some explanation of the particular contents (mindlessness, rote morality and legality) of its inflation. But this, alone, does not explain why this happening became an 'event', unless we are to suppose that all statements of the kind made by the little girl would provoke these particular reactions on the wide scale noted.

III. The Durkheimian perspective

1. Degrees of structural specification and their effect on members: Whether or not such roles as 'nurse', 'doctor' and 'patient' (each with its prescribed tasks and relationships of authority and accountability) exist in a given therapeutic community, at what time breakfast is served, by whom it is made, and the degree to which attendance is compulsory – these and myriad other social structural matters clearly have an effect on the behaviour and experience of the members of a therapeutic community.

For Durkheim, social structure is a social fact, one of:

> a category of facts with very distinctive characteristics: it consists of ways of acting, thinking and feeling external to the individual and endowed with a power of coercion by reason of which they (social facts) control him. These ways of acting are not to be confused with biological phenomena, since they consist of representations and of action; nor with psychological phenomena, which exist only in the individual consciousness and through it (1938, p.3).

In this view, the members of a therapeutic community are regulated by social structural rules which, at any single point in time, have an 'external' existence; they exist whether or not any individual member believes that they do, they are not of his or her individual creation and they substantially affect what he does, says, thinks or feels whether he conforms to them or not.

The most obvious purpose of social structure is to regulate what the people of a social system do, when and where, in relation to each other. Different social structural arrangements may be assumed to lead to different activities done at different times in different places. In what respects, if at all, do these differences affect therapeutic progress?

The central character in Kafka's *The Castle* (1926) can never find out the rules through which he can obtain his objective of entering it; similarly, the central character of *The Trial* (1925) cannot find a means of discovering the crime of which he is accused. The patient in a therapeutic community with little or no structural specification may be placed in a similar position.

The central character of Sartre's *Nausea* (1938), on the other hand, knows what he is supposed to be doing and being all too well. The social structural constraints placed upon him by a small French bourgeois town are experienced as so constricting and all-pervasive that he begins to lose touch with himself and his wishes altogether. The patient in a community that is over-specified structurally, may be placed in the same position.

In the 1950s and 1960s the work of Goffman (1961) and other sociologists showed that over-specification of hospital structures led to 'institutionalization' of patients. Their capacity for autonomous action became severely limited, and they ceased to be able to function beyond the hospital when their actions were no longer structured by it. In attempts to avoid these effects, some institutions sought less specific structures, and in some extreme cases, almost no formal structure at all; (for example, the Philadelphia Association Houses (Boyers, 1972). At least in some cases, this extreme absence of structure induced infantilization every bit as much as its highly specified opposite: given no structural signposts for organizing time, space and tasks, some already anxious and confused persons regressed to states of incoherence (Barnes, 1973).

One can conceptualize the effects of structure on members as follows: very high degree of specification in a social system's structure produces a state of extreme individual certainty. Also, very low degree of specification in a social structure produces a state of extreme individual uncertainty. Extreme individual certainty increases the likelihood of the experience of anxiety, since the individual has lost his or her autonomy in such circumstances, and is less likely to be able to be flexible and therefore reality-tested, in terms of responsiveness to his environment. Also, extreme individual uncertainty increases the likelihood of the experience of anxiety, since an experience of a largely unpredictable world reduces the individual's capacity to locate him or herself within it.

In psychoanalytic terms, the former case is likely to evoke any childhood experiences of an impinging environment which 'took over' the person, whilst the latter case evokes early experiences of a chaotic internal and/or external world.

A social system with over- or under-specification of social structure evokes levels of anxiety in its members which impede the performance of its tasks. In short, this view of the role of social structure in therapeutic communities is that it regulates overall level of anxiety of members: it controls the extent to which members know what to do, where, when, how, and why, and depending on the fixity, clarity, explicitness and sanctioning with which it specifies these things, members will or will not tend to experience anxiety at levels which impede their capacity to perform their tasks.

2. *Application of this view to 'the event':*
Numerous structural rules, roles and relationships with varying degrees of fixity, clarity and explicitness and sanctioning can be seen to have influenced the course of 'the event'. First there is a rule against sexual activity with small children. This rule is highly specified in that it is fixed and sanctioned in law. The rule's content is clear enough in practice (although some debate regarding what is 'sexual' is possible), and although mainly implicitly apprehended, since most people go through life without having it told to them explicitly. It becomes very clear and explicit what the rule is when it is broken.

Before anything happened at all in this case there existed this highly specified conception of what is permissible and appropriate in the minds of members regarding sexual activity with children. The little girl told her mother that this rule has been contravened; the adolescent boy subsequently claimed that no contravention had occurred, but it is clear that all concerned felt that the rule existed. This would seem to argue for a Durkheimian view of it as external to and coercive of, the actions of individuals.

With regard to the duty nurse's role and structural relationships, the tasks of his role when confronted with an alleged contravention of the above rule were not highly specified. What action should be taken was not fixed and inflexibly laid down, and it was far from clearly known what the occupant of the role should do (for example, whether he should inspect the girl's genitals). The fact that the mother looked to the nurse for help suggested that he was explicitly expected to know what to do; and the fact that the nurse came in for criticism subsequently suggests that his role was sanctioned to do something.

When this role, determined by the social structure, came into coflict with the rule against sexual activity with small children, the ambiguities of specification of that role left its occupant at the mercy of his personal feelings. Thus, in that individual, the interaction of the role, rule and person led to activities which were later criticized.

A further uncertainty existed in the degree of specification of the accountability of the nurse for what was happening and his authority to change it. Was he accountable for ensuring that no paedophiliac acts occurred during his shift? If not, for what could he be held accountable? To what authority, to do what?

He found himself investigating the girl's vulva, and before he could call a halt and institute some form of self-reflective moratorium, he found himself on the telephone to the duty nursing officer and the duty doctor, neither of whose role specification enabled them to act as fire breaks in the forest fire of morality and legality, which by now had been fanned into life from the original 'careless dropping of a match' by the little girl/adolescent/mother. The match had fallen on structural tinderwood, it would seem, and no adequate fire brigade existed which would recognize the extent and nature of the fire, or put it out. The fire was not properly doused until well into the next week, by which time the widespread discussion of the happening began to be seen for what it was: voyeuristic. In the meantime, the family had left the hospital.

3. Inadequate structuring of communication between staff:
Every Cassel patient has a particular nurse and psychotherapist concerned with his or her treatment. As Main (1946), and James (p. 78) and Tischler (p. 95) have described, effective communication between these two is critically important for successful treatment. In the case of the adolescent boy, it would seem that the organization of this communication was inadequate: if the boy was likely to 'act out' in general or in this way in particular, this should have been known beforehand by his therapist and his nurse, and therefore, by the duty nurse. With advance warning, this latter would at least have had a framework within which to understand the happenings going on around him. Likewise, a

more effective system might have enabled the duty nurse to know that the little girl could be 'very flirtatious' and that the mother feared damaging the girl herself. With such knowledge and appropriate back-up, the nurse could have used thought to control the fire.

The little girl said something to her mother which was anxiety-provoking. The social structure of the hospital was insufficiently specified to enable her communication to be represented in a therapeutically usable form. The adults involved were overwhelmed by anxieties and sought inflexible and unconstructive ways of protecting themselves – society's emergency firefighting suit of asbestos morality and legality.

Conclusion

A social structure exists regardless of whether its individual members believe it does. Paradoxically, it exists only if they do. We have seen that the way in which individuals interpret its prescriptions significantly affects what it is and what they do.

The two perspectives from which we have viewed its operation seem to conflict, from a scientific, theoretical standpoint. In theory, the 'event' cannot have been caused both by its inherently anxiety-provoking subject matter and by an ineffective structure. In practice, we have seen that it was the combination of the two in the particular individuals involved which enabled the happening to become an 'event' whose consequences were not therapeutically constructive in the case of the little girl's family, assuming that furthr therapy would have been desirable.

In the literature concerned with therapeutic communities (for example, Hinshelwood, 1979; Jansen, 1980), detailed examination of the effects of the different social components which make them up is rare. The implication of this paper is similar to that which was clear to Main as long ago as 1956: the *specifically structural* in therapeutic communities requires the constant attention and review provided by a group that has been deliberately delegated this task. Unless such machinery exists, it is hard to know how a community can have any degree of certainty that its social organization is affecting patients for better or worse.

Summary

An event in a therapeutic community is examined from the perspectives of the structural analysis of Durkheim and psychoanalytic functionalism. Although these two approaches might appear to be competing, analysis of the evidence shows them to be complementary from the clinical standpoint. The role of social structure in therapeutic communities emerges as requiring deliberate conceptualization if such communities are to be truly therapeutic.

[20]

Social Action Theory and Psychosocial Nursing

Gillian Chapman

The impetus for this paper arose from two main sources. Firstly, my own experience as clinical sister and course tutor and my observations of and discussions with other nurses in the hospital. Secondly, a felt need to offer a social model from which to derive descriptions and explanations of social events and structures related to nursing. It seemed important that a theoretical model suited to nursing and about nursing which is grounded in the experience of nurses be articulated.

It will, therefore, be argued that for the nurse group, the social model suggested here offers a basis for conceptualizing techniques able to cnhance nursing practice. Furthermore, for the psychoanalytical enterprise in the hospital it offers a theoretical model with the potential for a creative dialogue with psychoanalytic theory and practice. The essay will be divided into three main sections. The first is a brief outline of key ideas in social interactionist theories.

The second section of the essay describes the historical and philosophical traditions of social therapy within which Tom Main, Wilfred Bion and Maxwell Jones developed their notions of the therapeutic community. The 'coincidence' of interests between the social therapy movement and social interactionist theories mentioned above will be traced.

In the third and final section, current nursing models will be introduced. I will begin to outline a view of psychosocial nursing set in the context of the developments in social theory mentioned earlier in the introduction. A short case study will be presented.

Approaches in sociology as applied to medicine

Of the many approaches to medical sociology, such as structural functionalism, Marxism and feminism, that of symbolic interactionism, derived in Europe from the work of Simmel and Weber and the social psychology of G.H. Mead, seem the most useful. While the other theories help to place nursing work in a broad social context, interactionist work provides concepts which may help to inform nursing action.

Symbolic interactionism is a term used to describe a wide and disparate field of writers interested in describing social actions (Douglas, 1971; Berger and Luckmann, 1975; Goffman, 1974). These writers sought to combine the methodological principles of Max Weber with the psychological model provided by G.H. Mead. For Mead (1935), the self is a social construct; the way we act towards others and see ourselves as individuals is a result of the way in which other people react towards us. It is in these continual reciprocal social negotiations that our social world is constructed. Unlike Freud, Mead does not recognize the unconscious element in human existence, nor the importance that individual biography might have in influencing social interactions. The self is essentially unstable, reconstructing itself in the processes of social intercourse. It proved possible, therefore, to combine his theory with Weber's notion of *verstehen*, a preoccupation with the need to understand the actors' meanings through emphatic methods. It is through the meanings that actors attribute to their acts that we are best able to understand social actions. The methodology of choice for this approach is, therefore, participant observation. The observer joins in with the activities of the actors while 'bracketing off' any preconceptions he or she might have about their actions.

This approach in medical sociology led to the classical studies of the experience of treatment programmes for patients suffering from tuberculosis and poliomyelitis by Roth (1963) and Davies (1963). In England, interactionism was combined with ethnomethodological preoccupations with language to produce many studies of doctor/patient interactions and the ways in which disparities in power were managed through talk. Horobin and Davis (1977) and Wadsworth and Robinson (1976) have provided examples of this work.

Despite the insights which these studies have contributed to our understanding of the process of becoming ill, they have several limitations. At the methodological level there are problems concerned with realiability, generalizability and validity. It has been pointed out by Menzel (1978) that while human actions cannot be understood independently of the meanings which actors give to them, neither can they only be indentified with one particular actor's or group's interpretation of events. Human actions have a multiplicity of meanings according to the perspective from which they are viewed. The tendency of interactionists to identify with the underdog (in this instance the patient) has meant that their criticisms have centred on middle-level occupational groups (in this case the nurses) with little theoretical acknowledgment that these groups are themselves subjects of cultural and social constraints. Giddens (1977 a,b) explains this in terms of the lack of a general theory of society and its institutions in symbolic interactionism. Thus, the studies rarely take into account the structural elements of society through which actors articulate meanings and which, to some extent, determine what these meanings are taken to be. This is crucially important in relation to political and economic structures. Lichtman (1970), a Marxist, regards interactionism as inadequate insofar as it is overly subjective and voluntaristic, and lacks 'awareness of historical concreteness'. For Lichtman, interactionism 'ultimately abandons the sense of human beings in a struggle with an alien reality which they both master and to which they are subordinate'. In his view, interpreted meanings in society are channelled through the class stucture and are formed in class-controlled institutions. The work of Giddens, who sought to combine an interest in psychoanalysis and linguistics, and a social theory concerned with action and structure helps us resolve this dilemma. In a series of papers (Giddens, 1977 a,b, 1979) he seeks to develop a theory which, while acknowledging the constraining influence of social structure on individuals, also recognizes the importance of the self-conscious, knowing activities of individuals in reciprocal social negotiations which reproduce and maintain those structures. The sources of social transformation or change, in Giddens's model, lie in the unintended consequences of unconscious motivation on individual and group actions and the contradictions inherent in the unequal distribution of resources (power) within social organizations. It is his ability to draw on the work of Freud, Lacan and Habermas to inform his social theory, and the way in which he combines this with the methodological preoccupations of action theorists, which makes his work of particular relevance to the study of the therapeutic community. He seeks, for example, to examine the way in which language or talk not only acts as a vehicle for communication across time and space, but mediates between individual and social experience, embodying within it the actors' experience of social structure and social forms. It is not my intention to suggest that Giddens offers a full-blown psychosocial theory easily adapted to medical and nursing practice in a therapeutic community. Rather, I would suggest that he offers us a theoretical and methodological approach to the social aspects of individual experience which combines with psychoanalysis without reifying the patient. This attempt to restore intentionality and subjectivity to the actor may be illustrated by listing the central methodological preoccupations of action theorists about how to understand social relationships in organizations. Silverman (1976) notes that they seek to:

1) understand social action rather than merely observe social behaviour, social action arising, it is thought, from the meanings, that individuals attribute to social reality;

2) demonstrate the way in which meanings are established by shared social orientations, and once everyday practices become

institutionalized, how they are experienced by later generations as social facts;
3) examine the way in which particular configurations of meaning are sustained by continual reaffirmation in everyday actions;
4) observe the means by which individuals modify, change and transform social meanings;
5) maintain a concern to explain human action not only in the light of a pre-determined theory, which assumes a privileged position vis-à-vis truth (for example, 'vulgar' psychoanalysis or Marxism), but also in terms of the meanings which actors attribute to events, and their perceptions of the everyday world in which they exist.

Such an approach, I would argue, has a built in requirement that patients be seen as autonomous, knowing individuals whose actions are guided by social knowledge as well as psychic impulses. Overall, this preoccupation with understanding actors' actions in terms of meanings they attribute to them seems in keeping with the psychological and sociological tradition of the Cassel hospital. It emphasizes the humanistic impulse to respect a patient's account of his or her actions, and the patient's understanding or perception of personal or social events. I will trace the humanistic impulse in the care of the mentally ill in the second section of this essay. Here I dwell on the recurring patterns of care in the history of psychiatry, with particular reference to the social therapy ideal.

The social therapy tradition

In a previous paper (1984) I noted Sedgwick's (1982) argument that what is striking about the history of psychiatric medicine is its capacity to produce quite different rationalizations for a relatively constant set of practices. He has distinguished between two models of care in the history of psychiatry. The first, mechanical and instrumental; the second, concerned with moral and social management. The constancy and continuity of mechanistic medical practice is evident from the time of ancient Greece to the present day. What innovations there have been, have been derived from changes in technique or the hardware of technology rather than in basic approach. Sedgwick draws parallels between cold water douches, ECT, trepanning and psycho-surgery. He argues that the mechanistic impulse has given way, from time to time in some socio-historic epochs, to a profoundly humanistic impulse. Here, institutions are designed to combine some form of philosophical or moral treatment with management of the day-to-day living environment. The growth of the social therapy movement after the Second World War was just such an emergence of traditional ideas on moral treatment. Tom Main (undated) acknowledges this tradition and states, 'Elements of milieu therapy have been assembled from a variety of sources – political reformist ideals, psychoanalytic theory, social science and so on'. He goes on to contrast the principles of social milieu therapy, emphasizing 'humanizing' patient care, 'democratization', personalized relationships, as against 'depersonalized, mechanized, bureaucratic forms of organization in which patients were customarily dealt with as "things" or as infra-human creatures'. Main was to argue that social environments can enhance or inhibit an individual's capacity to function as an autonomous creative adult. Impoverished social environments, where an individual feels he or she is not involved in policy and decision-making affecting his or her life, leads to apathy, loss of enthusiasm, regression, narcissistic withdrawal, and primitive projective mechanisms for staff and/or other patients alike. In order to create a social environment conducive to 'mental health' and the capacity to function as an autonomous adult, there should be, he argues, clarity about the social/organizational structure of the institution. Staff and patients' roles, tasks, and responsibilities, and the relations between them, should be 'crystal clear'. Only in this way may interpersonal problems of functioning, communicating, and understanding, be examined in a supportive atmosphere of enquiry.

It is worth noting that Goffman, one of the earliest interactionist sociologists is not only quoted and used by Main, but was also highly influential in the development of the sociological models I outlined above. There is not only a 'co-incidence' of interest, but a unity of purpose between the ideals of the therapeutic community, and the concerns of recent sociologists in understanding structure and action; also, there is the role of language in mediating between the two. In the following sections I will begin to outline the way in which these ideas and concerns may help us develop a theory of psychosocial nursing.

Psychosocial nursing

An earlier presentation of material in this paragraph appeared in Chapman (1984). At the Cassel Hospital, patients are offered individual psychoanalytical psychotherapy, in the context of a therapeutic community facilitated and maintained by nursing staff. The use of language in various settings by patients, nurses, and psychotherapists is one therapeutic tool available to help severely depressed and suicidal people with self-acknowledged difficulties in coping with everyday life.

The participants in the community use talk to share and transform inner experiences and to make them available and discussable. It is through this therapeutic discourse that changes in inner experience and social actions are sought. The nurse's role is such that she mediates between the psychological and social experience of patients via the medium of language in interpersonal and group work. In the context of what Habermas (1970) describes as the 'systematically distorted communications' structure found around neurotic patients, sharing observations and explanations of social relationships and events in the community with the staff team is a crucial aspect of nursing care. However, talk is only one aspect of the nurse's role. Nurses participate in the community at the same time as observing it. Nurses act in the community both through talk, and by working alongside patients on day-to-day living. For example, nurses cook, clean, and facilitate all those activities centred on managing the core problems of living. This preoccupation with the use of everyday activities has also been noted by Bloor and Fonkert (1982) in their studies of other therapeutic communities. It is the multi-dimensional aspect of the nurse's role, the requirement that he or she respond appropriately to the varying dimensions of human experience, which separates the nurse's task from that of the psychoanalyst. I would suggest that the nurse mediates between the physiological, psychological, and social experience of patients through action as well as talk. At best, she is aware of these domains of human experience, both in terms of the knowledge base which informs nursing action, and the techniques used to understand and facilitate change either in the individual or the social environment. Awareness of the configuration or constellation of these domains is crucial to nurses' practice.

A description and analysis of a fairly typical nurse/patient encounter, and the potential theoretical and practical resources available to the nurse in solving the problem follows:

A patient arrives in the kitchen complaining of a headache, which he claims will prevent him from doing the cooking. It is one hour before supper, and he has not made alternative arrangements.

A nurse's response to this may vary. He or she may respond either spontaneously and intuitively, or thoughtfully and in a planned way. In either case, the nurse has a particular range of theoretical and technical resources available.

Using a mixture of commonsense knowledge and traditional nursing knowledge, the nurse may sympathize and offer an aspirin. Here, understanding and response is influenced by a physiological model of human existence. Action is determined by decisions about the severity of the event, the typicality of the event, and the likelihood or not of it being an indication of a more serious brain lesion.

The nurse may use a mixture of commonsense knowledge (headaches are caused by stress) and psychoanalytic knowledge (somatic complaints may express psychic conflict) and interpret the complaint: 'Are you reluctant to do the cooking this evening for some reason?' Such a response might include the offer of an aspirin.

The nurse may use observations and knowledge of social events in the community to inform not only the interpretation or understanding of the headache, but to guide nursing actions: 'I noticed that you were disagreeing with the servery sister in the catering meeting this morning about the menu. Do you think you should talk about your feelings about that? Shall we discuss with the Firm chairman how to get the supper cooked?'

It may be the case that the row between patient X and the servery sister was in part caused by them both being caught up in an external socio-economic conflict. That may be recognized too, for example: 'The row that you had this morning about the menu – yes, that is a problem we have inherited from the district. We can only afford stock items and a few locally-purchased luxury items'. Should it be observed that a patient perpetually becomes involved in conflicts like this, it might be considered pertinent for discussion with the therapist, as it may add insight into the patient's own intra-psychic processes.

I have made analytic distinctions between nurses' responses, in this rather artificial way, to demonstrate the complexity of the nursing task. In practice, as a lived experience, this is but one example of a small incident, a multitude of which constitute the nurse's day. What is more, it is important to note that patients too bring to the nurse/patient encounter a complex set of beliefs, ideas, expectations, and experiences. In combination a variety of such events, and other more complex events like facilitating the mothers' group to budget for and organize children's meals, constitute the nurse's lived experience in the community. These everyday practices and interactions constitute and reconstitute the social structure of the hospital. In other words, the everyday nature of the content of the nurse/patient interaction also provides the therapeutic context in which change is sought. These activities provide an environment (physiological, psychological, or social) in which patients and nurses may collaborate together with the psychotherapist in a mutual therapeutic endeavour.

As noted above, there are a range of contexts in which interactions occur, politico-economic, socio-cultural, and psychosocial. In so far as the nurse's task is concerned with a therapeutic endeavour, the context of prime interest in the interaction is the emotional and psychological one. Nurses seek to undertake their task within the context of a relationship with the patient, the quality of which is understood. Traditionally, psychoanalytical concepts have informed these understandings. The importance of individual biography and its impact on current behaviour, together with a psychoanalytical model of human psychosexual development, have formed the basis of the nurses' approach to understanding the patients for whom they care. Furthermore, concepts such as transference and countertransference help nurses gain insight into patients' response to them and their response to patients. However, these ideas are based on assumptions about the conscious and unconscious mental world of individuals and the way anxiety associated with core developmental tasks may evoke one or more defence mechanisms. While the notions of repression, regression, denial, displacement and reaction formation may aid the nurse's understanding of the inhibitory factors affecting an individual patient's capacity to enjoy everyday life, they do not of themselves provide him or her with a guide to nursing action in the social milieu of a therapeutic community. These notions form the conceptual tools which act as a resource for the therapist in the consulting room; they are not so readily available to nurses participating in the everyday realities of the community. For example, in the consulting room, work on content (what the patient says) and context (the transference) is readily and appropriately available for interpretation. Many of the variables which might affect the content or context are controlled out of the therapeutic situation. One example of such a variable is the way the therapist's personality, personal interests and skills, are unknown to the patient. The nurse is very much a person. She uses her personality and differing personal social skills as a therapeutic tool. This makes her vulnerable. While the psychotherapist might use a patient's comment about him or her as an opportunity to interpret the transference, this may not be suitable in everyday situations where nurse/patient encounters arise. For the nurse, comments/criticism are not so symbolically addressed and will need to be resolved with considerable thought and social insight.

Another example of the difference in approach to the same problem is illustrated in a real, not apocryphal, report of an incident involving pig-bins. The catering manager had complained to the patients that the pig-bins in the patients' servery had not been emptied. This was discussed in some detail in the patients' meeting; responsibility, blame and feelings about the job were aired. At one stage in the proceedings a therapist made the following, perhaps obvious, interpretation: 'Maybe the mess in the servery reflects the messy and depressed feelings in the community'.

The accuracy or appropriateness of this interpretation in a community meeting notwithstanding, it was not enough to result in patients taking action to clear up what was becoming a health hazard. It was received with silence. Later that day, the nurse had to find ways to negotiate with patients about how, together, the unpleasant task could be achieved. Psychoanalysis does not alone constitute an adequate knowledge base to guide/inform nursing actions such as these. What follows is a model of nursing which might confront some of these issues.

A MODEL OF NURSING

As noted earlier, the prime foci of the nurses' work are the everyday activities of living, which patients suffering from neurotic problems may find it difficult to enjoy. This finding is confirmed by studies in other therapeutic communities. It is of interest that in the last decade, academic departments of nursing have also developed models of care based on activities of daily living. Writers like Roper, Logan and Tierney (1980, 1983) have focussed on the ways that general nurses can plan and implement care using these concepts. They argue that nursing care involves four stages: assessment, planning, implementation, and evaluation.

At the Cassel Hospital, the assessment period starts with a domiciliary visit by a nurse and a patient from the community, and continues through a post-admission review called the 'triage'. Here, the nurses, using participant observer techniques stressing insight into their own subjective reactions to the patient, and empathy into the patient's reactions to them, seek to make thoughtful observations of the patient's strengths and weaknesses while at the same time developing a relationship with him or her.

These observations and insights are then formulated into a nursing care plan once discussed and agreed by the therapeutic team and the patient concerned. The following care study may illustrate this process further.

Mrs Smith: history

In a detailed report of her first domiciliary visit the nurse noted that Mrs Smith, a tall, slender 28 year old with one daughter and one son, lived in a small, cold council house. The daughter, six-year-old Jenny, presented as a robust, sensible child, but John, 4½ year old, was extremely boisterous and provocative towards his mother and sister. John had been in foster care and Mrs Smith expressed resentment about this. She had been separated from her husband for two years and he had only occasional contact with his children. While Mrs Smith viewed Jenny as a model child she viewed John as 'unmanageable and subhuman'. He also soiled, with urine and faeces.

Mrs Smith maintained close relationships with her own parents, but overall seemed to lack insight into her own possible role in John's disturbance.

The domiciliary visit is intended to help identify and assess problems associated with admission. In this case the nurse envisaged problems with the rest of the community tolerating the boisterousness of the children and predicted that Mrs Smith might use this to isolate herself from other adults. Mrs Smith's difficulty in acknowledging that she needed help was noted. As they were on supplementary benefit, it was thought that the family might need financial assistance to go home for the weekends. As she liked her council house, Mrs Smith, it was thought, would need psychological assistance in returning home. There would be a break in Jenny's schooling, and John's incontinence would cause practical and psychological problems. On the basis of her identification of these problems, the nurse designed care plans on the basis of her knowledge of hospital structures. (see Example 1). The plans were implemented and Mrs Smith's three-week assessment period was recorded in a detailed nursing assessment report which, combined with the assessment reports of other members of the therapeutic team, would form the basis of subsequent action (see Example 2).

Example 1: Care plans following domiciliary visit

Problem 1 (Community Tolerance): Mrs Smith's admission was discussed in the regular Firm meeting with other patients. Two rooms were chosen by patients for her stay which would give her easy access to the children and which were central to community life. Other parents with children resided in the same corridor. Patients and staff generally discussed the impact of a new family being admitted and some ambivalent feelings were acknowledged.

Problem 2 (Social Isolation): The patient who attended the home visit would act as a guide / mentor to Mrs Smith in the first few days by helping her understand the hospital's structures and expectations. An understanding was reached that Mrs Smith should attend all the meetings and groups designed to aid communication and act as sources of support for patients.

Problems 3 and 4 (Housing and Finance): The nurse liaised regularly with Mrs Smith's social worker regarding her financial and housing needs, confirming the importance of Mrs Smith's retaining her independence.

Problem 5 (Education): The nurse made provisional arrangements with the hospital school for Jenny to attend in the first week's assessment period. Arrangements to attend the local school would be contingent on the result of the triage, and the teacher's assessment of her educational needs.

Problem 6 (Soiling): The practical consequences of incontinence were discussed with Mrs Smith and laundry arrangements made clear. A child psychotherapist would become involved in treatment of the family.

Example 2: Nursing assessment

Background history: Mrs Smith separated from her husband after a long period of marital problems. She almost immediately entered into several new relationships, one of the men moving in with her and the children.

John was then placed into care because of possible physical abuse. Mrs Smith claims that this was done by her partner.

Mrs Smith spent a short in a psychiatric hospital, but no firm diagnosis was made. A GP then referred the family to the hospital.

The Social Services lost their case for custody due to lack of evidence, and John came home the week before admission.

Admission Day: The family arrived early, having been brought by their social worker. An anxious Mrs Smith and the children were impressed by the hospital building and its surroundings.

She was shy of the approaches of the other patients. The children ran uncontrolled round the hospital, resulting in Jenny falling down the stairs and grazing her forehead within hours of arriving.

Internal Family Functioning: Mrs Smith always seemed to be in the children's company or worrying about what they may be up to. She seemed to need them around her but complained loudly about them at the same time. The children tended to do exactly what they wanted until Mrs Smith lost her patience; then she would clamp down on them in a verbally and sometimes physically harsh way.

Jenny needed John to be the naughty one and ensured this by often 'baiting' him. They both played happily beside each other, but arguments occured quickly when they were both involved in the same activity.

Family social adaptation outside community: The whole family got on well with their social worker. Mrs Smith said she was isolated from the rest of the local community and blamed this on her previous affair with a next-door neighbour and John's bad behaviour. Her main social contact was within the church, of which she was a regular attender.

Within the hospital: The children settled quite quickly but Mrs Smith found it difficult to involve herself in community events. She used John's behaviour as an excuse for this. Asking for help was also a problem. She often had her own supper on the landing because she had not arranged anybody to look after the children.

Family relationship with the nurse: It did not seem to matter to Mrs Smith whether I was around or not although she did enjoy having someone to talk to about her problems.

Jenny was more detached from me than John for the first two weeks.

John to begin with always seemed pleased to see me but over the last week or so has been clinging to his mother more when we are all together.

In summary, the assessment showed that while the nurse felt she had a reasonable understanding of the children and their behaviour, she did not think Mrs Smith had shown much of her true nature. Mrs Smith showed a capacity to manage everyday living situations within the community, yet she left the impression of an angry woman hiding behind her children.

The nurse was struck by Mrs Smith's lack of communication with the therapist involved. Mrs Smith had described him as a chauvinist who looked like her ex-husband. She had also directed much of her contempt for nursing policy towards a male nurse. Jenny and John, too, seemed to her to represent the good female and totally bad male. John remained incontinent.

The nursing aims were, at this stage, to:

Encourage Mrs Smith to participate more in the life of the hospital as an individual.

Plan with Mrs Smith limits for the children and help her to apply them consistently.

Plan humane care to help manage John's incontinence.

Explore with the therapist concerned, approaches to John's and Jenny's relationship with their absent father.

The triage assessment, then, not only provided the therapeutic team with the opportunity to share ideas and formulate plans, but also to evaluate progress in the first three weeks. For example, Mrs Smith's therapist confirmed that she had demonstrated a willingness to explore her own difficulties, as opposed to those of her son, despite initial misgivings and some resistance. John was also considered suitable for therapeutic intervention by the child psychotherapist. A fuller nursing care plan was formulated as a result of that discussion, to complement the overall therapeutic endeavour. The nurse used her knowledge and understandings of the structure of the hospital and its everyday activities as the basis of care rather than, as the therapist might, her knowledge of the structure of the unconscious. The plans took the form illustrated below.

Example 3: Nursing care plans following assessment

Problem 1 (Participation): The nurse undertook to work alongside Mrs Smith where appropriate, for example in undertaking the managment of John's incontinence. In this case, it involved the nurse helping with the laundering of clothes and the problems and negotiations with other patients around the presence of soiled linen.

It was felt that by providing a practical framework of sharing, Mrs Smith might be offered the opportunity of an adult / adult relationship which might aid her viewing herself as an individual separate from her children (and vice versa). Similarly she was encouraged to work towards taking on one of the patient 'official roles'. By involving herself in the cooking rota and sharing responsibility for the budget allocated for children's teas, she would be better able to integrate with other parents, thus tackling some of the problems of isolation noted earlier.

Problem 2 (Limit-setting): Mrs Smith was encouraged to discuss with other parents in the parents' group the difficulties experienced in setting limits for her children, thus sharing and learning from them ways of resolving some problems. The nurse sought also to be consistent in her approaches to Mrs Smith and her discussions with the therapeutic team as a way of providing a safe psychological environment for Mrs Smith and her children.

Problem 3 (Incontinence): An action plan which included a quiet expectation that John regularly used the toilet, that consideration be given to his diet, and to his feelings was devised. It was felt that the problems of incontinence would be tackled better if a framework of action was provided which attenuated the harsh and punitive reactions previously taken by his mother.

Problem 5 (Maintenance of relationships): The nurse continued to liaise with Mrs Smith's therapist, the child psychotherapist and social worker, and consideration was given to Jenny's schooling by the hospital teacher.

Conclusion

Earlier in the paper I noted that psychosocial nursing shared some central preoccupations with the social action theorists. It would now be helpful to explain this assertion using Mrs Smith's care plans as an illustrative material.

Firstly, the nurse endeavoured to understand the meaning of experiences for the patient and her children together with other members of the therapeutic team. For example, she focussed on Mrs Smith's apparent anger and rejection of John.

Secondly, she sought to understand how particular configurations of meaning are sustained by continual reaffirmation in everyday actions. The perception of John as bad was confirmed and reconfirmed when he was successfully provoked into anger by his sister and then scolded by his mother.

Thirdly, she also sought to understand the means by which Mrs Smith tried to negotiate, modify, and transform her interactions and experiences with others in the community. Mrs Smith's resolving of her problems was associated with her children's behaviour and her own difficulties in relation to people (eating alone or on a landing).

Fourthly, the nurse tried to stay sensitive to Mrs Smith and her family's response to events in the everyday work of the community, by acknowledging the meanings that the family attributed to events.

I also noted that psychosocial nursing shares much with the model of nursing recently developed in the general fields. I described the various stages in the process from assessment, through planning and implementation to evaluation. Perhaps the problematic nature of evaluation in psychosocial nursing deserves special mention. It is similar to problems of evaluation found in psychoanalysis. At the hospital, the evaluation of care plans is continuous and flexible in response to changes identified by the patient, the nurse, the therapeutic team or the community. The period of treatment for most patients is nine to fourteen months. It seems self-evident, therefore, that, as time progresses, and the patient grows towards different ways of being, the original care plans become outdated. The striking feature of the psychotherapeutic endeavour and that of psychosocial nursing is its emergent nature. There can be few pre-set measurable goals if growth and change is to be a genuine result of a collaboration in which a patient is a willing and equal partner in self-discovery. Sometimes change may be the result of the unintended consequences of staff, patient, or community events. Care plans reflect this possibility by not being too rigid. Thus it is not the individual care plans which remain fixed but the daily structure and expectations of the hospital; that people talk about their experiences and feelings and transform these words into fruitful actions. Given the flexible and emergent nature of psychological change, evaluation of care plans is often subjective. While the objective of ensuring John's continence and the objective of seeking to establish some individuation with Mrs Smith may be tested, it is difficult to establish which aspect of the shared care has been causal in that change. Nurses take on the normal everyday activities of life, which by their nature constitute the commonsense taken for granted aspects of our social world. Evaluation of the efficacy of any given nursing care plan is therefore problematic and speculative. Firstly, if it is taken for granted it may become invisible; secondly, nursing and medical claims can only be modest. It is the patient who, after all, is responsible for his or her own life; he or she may lay claim to successfully changing it.

Summary

A theoretical model suited to nursing and about nursing which is grounded in the experience of nurses in a therapeutic community is outlined. The co-incidence of interests and intent between social action theorists, therapeutic community structure and psychosocial nursing is explored.

Finally, the concepts derived from this exploration are used to illustrate techniques in psychosocial nursing through the examination of the nursing care of the family.

[21]

Hospital Administration in a Therapeutic Community

Elsie Buckenham

Administration at the Cassel has always been a challenge, but equally its rewards are tremendous, involving as it does complete integration with the work of the hospital and the aims of its clinical staff.

Prior to 1974, the role of administrator was a combined one of group secretary with responsibility to the hospital management committee, and a principal administrative officer, responsible to the medical director for all administrative matters affecting the clinical work of the hospital. This made for conflict within the holder of the combined post, but over the years it formed a firm foundation for the building of the administration at the hospital.

After the re-organization of the National Health Service in 1974, such a division of responsibility was no longer possible. The method of administration at the hospital had to be continually justified to Health Authority officers, both by administrative and clinical staff.

The Cassel requires a competent administrator, fully versed in National Health Service regulations and the normal administrative skills, but with the ability and willingness to understand the treatment offered to the patients, and thereby to facilitate the work of the therapeutic community. In addition it is necessary for the administrator to forge good working links with the Health Authority staff so that, with the support of the clinical staff, Cassel methods and requirements may be explained convincingly to those not familiar with them.

Unless the administrator understands the treatment offered, much damage can be done. For example, the administrator may for some reason be inclined to be lenient with a patient over irregular receipt of that portion of his or her wages that are due to the hospital if he or she is continuing to work during in-patient treatment, when perhaps it is a necessary part of the therapy that responsibility in this connection be encouraged. Again, whilst it may seem good administration, doing too much for the patients' comfort (for example, arranging the redecoration of rooms), is not always in the interests of treatment.

For the administrator to be aware of all the pitfalls, it is necessary to be closely involved with what is going on in the community. The administrator attends weekly meetings with staff and patients, and with all staff, thereby gradually learning the complex work of the psychotherapeutic community, and being able to make a useful practical contribution by his or her knowledge of National Health Service regulations.

There must, however, be a mutual respect between clinical and administrative staff, as the administrator has responsibilities which cannot be delegated, and which the clinicians must respect. However, it is remarkable how much easier it is to reach satisfactory solutions to problems when the administrator *feels* consulted and respected instead of, as is so often the case in hospitals, seen as blocking progress for reasons not understood by medical and nursing staff, often because of their lack of interest in, and irritation about, adminstrative problems.

It is my experience that the therapeutic community cannot function successfully without the full support and understanding of the hospital administrator, and to obtain this it is necessary not to control the administration, but to care for it and integrate it into the work of the community. This makes hospital administration a most satisfying and rewarding experience.

Conclusion

Roger Kennedy

The task of this book has been to describe and discuss the Cassel Hospital's ways of working with troubled families and adolescents. This work involves a unified approach to psychotherapy and nursing, each of which have defined and equally valued roles. The work of both the nursing and the psychotherapy is to a large extent focussed on everyday activities and events within the hospital. The rationale for this has been discussed in several papers here, for example by Roger Kennedy, Alan Wilson, Brian Muir and Gillian Chapman. There have also been descriptions of the way that we use and interpret the individual and family transference reactions, and also how we deal with the complicated transference issues involving the whole institution. Our ways of working require relatively sophisticated understanding of psychoanalytical knowledge by both nurses and therapists.

Patients bring into the hospital complex and often very confusing ways of relating. They usually try, consciously and unconsciously, to recreate the pattern of behaviour and relationships that led to their breakdown outside the hospital. This may involve their considerable use of, for example, 'primitive' splitting and projection, which they repeat in relation to the staff. This causes considerable pressure on staff, who are, and need to be, backed up in their work by a body of psychoanalytical knowledge, of expertise in how to apply this knowledge, and by a structured staff support and supervision system. Our ways of working are constantly being modified and adapted to changed circumstances in staff and in relation to the needs of the National Health Service.

The Cassel Hospital has for many years been in the forefront of treatment innovations, for example, in admitting children with their mothers, and in admitting whole families. It has also made major contributions to applied psychoanalysis and the nursing process. Underlying the work is the assumption that the patient is a human subject with a life of his or her own, with conscious and unconscious intentions and motives, whose capacity to relate and take on responsibility is respected and encouraged. Such an attitude implies taking considerable risks. For example, many of our patients are actively suicidal for part or all of their stay. Rather than collude with their self-destructiveness, for example by offering medication (which has often had no long-term benefit in a number of patients), our aim is to help the patients face and understand their own feelings. In the case of parents with children in the hospital, there is an expectation that they will continue to take charge of their children. Taking clinical risks implies the capacity to cope with uncertainty, or as Alan Wilson puts it (p. 52) 'going into, inventing, the peril of experimental relationships between people and things, discovering the nature of danger and security, jeopardy and safety'.

Ways of understanding how the hospital has a therapeutic effect are often being revised. The paper by Oliver James and Alan Wilson (p. 315) is a way of attempting to understand the role of social structure in the life of the hospital, while Gillian Chapman's paper (p. 329) focusses more on the nursing process itself. Roger Kennedy (p. 27) has attempted to link classical Freudian psychoanalysis with the work of the hospital, while Brian Muir (p. 64) has offered a unified account of the various aspects of in-patient therapy from an applied psychoanalytical perspective, basing his account on classical analysis and its modifications. We feel that our understanding of the complexities of the hospital as an effective therapeutic institution, and of the complexities of the mental life of individuals and families, continues to evolve. The use of the nurse/therapist supervision described by Lydia Tischler (p. 95) is one recent instance of the evolution in practice. There are other projects in the offing: for example, we intend to set up a walk-in Family Consultation Service. This will be aimed at reaching families in distress that otherwise would not be referred, as well as helping with the flood of referrals and enquiries we receive from social service agencies in the Greater London area, who are having to deal, often unsupported, with very difficult family situations. We also intend to concentrate resources on research and treatment of severe child abuse, as this has become an urgent and increasingly recognized area for skilled work.

Thus, the Cassel has evolved an adaptable system of working with disturbed patients, which involves the use of psychoanalytic insight, and in particular, focal attention to the nature of professional relationships. We aim to provide a setting for self-reflection and for the registering and understanding of distorted communication and distorted relating. By having a solid staff structure, and by means of focussing on everyday realities, we seem able to tolerate and understand degrees of disturbance and situations of anxiety which many other workers in other settings find difficult to cope with. Indeed, we ourselves are often under considerable stress, and for this reason staff are encouraged to find individual therapy themselves away from the hospital, if they so desire, rather than use the hospital for their own therapy. It is difficult enough to cope with the patients' pathology. However, we do not encourage an attitude of detachment (which is counter-productive to any therapy, but especially so of in-patient therapy); the work requires considerable personal involvement and a capacity to rely on and trust fellow professionals.

There are a number of ways in which our methods can be applied in the mental health field, and perhaps elsewhere.

Preventive health care

A multidisciplinary approach is widespread in work with families, but nonetheless staff are often put under considerable stress, usually because they are subject to the same sort of splitting mechanisms and emotional pressure from families as we have described in our work at the Cassel. In our experience, the workers need to come together to discuss such problems, and we often facilitated such meetings as part of our work with referral agencies. But it is not just enough to meet; it is also important, as Trevor Hartnup writes (p. 127) that the workers 'clarify their individual powers, responsibilities and areas of work in order to find ways of working together'. If this proves possible, the circumstances are favourable for the patient or family to develop the capacity to deal with their own problems, which they had hitherto loaded onto the group of professional workers. Such work with families, if done early enough, may play a major role in preventing the next generation's breakdown of family functioning, with the attendant mental health problems and high financial cost.

An additional secondary benefit of our work with families is an increasing understanding of how and why families break down, and what interventions are therapeutically effective. This is ongoing work; it is our wish to set up a separate mother/infant observation and research unit, to help systematize our work and encourage further psychoanalytic research into early childhood development.

Psychiatric institutions

We are selective at the Cassel about which patients we treat and which we think may be susceptible to our treatment. It would also appear that we have considerable resources to deal with our patients. Both these points might make it appear that our methods cannot be directly applied to traditional, medically-orientated psychiatric institutions. In fact, the hospital runs both its considerable out-patient facilities and in-patient units on a relatively small and very stretched, dedicated staff. The number of hours devoted to out-patient work for the whole hospital is currently, in 1985-6, running at some 5,300 hours per year, and includes treatment of a wide spectrum of patients from all social classes. This treatment takes place in a hospital mainly staffed for in-patient work.

The effectiveness of any hospital service is not only a question of the amount of resources but of their effective use, and the degree to which coherent treatment plans are adhered to. However, there is also a need for a basic core of senior staff to supervise and facilitate the work. In addition we believe, as Elsie Buckenham has outlined (p. 348), that such work requires the backing of, and integration with, hospital adminstration.

We would suggest that our model of working with disturbed patients can be directly applied to psychiatric institutions and services, at least in a modified form. Our attitude of facing the patients with the consequences of their actions and of encouraging the normal process of everyday life to continue, could easily be built into a psychiatric treatment plan, as could the development of nursing care techniques.

What distinguishes psychoanalysis from other kinds of therapy is the use of the concept of transference, and in particular the toleration and use of the negative transference – which includes feelings of anger, fury and resentment shown towards any person or institution that tries to help and foster change. In the Cassel, both the individual and the complicated whole hospital transferences are faced, and not ignored. What the Cassel has shown is that these complex psychodynamic processes can be understood, monitored and used therapeutically within an institution, even with whole families and staff organizations. Our model and experience can be applied in a wide range of settings, including psychiatric hospitals and multidisciplinary teams in the community. This is unlike most current psychiatric set-ups which are often designed, on adminstrative and theoretical grounds, quite specifically to ignore precisely what we find therapeutic.

FUTURE COMMUNITY NEEDS

In the light of the increasing incidence of family breakdown, and our awareness of family disturbance, and also in the light of the increasing public concern and anxiety felt by professionals faced by very difficult cases of severe physical and sexual abuse of children, there would seem to be a strong argument for the development of resources such as the Cassel Hospital as a service, training, and (perhaps more importantly) a research institution. Child guidance clinics, social service offices and child psychiatry departments deal with the majority of problem families and a certain number of adolescents, but there remain a significant and increasing number of problem families where out-patient interventions have not succeeded. We firmly believe that the Cassel has a continuing and increasingly important role to play in both helping other professionals deal with these families in order to keep them in their own home and community, and to take on the treatment of those families who need our resources. There is also an urgent need for more research on family breakdown. The Cassel offers a unique opportunity for such research, since there is the possibility of many detailed observations from a whole day in the life of a family.

PSYCHOANALYTIC APPLICATIONS

We hope that the innovations of the Cassel can have an effect on psychoanalytic theory and practice. For example, the work of the hospital can provide information about family and adolescent structure and breakdown which can be of use in understanding individual psychopathology and the nature of childhood, adolescent and adult disturbance. Our work thus, at the very least, contributes to research into mental functioning by the study of certain forms of mental breakdown.

The issue of how analytic theory and techniques can be directly influenced is more difficult to clarify. On the one hand, the patients we treat at the hospital are often people who could not possibly deal with traditional analysis, let alone any out-patient psychotherapy. They often need the other 23 hours in the day, apart from the solitary hour of the therapy session, to be attended to and looked after. That is, they often, at least at first, need 24 hour treatment, five to seven days a week, not five hours a week treatment (which is the most provided by analysis). The implicit assumption of analysis is that the patient can deal effectively with what we explicitly call the 'work of the day' and, indeed, the 'work of the week'.

It is clear that the Cassel is deeply indebted to psychoanalytic theory and practice, as we have demonstrated throughout the book. It shoud now also be clear that analysis itself could learn from the Cassel: how to pay close attention to the everyday events, how such events can be charged with conflict, or used defensively to ward off conflicts, and how the complexities of life offer therapeutic possibilities, not just disturbances of the analytic frame. Analysis can learn the importance of what has happened in the day, not only for the investigation of dreams, but also for the understanding of the to and fro of the analytic relationship.

In the Cassel, the nurse provides an essential link with ordinary expectations and social reality, and usually brings therapy 'down to earth'. The nurse roots it in immediate and fresh situations. It would probably be of enormous benefit to psychoanalysts were they to take on themselves something of the nursing function in their own analytic work. It might help them to bring into focus the most immediately relevant conflicts in the patient's life.

Perhaps the work of the Cassel could offer models and encouragement towards seeing the benefits of such an elaboration of the analyst's work. The hospital's experience with difficult patients is especially useful in extending analytic knowledge into areas such as the treatment of the disturbed adolescent, the psychotic and the borderline psychotic patient. Finally, an application of our methods of thinking may enable the analyst to provide a more effective holding of difficult, psychotic patients, or to hold neurotic patients in times of acute crisis. Necessity has forced the Cassel staff to explore these areas, rather than to leave them as topics of theoretical interest.

Medical and nursing practice

There are radical implications for medical and nursing practice following from the fact that the Cassel gives an equal share in treatment of patients to nurses. Traditionally, in most branches of medicine, the doctor prescribes treatment and very often the nurse carries it out. There is no question of equal shares in decision-making and treatment plans. The medical organization and the entire hospital hierarchy are adapted to the special status of the specialist doctor who traditionally appears at 'special' moments such as on the ward round. But relatively little attention is given to the knowledge and expertise of the nurse, except in the loose sense of servant to the doctor and of caretaker while the doctor's treatment takes effect.

The patient in a hospital ward is often in a weak physical state and in a regressed, helpless and dependent state of mind. One of the most difficult tasks is to support the patient's functioning areas, particularly in patients who have a difficult family situation, or have severe psychopathology. The multiple caregivers in the hospital ward may only heighten the deprived patient's own feelings of being deprived and incapacitated.

One could speculate that there are at least two main transferences encouraged by the hospital ward organization. The father transference to the doctor, which is often in the form of an idealized father invested with hope and omnipotence, and a mother transference attached to the nurse, or what one could call the nursing transference. This latter element is invested with maternal holding functions, but also with all the patient's fears of breakdown and fragmentation of the holding environment. The nurse may be expected, by both patients and doctors, to magically deal with all these anxieties.

There is usually an extreme split between the nursing transference and the transference to the doctor. The doctor in particular may be quite unaware of the nursing transference and what the nurse has to deal with, because it usually suits the doctor to be considered as omnipotent. Knowledge of the nursing transference may or may not be relevant in a particular treatment. For example, it may be only of marginal significance in the healing of a broken leg. But it may be of vital significance in the treatment of the more psychologically vulnerable patient. At the very least such knowledge may help to understand the patient's whole attitude to treatment, and must inevitably help the nurses in their day-to-day work of dealing with the patient for 24 hours of the day.

In summary, we have attempted to provide a coherent account of a very complex situation: a busy, in-patient Family Unit, the members of which are treated by a number of different professionals. The basis of the treatment is a combination of psychoanalytic psychotherapy and psychosocial nursing. Rather than attempt to eliminate the intense thoughts and feelings revealed by patients in this setting, we have explained how the Cassel Hospital monitors and deals with such thoughts and feelings in a therapeutic way, by attending both to the transference of patients to the hospital and to individual nurses and therapists, and by attending to the countertransference of these nurses and therapists in a safe and supervised way.

In Vivien Biggs's paper (p. 292), she found that ex-patients on follow-up often spoke more highly of their interaction with other patients and the mutual support they experienced, than they did of their work with staff. It is difficult to be certain of the significance of this discovery, but it may be relevant to make some comments about it here, when we are looking back at what has been proposed by the contributors.

It is true to say that one of the main aims of our treatment is to help restore the patients to ordinary life, where they can relate to other people in more satisfactory ways. In this sense, the fact that patients retain the memory of human encounters with other patients is perhaps of cardinal importance, and indicates successful treatment. Before admission it is usually the case that the patient's own extreme pathology has interfered with the capacity to relate to others in this way. In addition, the fact that patients valued the community as the therapist rather than individuals as such indicates a correct perception by patients of the fact that the staff teams value the ideal of the hospital community, and in fact work together as a community, however hard it often may be.

It is hardly suprising that patients still show evidence of unresolved transferences to the staff, and still feel resentful of the help they received. In focal treatment of between one year to 18 months offered by the hospital, it is often not possible to resolve all transference issues. One may merely help to start off a process of psychological inquiry that hopefully continues for some years, and may help the patient deal more effectively with life crises as they arise.

Biggs's study also highlights the intense pressure that this sort of work puts on the staff. Of course, every analyst and therapist must bear the unresolved ambivalence of patients who are leaving treatment. But the hothouse conditions, the prevalence of primitive psychic mechanisms, the deep day-to-day involvement of staff in patient's lives subject in-patient staff to psychical assaults on their sense of adequacy and reality, which must be contained by the therapeutic structures of the hospital. Although the senior staff try to help metabolize staff anxieties, the work nonetheless remains traumatic for some.

Finally, both the editors and the other contributors to this book have found that the writing of it has helped us to focus more clearly on the work we are doing. It has helped us clarify some of the confusion inevitable in such demanding and complex work. We hope that our ideas will continue to develop in this way, and adapt to new demands.

Bibliography

Barnes, E., ed. (1967) *Psychosocial Nursing*. London: Tavistock Publications.

Barnes, M. and Berke, J. (1973) *Mary Barnes*. Harmondsworth: Penguin Books.

Bateson, G. (1936) *Naven*. Cambridge: Cambridge University Press.

Berger, R. and Luckmann, T. (1975) *The Social Construction of Reality*. Harmondsworth: Penguin Books.

Bion, W. (1961) *Experiences in Groups*. London: Tavistock Publications.

Bloor, M. and Fonkert, J. (1982) 'Reality construction, reality exploration and treatment in two therapeutic communities', *Sociology of Health and Mental Illness*, vol. 4, no. 2.

Box, S. et al. (1981) *Psychotherapy with Families*. London: Routledge & Kegan Paul.

Boyers, R. and Orrill, R. (1972) *Laing and Anti-Psychiatry*. Harmondsworth: Penguin Books.

Chapman, G. (1984) 'A therapeutic community, psychosocial nursing and the nursing process', *Int. J. Therapeutic Communities*, vol. 5, no. 2: 68-76.

Davis, F. (1963) *Passage through Crisis*. New Jersey: Dobbs Merrill.

Denford, J. et al. (1983) 'Selection and outcome in in-patient psychotherapy', *Brit. J. Med. Psychol.* 56, pp. 225-243.

Deutsch, H. (1933) 'Motherhood and sexuality', *Psychoanal.* vol. 2: 476-88.

Deutsch, H. (1947) *Psychology of Women Part II: Motherhood*. London: Research Books.

Douglas, J. (1971) *Understanding Everyday Life*. London: Routledge & Kegan Paul.

Durkheim, E.(1938) *The Rules of Sociological Method*. London: Hogarth Press.

Folkart, L. (1964) 'The Role of a Child-Psychotherapist in an In-patient Setting', *Child Psychotherapy* vol. 1., no. 2, pp.44-45

Folkart, L. (1967) 'Some problems of treating children in an in-patient setting', *Child Psychotherapy*, vol. 2, no. 1, pp.46-55.

Freud, A. (1958) 'Adolescence', *Psychoanal. Study Child* 13, pp.255-278.

Freud, S. (1900) *The Interpretation of Dreams*. S.E.4-5, London: Hogarth Press.

Freud, S. (1901) *Psychopathology of Everyday Life*. S.E.6, London: Hogarth Press.

Freud, S. (1911) 'Formulations on the two principles of mental functioning', S.E.12, pp. 215-226, London: Hogarth Press.

Freud, S. (1913) 'An evidential dream', S.E.12, pp. 268-74, London: Hogarth Press.

Freud, S. (1917) 'Mourning and melancholia', S.E.14, pp. 238-60, London: Hogarth Press.

Giddens, A. (1977a) *New Rules of Sociological Method*. London: Hutchinson University Library.

Giddens, A. (1977b) *Studies in Social and Political Theory*. London: Hutchinson.

Giddens, A. (1979) *Central Problems in Social Theory*. London: Macmillan.

Gluck, I. and Wrenn, M. (1959) 'Contribution to the understanding of disturbances of mothering', *Brit. Med. Psychol.* 32, pp. 171-182.

Goffman, E. (1961) *Asylums*. Harmondsworth: Penguin Books.

Goffman, E. (1974) *The Presentation of Self in Everyday Life*. Harmondsworth: Penguin Books.

Green, A. (1979) Second Lecture as the Freud Professor of Psychoanalysis, University College, University of London.

Habermas, J. (1980) 'Systematically distorted communications', in Connerton, P., ed. *Critical Sociology*. Harmondsworth: Penguin Books.

Hinshelwood, R., ed. (1979) *Therapeutic Communities*. London: Routledge & Kegan Paul.

Horobin, G. and Davis, A. eds. (1977) *Medical Encounters*. London: Croom Helm.

Jansen, E., ed. (1980) *The Therapeutic Community*. London: Croom Helm.

Jaques, E. (1955) 'Social Systems as a Defence against Depressive Anxiety', in Klein, M., ed. *New Directions in Psychoanalysis*. London: Tavistock Publications.

Jones, Maxwell (1953) *The Therapeutic Community*. New York: Basic Books.

Kafka, F. (1926) *The Castle*, E. and W. Muir, trans. Harmondsworth: Penguin, 1930.

Kafka, F. (1925) *The Trial*, E. and W. Muir, trans. Harmondsworth: Penguin, 1957.

Katan, A. (1952) quoted in Freud, A. (1958) 'Adolescence', *Psychoanal. Study Child* 13, pp.255-278

Kennedy, R. (1984) 'A dual aspect of the transference', *Int. J. of Psychoanal.* 65: 471-83.

Kernberg, O. et al. (1972) 'Menninger Foundation Psychotherapy Research Project', *Bulletin of Menninger Clinic*, vol 36.

Lichtman, R. (1970) 'Symbolic interactionism and social reality: some Marxist queries', *Berkeley Journal of Sociology*, 14: 75-94.

Lomas, P. (1959) 'The husband/wife relationship in cases of puerperal breakdown', *Brit. J. Med. Psychol.* 32: 117-723.

Lomas, P. (1960a) 'Defensive organization and puerperal breakdown', *Brit. J. Med. Psychol.* 33: 61-96.

Lomas, P. (1960b) 'Dread of envy as an aetiological factor in puerperal breakdown', *Brit. J. Med. Psychol.* 33: 105-12.

Macklin, D. (1978) 'Psychosocial Nursing' (unpublished).

Main, T. (1946) 'The ailment' in Barnes, E., ed. (1967) *Psychosocial Nursing*.

Main, T. (1946) 'The hospital as a therapeutic insitution', *Menninger Clinic Bulletin*, vol 10: 3. London: Tavistock Publications.

Main, T. (1956) 'The social structure of a mental hospital', in Barnes, E., ed. (1967) *Psychosocial Nursing*. London: Tavistock Publications.

Main, T. (1958) 'A fragment on mothering', in Barnes, E., ed. (1969) *Psychosocial Nursing*. London: Tavistock Publications.

Main, T. (1975) 'Some psychodynamics of large groups', in Kreeger, L., ed. (1975) *The Large Group*. London: Constable.

Main, T. (1980) 'Some basic concepts in therapeutic community work', in Jansen, E., ed. (1980) *The Therapeutic Community*. London: Croom Helm.

Mead, G. (1935) *Mind, Self and Society*. New York: Citadel Press.

Mead, M. (1950) 'Training in community relations', *Human Relations*, vol. 2, no. 2: 206-8.

Menzel, H. (1978) 'Meaning: who needs it?' in Brenner, J., ed. (1978) *Social Context of Medicine*. London: Methuen.

Menzies, I.E.P. (1959) 'The functioning of social systems as a defence against persecutory and depressive anxiety', *Tavistock Pamphlet No. 3*. London: Tavistock Publications.

Parsons, T. (1951) *The Social System*. Glencoe: Free Press.

Ployé, P. (1977) 'On some difficulties of in-patient individual psycho-analytically-orientated therapy', *Psychiatry* 40: 133-45.

Roper, N., Logan, W. and Tierney, A., (1980) *The Elements of Nursing*. London: Churchill Livingstone.

Roper, N., Logan, W. and Tierney, A., (1983) *Using a Model for Nursing*. London: Churchill Livingstone.

Rose, A., ed. (1977) *Human Behaviour and Social Processes: An Interactionist Approach*. London: Routledge & Kegan Paul.

Roth, J. (1963) *Timetables*. Indianapolis: Bobbs Merrill.

Rothman, D. (1971) *The Discovery of the Asylum; Social Order and Disorder in the New Republic*. Boston: Little Brown.

Rowland, J. (1938) 'Interaction processes in the state mental hospital', *Psychiatry*, 1:323-37.

Sartre, J-P. (1938) *Nausea*, R. Baldick, trans. Harmondsworth: Penguin Books, 1965.

Sedgwick, P. (1982) *Psycho-Politics*. London: Pluto Press.

Silverman, D. (1976) *The Theory of Organizations*. London: Heinemann.

Stanton, A., and Schwartz, M. (1954) *The Mental Hospital*. New York: Basic Books.

Tonnesmann, M. (1979) 'Containing stress in professional work', *Social Work Services Magazine* (D.H.S.S.), 21:pp.34-41.

Wadsworth, M. and Robinson, D. eds. (1976) *Studies in Everyday Medical Life*. London: Croom Helm.

Weber, M. (1964) *Basic Concepts in Sociology*. New York: Citadel Press.

Winnicott, D. (1956) 'Primary maternal preoccupation', in Winnicott (1958) *Collected Papers: Through Paediatrics to Psychoanalysis*. London: Tavistock Publications.

Winnicott, D. (1965) *The Maturational Processes and the Facilitating Environment*. London: Hogarth Press.

Winnicott, D. (1972) *Playing and Reality*. Harmondsworth: Penguin Books.

Index

This first edition of
The Family as In-Patient
was finished in February 1987.

It was typeset in 10½/13pt Garamond
on a CRTronic 300 and printed by a
Harris cold-set web offset press
on $80g/m^2$ vol. 17.5 Chantry Book Wove.

The book was commissioned by Karl Figlio,
copy-edited by Charlotte Greig,
designed by Carlos Sapochnik
and produced by David Williams
for Free Association Books.